Charles Firth is, according to Wikipedia, the _____
history of humanity'. In 1999, he and a grou _____
The Chaser – a satirical newspaper and websit _____
The team has gone on to produce various award winning things in television, radio and print.

His TV credits include *The Election Chaser* (2001), *CNNNN* (2002–3), *The Chaser Decides* (2004) and *The Chaser's War on Everything* (2006).

He is the author of thirteen books about himself, including *Me: A Memoir* (unpublished), *Me 2: The Sequel* (unpublished) and *You Ain't Seen Nothing Yet: The Best of Charles Firth* (unpublished), as well as numerous *Chaser Annuals* (published).

For the past couple of years, Charles has also been a freelance contributor to various magazines, including *Cigar Aficionado*, *Pipe Aficionado*, *Snuff Aficionado*, *The Monthly*, *The Bulletin*, *GQ Australia*, *The Nation* (Botswana edition) and most proudly, *The Australian Worker Magazine*.

In 2005, Charles moved to New York City with his wife Amanda, and has recently changed his name to Jihad al-Firth. He is currently working on a project, which he says is 'top secret'.

This is his fourteenth book.

AMERICAN HOAX

Charles Firth

Undercover in the USA
(sort of)

MACMILLAN
Pan Macmillan Australia

First published 2006 in Macmillan by Pan Macmillan Australia Pty Limited
1 Market Street, Sydney

National Library of Australia
Cataloguing-in-Publication data:

Firth, Charles.
American hoax.

ISBN-13: 978 1 4050 3762 4

ISBN-10: 1 4050 3762 8

1. Firth, Charles. 2. Firth, Charles – Travel. 3.
Imposters and imposture – United States – Biography. 4.
Political satire, Australian – United States. 5. Public
opinion – United States. 6. United States – Politics and
government – 2001—Public opinion. I. Title.

303.380973

Typeset in 12/16 Fairfield LH Light by Midland Typesetters, Australia
Printed in Australia by MacPherson's Printing Group

Papers used by Pan Macmillan Australia Pty Limited are natural, recyclable products
made from wood grown in sustainable forests. The manufacturing processes conform to
the environmental regulations of the country of origin.

To myself, with frank admiration.

CONTENTS

PHASE ONE
Shock and Awe

1

NEW REALITY

*Zeus most glorious and most great, Thundercloud, throned in
the heavens! Let not the sun go down and the darkness come,
until I cast down headlong the citadel of Priam in flames, and
burn his gates with blazing fire, and tear to rags the shirt upon
Hector's breast! May many of his men fall about him prone in
the dust and bite the earth!*

Homer, The Iliad

I arrived at the Council of Foreign Relations on Manhattan's Upper
East Side with one mission: to get a frank, off-the-record quote
from a senior White House official. I knew that if this book were to
have any chance of getting onto the *New York Times* bestseller list
I needed a juicy revelation from an 'unnamed source close to the
President' for page 221, which would excite the Sunday morning
chat shows for at least one news cycle and, more importantly, get
me a seat on the punditerati gravy train for life.

Ninety percent of the room were men, perhaps half of them over
sixty, the vast majority white: a cross-section of corporate America's
diverse senior management. Along a table on the far side of the
room were silver trays of lunch, all of it in bite-size portions, as if
even the food had been executive summarized. There were only a
few cucumber and watercress sandwiches left, and a single soggy
caviar one. The marinated chicken-on-a-stick was moving fast, but
there were plenty of beef balls. And the vegetable platter – an
alluring selection of raw cauliflower sticks, carrots, zucchini and
celery – was untouched.

I stood alone by the tall, dark wood doors while those around me stood chatting about the windy weather and joking about how crowded the function was. And it was crowded: one of the busiest of the year. Which was unsurprising, I suppose, given how powerful today's speaker was.

Getting in had been surprisingly easy. As soon as I had arrived in the US from Australia, I had put myself down on numerous press lists thinking that it might come in handy while I wrote my profound and earnest think piece about America.[1] But I'd never bothered to actually go to any event until now because they had all sounded painfully boring. Indeed, I had ended up putting a rule on my email software so that they all went into a separate folder marked 'Invites – p221', which I rarely browsed. Sure, various ambassadors, visiting heads of state and the occasional UN chief would speak at these things, but if anything amazing happened I figured I'd hear about it the next day. As it turned out, it's not as simple as that – the press pack who turn up to these events only report what's newsworthy. They never mention the caviar.

I had RSVPed to an email invitation from the CFR a week before; they had sent the final details, and when I turned up I just had to show a press card and my driver's license. No frisking, no metal detectors. Even the security detail was subtle. The security men were dressed in tailored suits, with no apparent earplugs or lapel mics; the only way you could tell that each room had two or three security people present was that they were about a foot taller than everyone else. Bit of a giveaway, but perhaps that was the point.

I had the honour of being assigned a spot in the overflow room, meaning that my hope of seeing raw power in the flesh was dashed at the door. Although some media were allowed in the main auditorium, there were about fifty members of the press who didn't

---

[1] This book.

make the grade. Next to me sat Jan Herman, a former *LA Times* reporter and now freelance blogger, a reporter from a Hungarian newspaper, and two reporters from the *Economist*. The real cream of American journalism.

In the corner of the overflow room was a black box with a few cables coming out of it. Occasionally a reporter would go over to it and plug in their tape recorder. In this room, they had no way of asking questions. All they could do was plug in their equipment and wait for the electronic spoon-feeding to begin. This was a disappointment to me – it meant that a juicy quote for page 221 was almost certainly out of the question.

At the front of the room stood a television. Jan Herman whispered to me, 'A TV screen? I could be at home.' I laughed. He leant over further and whispered something about the speaker: 'He's a war criminal.' I laughed again, but this time more ill at ease. Jan, a guy in his late fifties, had a recent and massive gash across his left cheek which was only just turning bruise yellow. It went through my mind that perhaps he was a plant, a secret security agent posing as a blogger, stationed to entrap people like me into expressing some sort of opinion that was banned under an obscure clause in the Patriot Act.

I decided to hedge my bets. 'In fairness, I think that if you're involved in running the world's largest superpower, by definition you're going to be a war criminal.' This amused Jan, who then proceeded to hand me printouts of stuff he'd written on his website outlining various radical left opinions. No wonder he'd only made it to the overflow room.

As Jan and I chattered away, the two young *Economist* reporters looked down on us with British levels of disdain. For all I know – for they never spoke to me once – they were American nationals born and bred, but they'd clearly been trained by the *Economist* in British reserve. They oozed a silent superiority. Which I suppose is the only thing you've got going for you if you never get a by-line.

The din of conversation subsided. Kenneth I Chenault, CEO of American Express, took the podium to introduce the speaker. As the introduction went on, it became apparent that the man who was about to share his wisdom with us had no clear career line. He had been a consultant in the 1950s, a CEO of a couple of companies in the 1960s, and then had fallen into government work, including roles as the White House chief of staff, US ambassador to NATO, director of the Office of Economic Opportunity and a four-term congressman. The breadth and diversity of his roles was impressive, but it also left me wondering what made this guy so special that he was able to become one of the most powerful men in the world.

'But now, without further delay,' announced Kenneth, 'let me present to you the Secretary of Defense, Donald Rumsfeld.'

*   *   *

In the six months since I had arrived in the United States, up until the moment Donald[2] took the platform, my plan for this book had been straightforward enough. I was going to write a weighty tome about the American Empire, called simply *Empire*. It was going to be over 1300 pages long and extremely earnest.

From my brief skims of other books with the word 'Empire' in their titles, my task seemed easy enough. Most Americans, it turns out, don't want to be an empire, and so scholars, keen to sell as

---

[2] It is a cardinal rule of books about America that if they're going to sell well beyond the Beltway then they have to exude a sense of being 'in the know'. For this reason, as you may have already noticed, I've decided to use first names for everyone I talk about in this book. This will hopefully create a sense that you are reading the musings of an insider. Think of this book as being a kind of internal memo to the most powerful people in the world. (I was thinking of using the nom-de-plume 'Anonymous', but unfortunately Robert Baer – Bobby (as I like to call him) – got in with that trick before me.)

many books as possible, have invented the concept of America as a 'reluctant empire'. Indeed, I'd noticed a formula to these books, and was planning to replicate it myself. It went something like this:

- Chapter 1: Start with a classical quote and drop in a quick allusion to Roman Empire
- Chapters 2 and 3: Detailed discussion about how great it is America won World War Two
- Rest of the book: America's current role in world and how it really isn't trying to be an empire. Really. Honestly.

And that's about it. Of course, if *Empire* was going to sell any copies at all, it was also important it include the quote for page 221 that would get it on the Sunday morning chat-shows and even possibly its own spin-off sitcom series on C-SPAN (for non-American readers – a very boring channel that is lavishly funded by the cable companies and partially subsidized by the taxpayer because even proponents of small government like seeing themselves on TV).

And so, like the rest of the books in its category, mine was originally going to be about such worldly matters as empire which was actually a thin marketing veil for an introspective look at America. I figured that so long as I also talked at great length about how the Internet (specifically Google) had changed the rules of the game, made a few references to 9/11 and dropped the name of at least one Kennedy, then the book should manage to get onto somebody's book club list and I'd be singing the sweet tune of lending rights and royalties for the rest of my life.

From the beginning, however, I had been running into troubles. Naturally I had started out tackling the most important part of any book: the photo on the front cover. For this I figured I would need a professional I could trust: the same guy that Tom Cruise would use as his wedding photographer. And so I looked up exactly who it was who did Tom and Nicole's wedding (the only true Tom Cruise wedding in my opinion), and found out his name is Dick Zimmerman[3], a trendy Hollywood photographer who doesn't do photos but what he calls 'Portraiture', which judging by the 'Portraitures' on his website means 'photos with a bunch of flowers in the background'. His CV reads like a list of Hollywood's A-List. He's photographed, sorry, portraitured Hulk Hogan, Lisa Presley, Robert Wagner and, of course, the 1984 Nobel Prize Winner, Desmond Tutu. There was no choice but to email Dick and line up an immediate Portraiture session:

Dick,

I'm writing to see whether you would be able to photograph me for the cover shot of my upcoming book Empire. *It's being published by Pan Macmillan.*

I noticed on your website that you photographed Desmond Tutu. I imagine this would be a similar sort of deal – I can't actually afford to pay you at the moment, but my book will almost certainly end up getting a Nobel Peace Prize, and once it does, I'll pay you back with some of the prize money. Did you do a similar deal with Desmond?

Oh, by the way, I noticed that you did a portrait of Tom and Nicole when they were together. Did you notice any tension in the relationship at the time? I'd love to know.

---

[3] Dick Zimmerman really exists. Indeed, everyone I mention in this book really exists (including me). Furthermore, everything I do in this book actually occurs. The only people who don't exist are the ones that I invent (which, without wanting to give anything away, is something that hasn't happened yet, but will shortly). To avoid any confusion, I will let you know if, at any point, the person I'm talking about, or the scene that I am describing, is not real. Unless, of course, it suits the narrative for me to make you think momentarily that what you're reading is real even if it's not, in which case, I'll let you know after that point that what you had read and thought was real was in fact fiction. If you're at all confused, don't worry, I am too. Needless to say, Dick Zimmerman exists, and this interaction that I describe actually did occur. Clear?

Hope you agree to do this project – I think it's the sort of thing that will be to our mutual advantage.
Regards,
Charles Firth

His response was quick and he acted like a true professional – he didn't spill the beans on Tom and Nicole or anything.

Dear Charles . . . Can you tell me what the theme of you book is and what it deals with . . . Do you have an outline or script I can read? . . . If I feel I can support your concept then I would be willing to talk further. The portraits of Tom & Nicole were wedding portraits . . . shot the day of the wedding . . . so no tension!
Best,
DZ

No tension? As if. But there was one problem: Dick wanted an outline for the book. Unfortunately, I hadn't got to that stage yet. So I phoned Dick and tried to explain to him how I hadn't actually come up with a hook for my book yet, but that an outline was redundant in today's marketplace of ideas anyway. He muttered something about being in Chicago and therefore being unavailable for the next month. So I hopped on a plane and went to Chicago.[4] As soon as I got there, I rang Dick, but unfortunately he had been called away to Los Angeles.

Over the next six months I tried half-a-dozen times to get a sitting with the great Dick Zimmerman, each time explaining that I didn't actually have any money but that I would cut any sort of deal he wanted over a share of the Nobel prize money, and every time he unfortunately happened to be in a city different to the one I was in. On the last occasion I tried, I could only get through to his assistant; I told her I was in New York.

---

[4] This is completely true.

'Oh Dick is in LA at the moment,' she said, disappointed at my bad run of luck.

'But I'm going to Los Angeles tomorrow,' I told her.

Without missing a beat, she said, 'Oh, well, Dick will unfortunately be in Sacramento all week.'

I began to suspect that Dick was giving me the run-around. The celebrity Portraiture market was more hierarchical than it first appeared. Desperate, I tried other celebrity photographers, but the story was similar: I had no CV, no background, no Nobel prize, no 'body of work' that made them want to bite. Dick Zimmerman and his elitist Hollywood friends didn't seem to want to give the time of day to some ordinary guy with no money. To Dick, Charles Firth was a nobody. I just didn't cut it.

Luckily, the six months I had spent trying to get a good front-cover photograph were not entirely wasted. During that time I also was working on the back cover. And here I had more(-ish) success. Take, for instance, a very reasonable request I made to George Monbiot for a quote or 'squib' for the back cover. For those of you who don't know, George is the ultimate Big Thinker. In his last book he proposed global elections, where everyone in the world would vote to elect people to a global parliament that would, presumably, then solve all the world's problems. Simple solution to complex problem. Exactly the sort of stuff that I thought should be in this book. Of course, knowing that George is a bit of a lefty (he writes for the *Guardian*, a left-leaning British newspaper for people who drink tea and oppose war), I modified my pitch somewhat to appeal to him. I thought it best to pitch the book as a reinterpretation of Karl Marx. My thinking was that if he was going to write a squib for the back of my book, he'd want to think he agreed with it.

Dear Mr Monbiot

Big fan of your work. I especially like the idea of using the World Social Forum as the embryonic mechanism to start a world parliament.

It's only with that sort of big thinking that the forces of progress are going to get anywhere.

The reason I write is that I was wondering whether you'd be interested in providing a quote for the back cover of my book.

It's about the American Empire and it says all the sorts of things that you'd agree with (in fact, you'll probably wish you wrote the book yourself). It will argue that America is a voracious empire driven by the forces of capitalism which solves its crisis of over-accumulation by seeking accumulation through dispossession (I'm cribbing from David Harvey; basically it's a sort of modern-day Rosa Luxembourg meets John Maynard Keynes – but easier to read). It will also include a few action sequences where I go to Iran and Iraq to tour the most evil places in the world (you're welcome to come if you want to tag along).

I haven't actually written the book yet, but I was kind of hoping that you'd be able to provide a quote without actually reading the manuscript. Something like 'Charles Firth's book is incredibly profound, enormously thought-provoking, but above all, extremely easy to read. I recommend it to latte-sipping readers everywhere.'

In return for doing this I promise I'll provide you with a quote for the back of your next book.

I look forward to your response.

Regards,

Charles Firth

The key with letters like this is that you've got to talk to people on an equal footing – pundit to pundit. I admit it might sound a little sycophantic in parts, but that's actually how it works – punditry is all about the backslapping. So bearing in mind that I spent literally hours slaving over every word to craft a letter that sounded completely authentic and pundit-like, what did he reply with? I'll show you. It's not as if it'll take you very long to read.

Hi Charles, thanks for asking, but I'm afraid I don't do quotes. Good luck with it though. I'd like to see the end product.
Best wishes, G

'I'd like to see the end product'?? What a brush-off! I mean, it wasn't as if I was asking for his left kidney. Of course, what George didn't realize was that I'd be able to get a great squib out of it anyway – break it down and add a few ellipses, and hey presto: 'Charles . . . the . . . Best' – George Monbiot. But still – it was becoming clear there were insiders and outsiders in the pundit industry. Frankly, George made me feel like a bit of a nobody.[5]

The more emails I sent, the clearer it became that the punditry community was not going to be any help. Paul Krugman, Paul Kennedy, even Thomas Friedman gave me the cold shoulder. In a way I suppose I should have taken it as a compliment – I was a young commentator, nipping at the heels of the old guard, doing ground-breaking research while all they could do was wallow in their fame and success. If I had been in their position, I'd probably have done the same.

Nevertheless, as I sat in that overflow room at Donald Rumsfeld's lecture, my doubts about my original plan to write a weighty tome began growing. It was finally dawning on me that the established commentariat elites were unwilling to give space to an unknown outsider with no qualifications.

Donald Rumsfeld, it turned out, was a pretty shoddy speaker, but his message was exhilarating. The speech was called 'New Realities in a Media Age' and its central contention was that the problems in

---

[5] It's not even as if George was my first choice for a squib. My first choice was, of course, Edward Gibbon, the guy who wrote the definitive account of empire *The History of the Decline and Fall of the Roman Empire*. As it turned out, Edward Gibbon was incredibly hard to contact (he didn't even have an email address), so I eventually ended up having to post a letter to his publisher (Penguin Classics), but he never even replied.

Iraq and the Middle East stemmed from bad marketing. America simply wasn't getting its message across.

'Today we're engaged in the first war in history – unconventional and irregular as it may be – in an era of emails, blogs, cell phones, BlackBerrys, Instant Messaging, digital cameras, a global Internet with no inhibitions, hand-held video cameras, talk radio, 24 hour news broadcasts, satellite television. There's never been a war fought in this environment before,' Donald told us.

He painted a stark picture of America's inability to cope with this information revolution. The way he saw it, the product that they'd launched (ie, the war on terror), was meeting resistance in the market-place. Unfortunately, despite early indications of a strong market acceptance, the pitch had poor follow-through, and there were logistical problems in the actual deployment of the product in key segments which meant that other competitors had come in with a different product (ie, Islamic fundamentalism).

'Our enemies have skillfully adapted to fighting wars in today's media age,' stumbled Donald, 'but for the most part we, our country, our government, has not adapted. Consider that the violent extremists have established media relations committees – these are terrorists and they have media relations committees that meet and talk about strategy, not with bullets but with words.' In Donald's narrative, Karl Rove was being out-Roved by the terrorists themselves. 'They've proven to be highly successful at manipulating the opinion elites of the world. They plan and design their headline-grabbing attacks using every means of communication to intimidate and break the collective will of free people.'

Donald went on to explain that Islamic fundamentalism was spreading because it was being promoted on all the top-rating satellite channels in Iraq and across the Middle East. If America could make inroads into this market, and steal substantial ratings away from those channels, then the product they were trying to sell would gain greater acceptance.

'What complicates the ability to respond quickly is that, unlike our enemies, which propagate lies with impunity with no penalty whatsoever, our government does not have the luxury of relying on other sources for information – anonymous or otherwise. Our government has to be the source, and we tell the truth.' A parlous state of affairs – to rely only on the truth in this day and age.

Luckily Donald had a solution. Rather than continuing to rely on traditional media outlets to get America's message across, the Pentagon, he announced, was setting up a New Media Unit to produce content that subtly integrated America's message into dramas and soaps, and online social networks. The Defense Force was getting into the business of blogging.

'Soon after the devastating earthquakes in Pakistan, I had occasion to fly over the areas where entire sides of mountains had collapsed because of the quake, and entire cities and villages were gone and just rubble, where the roofs had all just collapsed down to the ground and there were no walls left.'

And so what did Donald do? He dispatched a 'rapidly deployable communication team' – a crack squad of highly trained elite spin-doctors – 'to go into the disaster area.[6] And operating in conjunction with other federal agencies and the US embassy, they worked directly with the commander who was in charge of the humanitarian effort there to help focus the attention on the US government's truly extraordinary commitment to helping the Pakistani people.'

And thus a natural disaster which killed 79 000 people was a public-relations triumph for the US, something that was confirmed after pollsters were also dispatched to the disaster zone. 'Public

---

[6] By the way, if you're still in any doubt about whether I'm making this up, I promise I'm not. http://www.cfr.org/publication/9900/. In fact, to avoid any confusion, I've set up a website that documents all the primary evidence (emails, weblinks, blog entries) I used to write this book: www. AmericanHoax.com.

opinion surveys taken by private groups in Pakistan before and after the earthquake suggest that public attitudes in that country regarding the United States changed dramatically because of the new awareness by the Pakistani public,' boasted Donald.

In fact, the campaign was so effective, it even boosted merchandising opportunities. 'It was not long before the favorite toy in Pakistan was a small replica of a Chinook helicopter – they were just everywhere in that country – because of the many lives that our helicopters saved and the mountain of relief supplies that they delivered.'

As Donald proudly waved his hands above the podium to convey the size and shape of the little toy helicopters he'd helped bring to market, I had an epiphany. In a world of Pentagon-funded crack squads of spin-doctors, writing a weighty tome was entirely the opposite of what I should be doing! If the US Defense Secretary could stand in front of a crowd with an entirely straight face and boast about sales of toy helicopters riding on the back of disaster aid, then a work of nonfiction was going to be completely insufficient to describe the reality in which he and his fellow Americans existed.

2

A 2.0 BOOK IN A 3.0 WORLD

I call this new phase Globalization 3.0
because it followed Globalization 2.0
Thomas Friedman, *The World is Flat*

In the olden days of what commentator Thomas Friedman calls Globalization 2.0 (that is, before the World Wide Web) it could take pundits months or even years just to write one book. It's hard to imagine now, but Edward Gibbon spent twelve years writing *The History of the Rise and Fall of the Roman Empire*. Compare this to Thomas's latest book *The World is Flat*, which he wrote while waiting in the check-in queue at JFK airport. With advances in information technology, books can now be written, printed, distributed and remaindered all within a matter of weeks. Sometimes the writing is removed from the process altogether. Thomas has outsourced his next book to an Indian transcription service, which will deliver a completed manuscript that is twice as pompous for one-tenth of the price he would have charged. Likewise, for her next book, *GenderShock!*, Naomi Klein apparently just wrote out a list of bullet points and then used the AutoRender function in Microsoft Word XP. Of course, Noam Chomsky is well ahead of his time and hasn't written any of his books for years.

In the 1980s Paul Kennedy spent a lot of time writing *The Rise and Fall of the Great Powers*, essentially arguing that America's demise was imminent. Back then, Kennedy was expected to back up his abstract assertions about the American Empire with rigorous historical analysis. He spent years pondering primary evidence, weighing the data and synthesizing facts. In short, it was a job that only a jolly smart fellow from Oxford with a PhD in extreme cleverness could ever hope to undertake.

Anyone who attempted to follow Paul's writing methods these days would be committing commercial suicide. If that book was published today, as soon as rival publishers got a whiff of its success, they'd rush off to print similar titles that would fragment the readership and steal valuable market share. *Falling Great Powers* by Peter Kennedy, *The Rise and Rise of Great Powers* by Paul Kenneth, and of course an attack-dog book *Why Paul Kennedy is a Nerdy, Skinny Pseudo-Intellectual* by Molly Franken.

Nowadays, Paul Kennedy would be advised by his publisher to take a slightly different tack. In the time it took him to write an old-style rigorous book, nowadays he could have written five books without leaving his search engine. Sure, they might not be as individually full of knowledge as the one he did write, but even if he only sold half as many of each book, he would still have sold two and a half times more copies in total than he did with *Rise and Fall*.

Take, for instance, the Homer quote that kicked off the first chapter. Whereas in previous eras it might have taken a classical education to recount that obscure quote, I actually took it from the first website I ever visited to write this book. I typed in 'quote homer illyad' into Google, and then Google said to me 'Did you mean: quote homer iliad' and so I clicked on the correct spelling and the sixth entry read 'Homer – The Iliad Quotes – Literary Quotes About Homer – The Iliad . . .' That sounds perfect, I thought, and pinched the first quote I came across on the website.

By massively cutting down the effort required to produce a book, Globalization 3.0 has substantially lowered the barriers to entry into the marketplace of ideas, which previously excluded thousands of writers. Writing books is no longer the exclusive domain of the 'expert' but is open to anyone who has a strident opinion. This is all good news – especially for those of us who aren't jolly smart fellows from Oxford. As far as Donald was concerned, however, the US military was yet to catch up.

While the Pentagon remained stuck in the plodding ways of Globalization 2.0, the Islamic jihad movement was exploiting Globalization 3.0. 'Regrettably,' Donald told us, 'many of the news channels being watched through these [satellite] dishes are extremely hostile to the West. The growing number of media outlets in many parts of the world still have relatively immature standards and practises that too often serve to inflame and distort, rather than to explain and inform.'[7]

A few months previously, the Lincoln Group and the Pentagon had been criticized by Congress for paying Iraqi newspapers to run pro-American news items. But, Donald said, that was exactly what the US should be doing more of. If America was just prepared to get its message out there a bit more – get a few more pro-war billboards up around Baghdad, a few more opinion pieces about the benefits of US occupation in the Baghdad press, a few more pro-US military viral emails in cyberspace – then victory would be theirs. If only the US military could come up with video podcasts that rated better than the bin Laden tapes, then everything would be fine. And in that battle for hearts and minds, the problem of the war was in the way it had been framed. There had been too much focus on the war itself, rather than the noble ideals it was being waged for. Donald had decided to win the war one opinion piece at a time.

Donald's message struck a chord. I had been trying to write a 2.0 book in a 3.0 world.

In the segmented world of BlackBerrys and blogs, content must be tailor-made for each audience. Rumsfeld understood that Iraqi citizens wouldn't pay much attention to a press release from the US Army, but they would pay attention to the same message if it was dressed up as an opinion piece in their local paper and had the by-line of someone who sounded vaguely Arabic.

---

[7] In case you're confused, he was talking about the Islamic media, not Fox News.

By the same token, a book about America written by unknown Australian 'Charles Firth' was simply never going to engage Americans or make it onto any *New York Times* list, except maybe 'Best Looking Author'. And the people I had been contacting clearly knew that – why bother speaking to an effeminate outsider with a nasal accent?

Furthermore, my idea that the book would be 1300 pages long and very, very earnest ran counter to Donald's wise understanding of how the media worked nowadays. In a world of a billion blogs the truth is arrived at not through 'research' and 'fact-finding' but through thousands of opinion pieces based on information sourced through an Internet search engine.

Clearly, I needed my own crack squad of commentators who could be deployed to pass opinions swiftly enough in this 24 hour world of global communications. And so, as Donald started taking questions, I decided to scrap my earnest tome on empire and embark on what I hoped would be a much easier and, above all, better selling hook for my book.

I would invent five characters – Americans – who would each represent a different segment of American life. These characters would have the CVs and back stories to allow them to seep seamlessly into the background noise of American commentary – and to get an insider's glimpse of America that I could never hope to attain from the outside.

One of them would be a right-wing economist who would try to make it in the world of blogging. Another would be a national security insider who would get a glimpse of the shadowy world of America's defense policy. Another would be a bleeding-heart left-liberal advertising executive who could infiltrate the vibrant world of American left-wing activism. And there'd be a couple of other characters who would cover the various ethnic, class and gender minorities that I'd forgotten to cover with the first three.

I would then unleash them into the blogosphere; they would be able to attend events (if I could just get my American accent up to scratch), and – most importantly – they could go to lots of bars to talk to ordinary Americans in their own tongue. In a world where you only need an email address to exist, why should I limit myself to looking at America with only one pair of eyes?

Implicit in the hook would be a test. Since all the characters would have a standing start, and have only six months to interact with America, whichever character got the furthest would clearly have the most successful opinions about America. After all, as Donald had taught me – it's the battle for the hearts and minds that matters most. And to make sure I arrived at the most accurate result, I would treat my mission like a Barbara Ehrenreich book[8] – it would employ rigorous, scientific methods that were in no way deeply flawed.

In a world where opinion is valued so highly, being able to declare a winner in the final chapter would allow me to draw some incredibly profound and thought-provoking conclusions about America, which would then propel this book into the most highly prized of all publishing categories: the evergreen.

Finally, if the competition was to be a fair one, I decided it must stick rigidly to the modern rules of opinion-gathering. Thus, all the real Americans and institutions that you meet in this book were selected through one process: they were the first result on a Google search. So if at times it feels as though this book is a little light on non-Google-based research, it's not because I'm lazy. Far from it. It's because I'm making an important point about modern research methodology.   * * *

As the talk drew to a close, it became apparent that Donald liked being realistic – and not just about the 'realities of the new information

---

[8] For those of you who don't know, Barbara Ehrenreich has written a couple of books in which she goes deep undercover to get jobs in working and middle America, and experiences cleaning toilets first-hand. Let me make it very clear that I have no intention of doing anything like that, although Barbara is welcome to come and clean my toilet any time she wants.

era'. During the Q&A session he was asked about locking people up without trial at Guantanamo Bay. Donald went straight to the point: 'We shouldn't close Guantanamo. We have several hundred terrorists, bad people; people if they went back out on the field would try to kill Americans. That's just a fact. And to close that place and pretend that merely there's no problem, it just isn't realistic . . .' At times he was almost shouting with the conviction and passion of someone who has dedicated all 68 years of his life to the single issue of being realistic. Rumsfeld's speciality, it turned out, was a single commitment to the idea that the ends justify the means.

It suddenly became apparent what was so special about this company executive turned political apparatchik turned corporate consultant that allowed him into the inner sanctum of the White House. Donald, it turns out, is a true believer. A true believer in being realistic. Donald thumped the table. As he did so, his hand caught the microphone, sending a large, fart-like noise through the television speakers. A woman behind me sniggered. As I looked around, Jan and I made eye contact. His eyes widened and he smiled broadly. It felt as though we were watching a teacher get angry in assembly, with the comfort that there was nothing he could do to punish us.

Only the *Economist* journalists – the prefects – remained emotionless. Donald waited until the microphone stopped rattling and then returned to his hokey brand of realism to justify his decision to lock up hundreds of men without trial. 'The idea that you could just open the gates and say, "Gee, fellows, you're all just wonderful" is not realistic. We live in a tough world.'

Despite my best attempts, I didn't manage to get an exclusive quote from the man for page 221. At one point during a particularly boring question, I snuck into the toilet right next to the main auditorium in which the conference was being held. Unfortunately the doors were closed and there were two tall people loitering around outside. I briefly considered pretending to be a secret service agent by flashing my metrocard while self-importantly whisking through the doors, but I decided it probably wasn't the best idea. I simply wasn't tall enough. So I asked if I could go into the main auditorium. 'No, sir,' the tall guard said. 'Please,' I asked meekly. He didn't reply.

We all filed out pretty quickly after the thing ended. It was 2.30 pm and everyone had to get back to work, although I suspect most people were going to spend the rest of the afternoon chatting by the water cooler: 'I saw Donald Rumsfeld talk at lunch,' and so on. Even pasty old men like Donald have one of the trappings of celebrity: gossip-worthiness.

As I walked up the pavement, five black vehicles with blindingly bright flashing halogen headlines raced down the street, led by a police car in full wail. Which struck me as odd. Did Donald Rumsfeld go everywhere with a police siren wailing? Wouldn't that get on your nerves after a while? I was glad, I reflected, that I had chosen to become a commentator (or, indeed, five of them). Nobody tries to kill pundits – there's no point. Even if you make it into the main auditorium, you end up asking fairly lame questions in order to keep your seat in there. As Jan the blogger explained, the guys in the main room were 'consensus journalists'.

Donald had spent 90 minutes in front of the media, feeding us the idea that we could change the world. Did Donald himself believe his New Media Unit was the answer to America's woes? Maybe, maybe not; but in the end, I could see Donald thinking that a few fibs to the press didn't matter – it was just a means to the more important goal of keeping the media on side. He had to be realistic.

It was a seductive line of thought. He had opened my eyes to the way the world works. All I had to do was invent five characters and unleash them on America. And if along the way the characters had to tell a few fibs in order to get their opinions out there, it wouldn't matter. I had to be realistic.

3

OPEN SOURCE REALITY

One night, a few months later, there was a moment, lasting two minutes and twelve seconds, when I thought the whole project had come undone. One of the characters I had made up, 'Edward' – a conservative economist from upstate New York – had just finished writing an op-ed piece about a US Congress bill to ban torture. It began:

> It's been a long time coming, but President Bush is now officially out of the Conservative Movement's good books. The nail in the coffin: Bush's needless kowtowing to Senator McCain over a Congressional ban on torture. Don't get me wrong – we all hate torture – especially those who have experienced it. But the ban, supported by Bush, is the silliest piece of legalism since the notorious Civil Rights Act of 1964.

The piece went on to argue that banning torture was impractical and, above all, economically inefficient.

Edward was quite pleased with the piece and he had posted it on several (real) conservative websites. The response to the piece had been warm, though some people on Townhall.com – a large, well-respected conservative website – had criticized Edward for expecting too much of the President. 'No leader has ever done everything that pleased everyone in his party, not even Reagan . . . yet you seem to continue to demand perfection from GW,' wrote one blogger, Malia.

Three of the websites Edward had posted the piece on were run by Neal, a retired engineer from Arizona who, mysteriously, would not let anyone know his last name. Edward had spent the past month grooming Neal as a contact, and Neal had responded by mentoring Edward about how to make it in the world of conservative commentary. He had recently put Edward on an email list of conservative bloggers and pundits who shared tips and discussed strategy.

That fateful night, Edward and Neal had struck up an exchange, because Edward was having technical difficulties with his own website. Neal had written back warning Edward against using the preview function because of a software bug. In my enthusiasm about how close the entirely fictional character of Edward was getting to Neal, I quickly emailed back a friendly reply:

> *Oh, right. It kept returning different looking text. Thanks for the tip.*
> *Charles*

It was only as I hit the send button that noticed that I'd absent-mindedly signed my own name. Panic immediately engulfed me. Had I just burnt this extremely promising lead? Indeed, had I burnt Edward? Neal knew other people I had met in the course of my research. If they got wind that the person they knew as Charles Firth – a naïve young Australian who was trying to write a book about America – was also going around masquerading as a gung-ho movement conservative, then the whole thing could come tumbling down. My names – both Charles and Edward (and perhaps some of my other names too) – would be mud. The tangled and increasingly hard-to-keep-track-of web of lies was threatening to unravel completely.

I knew I had to salvage the situation. It would be too risky to just let it slide and hope Neal didn't notice. I needed to take quick action and make the error seem like a slip of the mouse. Suddenly a thought struck me: Charles Krauthammer, a Pulitzer-prize-winning conservative columnist, had been in the press in recent weeks justifying the use of torture. There was no time for a second thought: he would have to become embroiled in my scheming.

Oh right. It kept returning different text. Thanks for the tip.

Charles Krauthammer just emailed me about my article. Isn't that incredible? I don't know which blog he saw it on (I also posted the piece on Townhall.com).

Ed

Neal received the email and didn't bat an eyelid. The project was not over. Indeed, it had only just begun.

* * *

Probably the hardest task in creating the characters was also the first task: to find an appropriately bland name for each of them. For the first one, I didn't want to stretch anyone's credulity too much. I wanted him to be someone who would blend into the background noise of the American punditerati. And so, after weeks of searching around to find a name that evokes only bland reliability, a name that reassures you that nothing particularly offensive nor memorable will ever pass this person's lips, I finally found the perfect solution: Edward McGuire.[9]

Every day Edward is reminded that his career peaked ten years ago. A bulky man with a slightly receding hairline, he has in recent years taken to sporting a patchy ginger beard that makes him look as though he is in the first throes of puberty even though he is 41.

The reminder of the decline of Edward's career comes in the form of a black Dodge Ram that he bought after a particularly juicy consultancy gig in 1996, which involved traveling all around Asia preaching the virtues of market liberalization, until the Asian economic crisis hit and Edward's career crashed faster than the Indonesian stock market. He has wanted to replace the Dodge ever since a newer model came out in 1997, but he hasn't had enough work to justify it.

---

[9] You can email him at edjmcguire@yahoo.com

Nowadays, Edward lives with his wife and two sons in Ithaca. This is because he quite rightly thinks that if people see that he lives in Ithaca they'll assume he is somehow associated with Cornell University. He isn't, although he is on all the email lists to receive invitations to public lectures and university events. In this way he can name-drop Cornell academics when he is talking to people about his work. Though he would never admit it to himself, this is how Edward has lived his entire life – by being proximate to power and knowledge, without possessing it.

Ed, you see, started out as a classic Reagan conservative, a freshman at Ithaca College the same year Ronald came to power. But Ed was actually never very good at academia and within a couple of months he dropped out to run a small satirical newsletter he founded called *Reaganomics Review*. While editing the newsletter he was the darling of radio shock jocks and had dozens of op-eds written about him. In 1984, the *Ithaca Chronicle-Gazette* labeled him 'Reaganite of the Year' – a label Edward wore proudly, despite its derisive intention.

When the administration deregulated the radio industry and dropped the 'Fairness Doctrine' on radio broadcasts, Ed joined the first wave of conservative commentators to take to the airwaves en masse. He set up a gig on his local radio station called 'In the Balance' where he would find examples of anti-Reagan journalism and then insult the authors on air, often delving into details of their private lives. Ironically, a few months after it began, the show was axed after the same deregulation led the station to be sold to a major radio network and all local programming was abolished.

Like Alex Keaton on *Family Ties*, Edward's cheeky conservatism was one of the first responses to what was later called the 'political correctness' of the Left. At a time most people were mocking Reaganomics, Edward was deifying it, but with an edge of sarcasm. Edward's critique of Reaganomics was that it didn't go far enough – that the deficit could be much bigger. Many people thought this a satirical jibe at supply-side economics, but arguably Edward was proved right many years later with the proportionately larger deficits of George W Bush, which allowed Edward to claim to have been right all along. If anything, Edward's training has made him an expert at double-edged commentary – it is never quite clear whether he is saying one thing, or the exact opposite. Edward always enjoys this wiggle room, which makes up for his gaping lack of authentic intellect.

Nowadays, whenever he tries to score a consultancy gig, Edward more than often finds that he is passed up for younger, hungrier, better qualified consultants. In his youth he would have absorbed each rejection, but now he is increasingly railing against the world, and finding himself at odds with those he once looked up to – sometimes he even finds himself thinking that the great conservative thinker William F Buckley is a second-rate know-it-all. Edward has the feeling that he has given more to the conservative movement than it has given back to him. And that wasn't the deal.

After a decade of career stasis, Edward has realized that he wants to recapture the adrenaline rush of being at the center of everything. That is why he's come out from the shadows. He is not quite sure how to do it, but his plan is to re-engage with the world of conservative commentary. That world has moved on since his day and now all the most interesting stuff seems to happen online – so Edward has a lot to learn. But perhaps if he can master that art then he'll finally be able to sell the increasingly out-of-date Dodge.

Almost as soon as Edward came to life[10] I found that I had a soft spot for him. This came as a complete surprise. On the surface,

---

[10] That is, the moment his email address had been set up – thus giving him a verifiable identity that would ultimately lead to him being offered countless credit cards with 23.9% APR, granted special 'only valid for edjmcguire@yahoo.com' car insurance discounts, and invited to Republican Party fundraisers. In a strange way, being advertised at became a very real validation of his existence.

I thought that I would hate Edward. He was lazy, incompetent and, worse, an economist. But perhaps that was what made him so endearing. I'd never known an economist very well before, so it came as a shock to me that Edward earnestly believed all the things he wrote. When he tried to convince me of the economic efficiency of torture, I thought he was joking, but then he produced a spreadsheet that had been written by two Ivy League econometric students which actually *proved* torture was economically justified. Edward never understood why I found the fact that he debated moral issues with spreadsheets so amusing. I don't think I ever really understood why he wanted things like torture to exist anyway. But, perhaps because we understood each other so little, he was a willing ally in helping me penetrate the American conservative movement.

As a result of this fondness, I wanted to make Edward's existence undeniable. Since the only tool that anyone uses nowadays is Google, I figured the only corroborating evidence that Edward needed to prove his existence was to make sure that his entry topped the Google rankings. For this, there is one tool in cyberspace that is truly awe-inspiring. It's called Wikipedia and it describes itself as the 'free encyclopedia that anyone can edit'. With more than 4.9 million entries across 157 languages it is fast becoming the largest encyclopedia in the world, and it is one of the ten most visited websites on earth.

At the time of Edward's cyber-birth, the site – run by the prestigious-sounding WikiMedia Foundation – was still thought of as a leading and innovative example of the noble quest to gather all the world's knowledge and put it into cyberspace. Indeed, a February 2006 study published in the respected journal *Science* claimed that Wikipedia's unique method of collaborative knowledge-gathering – where anyone could edit any page – had, on average, resulted in fewer errors than the Encyclopedia Brittanica. However, Wikipedia has since been rocked by several scandals in which irresponsible people have recklessly exploited the gaping openness to perpetrate hoaxes for their own selfish ends.

So let's look up Edward McGuire on Wikipedia, and see what it has to say.

Born in 1961, Edward McGuire is a non-partisan strategic economist – often on the side of controversy. McGuire was the winner of the 1995 Greenback Letters Essay Competition for a piece entitled 'Ready, Set, Soar' that persuasively argued America's economy was positioned to take full advantage of the peace dividend following the collapse of the Soviet Union. The subsequent Internet boom confirmed his central thesis.

So far so good. I thought it was important right from the start to establish Edward's credibility by making up an award that he had won. And I was also quite delighted by how prescient Edward could be since his bio was able to benefit from the rare privilege of 20/20 hindsight. It went on:

McGuire came to national prominence amongst conservatives when in 1982 he became editor of the nationally distributed satirical news-letter Reaganomics Review which gently ribbed the supply-side deficit financing of the Ronald Reagan's budgets. Even as early as 1982, McGuire was arguing that Japan – not the Soviet Union – posed the United States' greatest medium term strategic threat.

Since the 1990s, McGuire has traveled the world, working with colleges that offer management courses in business administration. He has run training courses specializing in Strategic Economics in places as diverse as Jordan, South Korea and Argentina.

McGuire is currently writing a book which attempts to provide the world with the first econometric analysis of freedom. McGuire lives in Ithaca, New York with his wife and two kids.

Hey presto! Thanks to the gaping openness of the WikiMedia Foundation, and its dedication to content over facts, I had suddenly given Edward McGuire a verifiable past. Furthermore, follow the links and you'll find Wikipedia has this to say about the *Reaganomics Review*:

The Reaganomics Review *was an American <u>conservative</u> satirical newsletter published between <u>1982</u> and <u>1985</u> which gently ribbed the supply-side deficit budget financing of the <u>Reagan</u> era's brand of economics – dubbed 'Reaganomics'. Originally edited by <u>Edward McGuire</u>, the publication was influential in shaping the opinions of a generation of conservative theorists in the Midwest and was arguably instrumental in bringing those conservatives into line with mainstream conservative thought. It was an early champion of free-market liberalization and <u>globalization</u>, which was only just gaining ground at the time.*

Writers for the Review *viewed the deficit budget financing as suicidal from an economic perspective, but were supportive of the strategic nature of the expenditure. The later victory by the United States in the <u>Cold War</u> makes many of their articles remarkably prescient.*

It had a robust letters section which allowed many young conservatives their first chance at serious, public political discussion, including Ann Coulter and Kimberley Mills. But it was the controversial publication of the 'Greenback Letters' that made Reaganomics Review *popular. The letters purportedly came from a senior policy advisor at the <u>White House</u>, though many now believe it was an invention of the youthful editors (who were in their twenties at the time), especially since the identity of 'Greenback' has never been uncovered. Nevertheless an essay competition now exists to pay homage to the Greenback Letters' extraordinary blend of shoot-from-the-hip common sense and informed economic analysis.*

Not only was Edward McGuire a cross-referenced economist, but the largest encyclopedia in the world had called the journal he founded 'remarkably prescient'. What a genius! I'd hire him.

In case that you think this is exploiting a highly ethical project – the WikiMedia project – for my own, admittedly less ethical, ends, then remember that it was perfectly possible for anyone, at any time, to modify any of my Wiki entries and correct them by, say, pointing out that none of the people, events or items described actually existed. In fact that's the whole idea behind WikiMedia.

In fact, if you click on the 'history' tab of an article, you can see a list of everyone who has edited each entry. And if you look at the 'history' tab of the *Reaganomics Review* entry, you'll see that not one but TWO people have edited the entry since I put it up. See, I hear you say, the Wiki system works! But take a look at their edits. Feyday came along and didn't, say, point out that the whole thing was a complete fabrication. Instead he usefully changed the entry from 'Reaganomics review' to 'Reaganomics Review'. And then Jeffq came along and corrected my spelling and punctuation, and added a couple of links.

Not only that but a short time after Edward's entry went in, another Wiki enthusiast trawled through all the Wikipedia's entries in order to compile a comprehensive index of famous American economists and, thoughtfully enough, included Edward's name and entry in it.[11]

So how could people anal enough to dedicate their time to compiling all the world's knowledge in pedantically well-spelled and properly formatted fashion overlook the broader issue of the topic's complete fabrication? Surely they could've spent a little less time fixing up the capitalization and more time, say, making sure the article was true. That was a question that had been worrying me well before Edward's name was put up on Wiki, which is why

---

[11] In case the Wikipedia entries are deleted by the time you read this, I've put screen caps on all the pages from Wikipedia on this book's very own website: www.AmericanHoax.com. That address again is: www.AmericanHoax.com. Check out my range of *American Hoax* merchandise while you're there.

I decided I needed a back-up plan that would fool even the most resourceful Wiki editor.

At the end of the article I knew I had to provide a link to a site outside Wiki, a site that was not immediately about the *Reaganomics Review* or Edward McGuire (that might come across as too suspicious), but something that would corroborate their existence. And so in half an hour one afternoon a long-running and highly prestigious Greenback Letters Essay Competition was born. Now, I won't bore you with all the details of the $40 000 competition – you can browse the website http://abbott.faithweb.com in your own time – but its introduction tells us that:

> *The Greenback Letters Essay Competition has been running since 1985, and was established to promote clear, confident writing in the areas of public administration and economic policy. Awarded every two years, it aims to encourage long-term strategic thinking about the United States' economic policy.*

The competition, in short, was eerily close to the sort of thing Edward would be interested in. Sure enough, if you look closely at the list of winners, you'll see a name you recognize right in the middle of the pack.

2003 – Guy McConnell, 'Marketing the United States Abroad'
2001 – Jeffrey Muriel, 'The China Question'
1999 – Kimberley Mills, 'The Alarm Bells of Freedom'
1997 – Martin Fitzgerald, 'It's the Middle East, Stupid'
1995 – Edward McGuire, 'Ready, Set, Soar'
1993 – Amanda Bundchen, 'The Way Back for US Hegemony'
1991 – Stephen Marsh, 'Berlin Rising'
1989 – (Not awarded)
1987 – Ahmed Al-Ansari, 'Oil's Well'
1985 – E Simon Woolley, 'Prospects of American Power'

Edward prides himself on winning such a prestigious competition. Every bio about him on the web mentions it. If you look him up on Townhall.com it's one of the first things mentioned. Maybe one day, if the public demands it, Edward may even put 'Ready, Set, Soar' up on the web for all to see. It promises to be chillingly prescient.

Of course, now that Edward was a living breathing character he needed something to do. Clearly, the place for any budding conservative commentator to start out was one of the thousands of conservative websites that churn out a seemingly endless stream of opinions each day. Edward figured that there was no limit to the amount of content these websites could absorb. And so, one night, with Fox News on in the background, Edward sat down in his pokey study on the second floor of his semidetached house in Ithaca and started browsing through scores of websites, from Common Conservative.com ('Practical Conservatism for the Common Man') through to NewsBusters.com ('Exposing and Confronting Liberal Media Bias') and PeoplePolitical.com ('Where it's okay to be RIGHT').

'Pretty hokey,' I said to Edward as he logged onto PeoplePolitical.com.

'What do you mean?' said Edward defensively.

I explained that I was surprised by how hokey the slogans were and just how amateurish the design of most of the sites were.

'They're authentic,' he explained. 'They're just not as well funded as the liberals in the mainstream media.'

If Edward was right, then it appeared to me that an arms race in authenticity had broken out, each site competing to be more 'authentic' than the next. Common Conservative, for example, was little more than a sparse single page, with the headline and by-line of each article, and a link to each article. The design skills seemed to extend only to the use of the bold and italics function which was used intermittently in no discernible pattern. Underneath the title graphic of the website, ran a small statement of purpose.

Our website offers Republican and Libertarian perspectives on the modern political battlefield. We attack liberalism with both barrels blazing. No syllable-writing contests. No snooty highbrow smugness. Just commentary written by regular people like you.

Even after seeing dozens of websites like this, it still wasn't clear to me whether they were being designed to look home-grown or whether they were indeed as hokey as they looked. Edward, of course, assured me that they were simply done by people like himself – who just wanted to share their views and weren't concerned with being slick. And, he pointed out, not all of them were like that. TownHall.com, for example, was a very professional looking website run by an organization called the Heritage Foundation. It was clearly run by professional webmasters and even included a 'Soapbox' section where amateur pundits could post their own articles.

One of the commentators that kept popping up on numerous websites was Vincent Fiore, who came across as the ultimate opinion follower. In the week when every other conservative commentator was complaining about George Bush's Supreme Court nomination, Vincent wrote an article 'Did Bush Blink on Supreme Court Pick?' In the week when every conservative commentator was complaining about anti-war protestor Cindy Sheehan, Vincent wrote a column entitled 'Go Home, Cindy'. All he seemed to be doing was regurgitating that week's spin, and yet somehow his articles seemed to dominate the front page of so many websites. Regurgitating spin was something Edward knew he could do.

Edward glanced at his Executive™ Travel Clock that he'd bought in a Skymall catalogue on the flight home from Indonesia back in 1996. It was edging past midnight in New York (11 am in Jakarta). His wife and kids had gone to sleep hours ago. Even so, Edward logged into TownHall.com's 'Soapbox' and posted his first article.

4

BRAND WARS

It was only shortly after moving to America that I discovered most Americans hate the notion that they're an empire. 'I'm writing a book,' I told Paul, a tall man, with strikingly dark eyes. His mop of messy dark hair worked well against his tanned skull. Paul was a 28-year-old marketing executive who was almost – but not quite – as crap as me at pool.

We were in a dive in the East Village. It was early evening and there were half-a-dozen other patrons sitting on wonky wooden stools along the bar. Tacked to the walls were old snapshots of bartenders standing next to celebrities who had visited the joint. The most famous one was Alec Baldwin, whose beaming smile looked at least 40% genuine. It was the type of bar that should have been filled with smoke – especially beneath the white glow of the pool-table light – but New York's recent smoking ban gave this genuine dive of a bar a slightly inauthentic atmosphere.

It was my first night out in New York and I needed some company.

'What's the book about?' asked Paul, whose current job was to sell Cingular brand mobile phones to people in the 13–18 year old bracket. At college he had studied 'all the greats' in his marketing course. Paul told me that he held the most admiration for the tobacco companies. 'It was wrong. But they did it so well!' he exclaimed, only half-joking.

'Umm. The book. The book's about the American Empire,' I told him.

'America's an empire?' Paul asked in genuine disbelief.

'Yeah, I think so.'

'It's news to me.'

Valuing his companionship, and not wanting to get snubbed on my first night out, I decided to leave it there. But it was a genuine revelation. Here I was, talking to a man who was living in the heart of liberal America. It would be hard to find someone the right-wing shock-jocks would be more likely to call 'French' than Paul. He grew up in Boston, the birthplace of liberal America; he lived on the lower east side of New York, the crotch of liberal America; but both he and his girlfriend repeatedly denied America was an empire.

Having surveyed two Americans and come to the scientifically valid conclusion that 100% of Americans did not think of America as an empire, I asked Paul whether it was alright to put him in the book. 'Yeah, as long as you make me a bit taller with darker features.'

As we bar-hopped across lower Manhattan, from the dive bar to the KGB Bar – which traded on gulag chic and cheap vodka (of course) – to a hole-in-the wall wine bar on 2nd Street which charged $13 a glass for Australian merlot, the conversation/survey became wedged in my increasingly drunk brain. 'One of the Great Tasks for the American Punditerati in the 21st Century,' I slurred as I knocked over a glass of the house rioja ($11), 'is to work out a way to reconcile America's image of itself as "not an empire" when it has 950 bases in 170 countries across the world.' Paul and his girlfriend stared at me blankly. Paul ordered another rioja from the bartender.

Of course, it's not surprising that 100% of Americans surveyed would consider their country anything but an empire. For the past 200 years America has repeatedly re-branded itself in order to avoid having to look at itself as an empire – with impressive results. The first brand of non-empire was the Monroe Doctrine two hundred years ago which, innocently enough, claimed that any time America's military intervened in South America, it was only doing so out of self-defense; the Cold War told the story of Communists taking over the world, threatening America's way of life in all reaches of the globe, which also happened to place America in the immediate path of all sorts of conflicts all around the world. Every event was interpreted through the overarching narrative: that America was under threat. It was, in short, a great piece of marketing.

But since the end of the Cold War America's opinion leaders have struggled to come up with a convincing story about why America remains a non-empire. A lot of them understand the project, but none – not even Thomas Friedman with his Globalization 3.0 – have so far hit the nail on the head. They know their task: what they have to do is convincingly blur the distinction between the defense of America and defense of the American way of life. They have to make Americans at home feel threatened by events happening many thousands of miles away.

The War on Terror is the latest storyline that immediately makes Americans feel threatened no matter where the terrorists are hanging out. Understandably it worked in the aftermath of 9/11 because it was pretty easy to draw a line between Osama living in Afghanistan and his attempts to kill American office workers. Problem is it has since run into trouble in Iraq. The link between Saddam, WMD and terrorism is just too tenuous – and the political consensus has started to break down. The White House tried to fudge some idea about the WMD falling into terrorist hands, but it didn't work. The story didn't fit properly. The War on Terror needs to be rebranded – and fast.

Luckily, there is an upside to all of this. It means there is a massive opportunity to be the guy who comes up with the marketing catchphrase – ideally one that encapsulates the way America conducts itself over the next fifty years. Get it right and you can shoot straight to the dizzy heights of the guy who coined the phrase 'Cold War'. In terms of kudos in wine bars, that's better than being the guy who invented the term 'extra mild' to describe cigarettes that contain 8 mg of tar.

May I therefore introduce my second character – Dr Andrew O'Keefe – a charming and fit 50-year-old conservative scholar with one mission in life: to work out how to describe America's role in the world without mentioning the word empire. Dr Andy's guiding principle is that America is just an honest broker trying to make it in a dangerous world. If anything, he believe it is America who has been exploited by the rest of the world.

Always the self-improver, Dr Andy's journey begins in the self-help section of his local Borders. Many a time Anthony Robbins has helped him with a flash of inspiration about how to justify the invasion of a country, or how to avoid Congressional oversight of a certain military mission.

Dr Andy is much higher up the food chain than Edward has ever climbed. He is the Emeritus Director of the Lamarck Institute, a small think-tank based in Alexandria, Virginia – a short drive from DC. The Lamarck Institute mainly conducts private research for defense contractors attached to the Pentagon. However, unlike many defense contractors, Dr Andy is not an ex-army officer or former marine. Having grown up during the Vietnam War, he was lucky enough to avoid the call. Or perhaps it wasn't just luck: nobody seems to know his birth date. Indeed, there is a lot about Dr Andy that remains secret, such as most of his work. If you go to the Lamarck Institute's website (www.thelamarck.org), you will see that many of the research papers can only be accessed by patron donors who have received a specially encrypted CD-ROM to access the website.[12]

A tall, lean man with a square face, Dr Andy jogs four or five times a week and has a black belt in the Israeli martial art of Krav Maga – a particularly vicious form of hand-to-hand combat. Dr Andy likes to think that this compensates for his lack of military training, but in fact he is overcompensating: many of his ex-officer friends are far fatter and less agile than he is.

---

[12] This has two advantages: 1) Dr Andy can appear to be very prolific without me having to write anything for him; and 2) It lends an air of mystery to him that increases his gravitas, don't you think?

Dr Andy majored in both Cryptography and in Marketing at Harvard, and his doctoral dissertation was entitled 'Pearl Harbor: the Greatest Product Launch in Military History?'. Unfortunately even today nobody knows Dr Andy's precise argument in the PhD because it was sealed as 'Top Secret' shortly after he submitted it for marking.

Since university, Dr Andy has had only one work-related success that is sufficiently declassified to allow him to drop it into dinner-party conversation. And it is this: during the US's overthrow of Noriega in Panama, he came up with the idea of rebranding the invasion as an 'intervention'. This idea won him a 'Silver Penta Gong' at the annual Defense Force's Night of Nights in 1990.

One of the reasons why Dr Andy has found himself back in the self-help section of his local Borders is that for the first time in his successful career he has felt himself being edged to the outer. In the field of foreign relations, having a PhD and an emeritus directorship is proving simply not enough: increasingly everyone Dr Andy is competing against on the lecture circuit is an ex-military officer who has been on tours of duty. There's no showbiz in a rigorous old PhD.

If you were CNN, who would you rather hire: Dr Andy O'Keefe, unknown academic, or say, Ken Robinson, ex-Army Ranger and now Hollywood producer, who can speak about the two decades he spent in all the hotspots across the globe, from Iraq to Iran to Venezuela? The answer is Ken Robinson – which is why he's their intelligence analyst while Dr Andy gets rejection letters from the *Pittsburgh Gazette-Post*.[13] Unless you've tried to overthrow at least one Venezuelan president, CNN's not interested.

As he stood in the bookstore, Dr Andy decided it was time to undertake the 13-step process to truthfully analyze his Self-

---

[13] Actually, that's a sort of lie. All he received was an automated rejection letter from their email server. Andy didn't know how to take that – is that better or worse than human-based rejection?

Actualization Quotient (SAQ), as one book suggested. And as he did, it quickly became clear to him that he never wanted to be a pundit anyway. With a lifetime of classified work behind him, the SAQ allowed him to SelfGlimpse™ that limelight can be fleeting. His SAQ revealed the Inner Knowledge that one word in the right ear was worth a thousand on paper. However, it also revealed that Dr Andy had one Belief Rabbit that he must pursue if he was to find his Inner Greyhound. His Belief Rabbit was this: that the way America looked at itself was broken, and that he had the opportunity to fix this. If he could come up with a way to justify America's foreign policy without mentioning the word empire, then that would be a lasting contribution not only to his own legacy, but to his country.

Dr Andy emerged from the Borders in downtown Alexandria a changed man. Holding copies of *Where's My Rabbit?*, *Don't Think of a Rabbit* and *Who Smelled My Rabbit?* he beamed at me as he got into his gray 2006 Lexus. This was good news. For the previous few weeks Dr Andy had been searching for a reason to exist. Always a perfectionist, he had repeatedly told me that if he was going to be in my book he wanted to do something bold and inspiring. Unfortunately, he claimed that most of his ideas were so classified he didn't have clearance to think about them, let alone put them into practise. Despite Dr Andy's impressive CV, I feared he was turning out to be a bit of a dud. I had begun to wonder whether he was using his security clearance to mask the fact that he actually didn't have any good ideas. As it turned out, that was the very least of my worries.

'At some point in your life you have to step up to the mark or get out of the game,' Andy told me earnestly as he drove me back to his apartment. 'There is a fifteen-minute moment when your true strength of character is severely tested. In the face of extreme duress, some people crumble and make expedient decisions they will regret for the rest of their lives; others, like me, make heroic decisions that will project them into the annals of history.' He sounded a little messianic, but I hadn't seen him in such a good mood for weeks, so I decided not to dampen his spirit. I thought to myself what a stroke of genius it had been to let him go to Borders for a few hours. It had totally transformed him.

'I have made such a decision,' Dr Andy said. 'I have decided to go to Iraq.'

Inside me something stirred. It was my Belief Rabbit and it was having a heart attack.

5

THE MESSAGE IS IN
THE MEDIAN

Darryl sat and waited in Terminal 3 at Los Angeles airport. A month before, an effeminate Australian guy who couldn't do an American accent to save his life had phoned and told him that he was going to write a book about him, but nothing had materialized. Then suddenly last weekend the man had rung again and told Darryl that he'd be arriving on Tuesday at LAX, and could he meet him there? Luckily it was fairly easy for Darryl to take Tuesdays off, so he'd caught the eight-hour Greyhound bus from Phoenix to LA to meet Charles Firth (coincidentally enough, that effeminate Australian happened to be me) at the airport.

I walked through the final long corridor of cascading automatic doors which provide a misleadingly efficient introduction to the LAX baggage claim area. In a previous era when going through such high-tech glass enclosures, I used to worry about whether I had accidentally stashed a couple of kilos of cocaine in my hand luggage. But now I was more worried about whether my sweaty palms betrayed me as having some sort of subconscious but highly illegal connection with al-Qaeda.

Over the phone, Darryl had described himself to me as a chubby man with a mop of mousy hair. Unfortunately, this being Southern California, there were about ten men fitting that description in the baggage claims area alone. After a couple of false starts I approached a man in a NASCAR T-Shirt with a highly airbrushed photo of a driver looking deadly serious.

'Darryl?'

'No. Sorry pal.'

I turned to walk away.

'I mean . . . yes. That's my name!' he said and laughed.

I turned back to him and put out my hand to shake his, but instead Darryl stepped deep inside my personal space and hugged me. Being somewhat taller than me, he pressed my face into his armpit. It lacked deodorant.

He was carrying a 64-ounce container of frozen cola from his local 7-11 which he spilt down my shoulder as he hugged. As he pulled out of the embrace, his official Barry Bonds[14] baseball cap fell off. He bent down to pick it up and his tracksuit pants stretched to reveal the tip of his considerable arse cleavage. The rest of his frozen drink spilt across the white linoleum.

'Oops. Let's get out of here.'

He made a dash for the exit, almost slipping on the freshly iced floor, and blithely leaving a trail of sticky footprints for someone else to clean up. With no other choice, I tiptoed around Darryl's wet patch and followed after him.

Having brought to life two middle-class conservatives, I'd come to LA because I figured it was time to formulate a character on behalf of the vast swathes of Americans who, in a previous era, would have called themselves working class. Unfortunately, within hours of meeting him, I was disappointed to learn that, like many Americans who scrape by on minimum wage plus tips, Darryl in fact considered himself middle class. He even wore Nike shoes (sticky ones) to prove it.

---

[14] Barry Bonds is a baseball player who recently surpassed Babe Ruth's home run record. Darryl is a passionate supporter of this controversial big hitter. He can talk forever on the topic if you're foolish enough to get him started. To Darryl it is irrelevant that Barry Bonds took performance-enhancing drugs to pass Babe Ruth's record. Darryl himself has failed several workplace drug tests over the years and considers the fact that Barry Bonds got away with it for so long a worthy achievement in itself.

Being a member of the working class, I'd assumed he would be the book's friendly, genial character. You know, a down-to-earth, salt-of-the-earth type of guy, who provided the slip-over-on-the-white-linoleum-floor slapstick while the more serious characters got on with the business of running the world. After all, surely including Darryl at all in the book was good enough. Generally people like him don't even make it into the footnotes of important history books, or at least ones that aren't written by Howard Zinn.[15]

But almost immediately my rendering of Darryl was leaving a lot to be desired. Rather than the fully fleshed-out character that would win me a Booker prize, Darryl was a litany of boring clichés – little more than a cross between Chris Farley and John Candy. It became very apparent that all my reference points for affable working-class Americans came directly from stereotypes portrayed in early 80s comedies.

Of course, you might think that represents a failure of imagination on my part, but I prefer to see it as some sort of profound metaphor for the way people like Darryl are invisible in this celebrity-obsessed world. Or perhaps it is timidity – I've never had the guts to walk up to the tough guys in the dive bars in the Deep South and ask them whether they're interested in being my friend. Whatever the reason, Darryl ended up being a male version of Paris Hilton if she didn't have any money and nobody knew who she was. That is to say, utterly uninteresting.

In order to help me flesh out Darryl, so I could create his character without my knowing anyone like him, I came up with a highly scientific system: the Statistical Character Generator. The SCG creates a character based entirely on the median of all the polling

---

[15] Howard Zinn is one of those incredibly worthy commentators. Most famously he is author of the *People's History of America* which you're supposed to find illuminating because it's all about the people who *weren't* making the Big Decisions when all the Big Decisions were being made.

done within a given demographic. In other words, Darryl is the demographic Everyman. Given the habits of low-income white men, his favorite show is *American Idol*, and he buys Coke from drink machines but Pepsi from the supermarket. He is loyal to his brand of margarine, and he always votes for the president who wins.

Being an SCG character, Darryl is completely malleable in his opinions and consumer preferences – just the way demographers like to think of everyone. His favorite fast food joint is Chipolatas, but if you put together a convincing marketing campaign for KFC, he'd be there in an instant.

Darryl, 31, was born in the very middle of America, in St Louis, Missouri. His father was a bus driver. To make ends meet, Darryl's mother worked in a Duane Reade drug store, four days a week. His family's average income was always under $30 000 per year, putting him squarely in the bottom 30% of households by income.

Unfortunately, Darryl is one of the 30% of Americans who use the Internet less than once a year. This means that it will probably be an uphill struggle for him to compete against the other characters in the battlefield of ideas. But that is alright because Darryl's political desires are not to participate but merely react to whatever message politicians put on the agenda. In other words, he behaves in exactly the way pollsters and politicians assume people behave. The considerable contempt that Darryl harbors for politicians comes across in the polling as a kind of folksy disinterest in the political process.

Because the vast majority of the data used in my ground-breaking SCG process came from consumer polling, Darryl's desires were somewhat consumer-focused. In fact, I was a little bit worried that, according to the figures, his overriding desire – above even finding love – was to own a large car. But for Darryl that made total sense. The kudos that flows from owning a large car would bring, he assumed, an attractive woman to ride in the passenger seat, and ultimately, he would end up owning a family mini-van – complete with a good-looking set of children to ride in the back.

Unfortunately, Darryl's consumer desires were mitigated by the fact that, as an average American, he owed $12 000 in credit card debt. It was spread across three cards, all of which were currently maxed out. He rarely missed a payment, but the payment was usually the minimum amount – with a 23% interest rate he was paying $200 a month and going nowhere (certainly not in a car). Behind accommodation, interest payments to finance companies were his second biggest expense. He spent about $5 a day on food: cereal, 99c meals, noodles, KFC and pizza were all staples.

Almost immediately, Darryl and I didn't get along. Frankly, I had expected him to have some sort of car – this was America, after all, where even working-class characters could afford their own wheels. But Darryl's statistically-accurate (but extremely inconvenient) gambling habit meant that he'd had to sell his car about a year ago.

I told Darryl that he was in charge, that he should just behave normally and I'd tag along to find out what it was like to be an ordinary American consumer. Darryl explained that he didn't 'normally' come to LA and that if it were his choice he'd head straight to the Greyhound terminal downtown and catch an overnight bus back to Phoenix. There was one leaving at 2 am and it would be easily the cheapest thing to do – the bus fare cost $40, and a motel would set us back at least $50.

As much as I enjoy the gritty reality of uncomfortable travel, the thought of spending another five hours on the bus after catching a ten-hour non-direct flight from New York was not entirely attractive. When I pointed this out to him, Darryl just shrugged and walked over to the hotel-directory board. After a quick survey he rang the cheapest-looking Super 8 motel. A man with a thick Asian accent answered, telling Darryl to go and wait underneath the red 'hotel shuttle bus' sign, which we did.

As we waited I explained to Darryl the reason that he'd been selected to be one of the characters in this book: 'You're an ordinary American.'

Oddly enough, he was insulted. He explained that even though he was an SCG character, now he'd been created he planned on taking on a life of his own. 'Just because you've got some fancy figures about me doesn't make me a simpleton. I'm still a human being,' he said as he munched on his favorite new snack – a packet of bite-sized Oreos, a sugary treat that could be consumed in much the same way as a packet of chips, but with a far greater risk of diabetes.

Darryl claimed that far from being a slapstick sideshow, he intended on proving that an average consumer was just as important in a tale about America as a national security insider or conservative economist commentator.

'But Darryl, you don't even use the Internet,' I said, trying to manage his expectations about what he could realistically achieve with no money and a central desire that required tons of the stuff.

Darryl was defensive. He'd had some contact with the Internet before. One of the regulars at the bar often brought in print-outs of emails he received, like '100 Things You Shouldn't Say to Your Wife'. Some of them were pretty funny.

'Besides, the point is: fuck you,' he said. 'I'm not ordinary. I'm Darryl Summers. I'm as real as anyone else.'

I decided to change the topic. 'What are you going to do tomorrow? I reckon we should do something in LA before we head back to Phoenix.' He lifted his eyebrows at my use of the word 'reckon'. I explained to him I wanted him to do something that he would normally do. Darryl didn't have many ideas. He usually just hung out at home.

But there was one thing that got him out of the house. Being a statistically-accurate median character, Darryl particularly loved the most popular participation sport in America: ten-pin bowling.

He would take me to do something which sociologists have claimed is a sign of the inherent alienation of modern capitalism –

bowling alone.[16] And we would do it at the cheapest alley he knew in LA, in the heart of South Central – home of the LA riots.

'Wow!' I said to Darryl. 'Wow!' I wondered whether a trip to Iraq and South Central LA in the one book was a bit of Dangerous Situation Overkill. My stomach was rising up through my chest and grabbing the back of my neck. 'Are you sure you wouldn't prefer to go to Disneyland?'

---

[16] This is true. Sociologists spent most of the 1990s musing about the social significance of the decline of league bowling and the consequential rise of people who chose to bowl on their own, wondering whether it pointed to the tragic alienation inherent in capitalism or some other decline in the fabric of modern society. But apparently no-one analyzing this phenomenon ever bothered to actually go bowling alone. Until now.

6

EMAILING FOR CHANGE

In contrast to the rugged looks of Darryl, the fourth character, Bertrand Newton, is a short, deeply middle-class man. His dark-rimmed beady eyes and rough-shaven look is supposed to exude a kind of up-all-night importance, but instead just makes you suspect he smells a bit. Bertrand talks constantly on his BlackBerry, and even takes his laptop to nightclubs so that he can strategise 24/7. He carries his computer in a very small, purpose-made laptop bag, so that you know immediately his laptop must be very small. In short, the Bertrand that I have invented to uphold left-liberal[17] opinions in this book is not the sort of person you'd ever feel sorry for. If he stubbed his toe, it would probably make you smile. And yet it was only a short time after Bertrand Newton first came to life that I started to feel sympathy towards him.

It was late afternoon in the dead of winter. Bertrand had no desire to leave the warmth of the Drop Off Service bar on Avenue A for the dirty sludge of New York's half-melted snow. The bar was 'faux dive'; you could tell it was faux because the place was impeccably clean. Bertrand came to Drop Off Service because he didn't stick out amongst the twenty-something crowd, but he stayed for the free Wi-Fi. As he sat peering out into the unwelcoming slush, he

---

[17] There is a rather large translation issue here. The term 'left-liberal' has a significantly different meaning in America than it does in Australia or England – or even in Canada. As far as I can work out, in America the term 'left-liberal' refers to someone who's not particularly left-wing but adopts that name in order to *decrease* the amount of influence they have over any given debate in order to lose it in an heroic but ultimately futile fashion. I have no idea why they do this.

decided to put a toe into the Left's online world and post his first opinion on the *DailyKos* – the Left's largest website, which claims to have 500 000 readers a day.[18] The article he had written was 'Why the Democrats Will Lose in 2008', a 700-word treatise arguing that without an effective strategy (running lots of ads), the Democrats were doomed to remain in semi-permanent opposition.

> *But just like it takes years to establish a brand, political ideas take years to penetrate the population. Without a full scale roll-out of targeted advertising, the Democrats might just as well pack up and go home now . . .*
>
> *This is why I have set up AdBack, a non-profit organization which is dedicated to changing the world one advertisement at a time. It is only by realizing that the agenda is ours to grasp that we will win in 2008.*

After only minutes, Bertrand's foray into liberal strategizing was greeted by a barrage of attacks, most of which were dismissive one-liners about why Bertrand was wrong . . .

- Nathaniel Ament Stone: *God, I'm sick of these types of diaries 'Why Dems will lose', 'Why the Dems suck', 'Why Dems will never win an election again'. You must be quite the fortune-teller to know what politics will be like in 2 years and 10 months.*
- *Newsflash! There is an election this year that could use some attention.*
- DiHinMI: *If you're going to pontificate on politics, you may want to start following it.*

Bertrand's stomach knotted as he endured the angry scattergun of insults designed to make him feel small and the writers feel large. He was ruffled by the hostility. It wasn't that he couldn't stand the heat – he had been involved in politics for the past decade, starting

---

[18] Although I suspect it's in much the same way as I claim to have 50 trillion fans world-wide.

with his controversial involvement in the 'No Blood for Oil' coalition at the Berkeley Campus of the University of California in 1991. The coalition had argued constantly with the Californian Peace Coalition that their demands weren't radical enough. Bertrand had always looked back at those days with fondness. The high point in the campaign – and perhaps his life – had been when he'd moved to rescind a motion that was on the table modifying an amendment to the original motion which, had it passed, would have made the motion end up with almost exactly the same wording as it had at the start of the debate. Several of Bertrand's enemies within the CPC had been confused about the meaning of his last-minute rescission, and the motion had passed despite its overwhelming unpopularity. It was shortly after this that Bertrand and his 'No Blood for Oil' buddies had been expelled from the CPC, splitting the movement irreparably.

But even with his experience in acrimony, Bertrand was a little surprised by the venom that a first-timer attracted on the DailyKos. The message was clear: you may think you're smart, but we're smarter. Bertrand comforted himself with the knowledge that it was, in fact, the other way around.

Bertrand was in his early thirties and yet he had already retired from his initial career path, which was advertising. During the Internet boom he had made a lot of money copywriting ads for dot com companies that no longer existed. And unlike his colleagues, he had not spent the enormous wads of cash on cocaine. In advertising circles he was best known for coming up with a spectacular Super Bowl commercial for a website that depicted over 400 skydivers plummeting to earth in formation while throwing fistfuls of $100 notes out of pink and yellow bags attached to their waist. The 30 second commercial ended with a black screen and the slogan in white text 'The Sky's the Limit'. It was hailed in the press as being 'avant-garde' and 'edgy', and won several Silver Promax awards, especially because it didn't even mention the website's name.

Bertrand's talent lay in his absolute belief that ads were the high art of late 20th Century culture. He believed that since advertising was the most well-funded creative pursuit it attracted the best minds, harnessed the best resources and therefore was the art form that subsequent generations would remember the society by. After quit - ting advertising during the post-boom downturn, Bertrand found himself at a loose end, but with millions of dollars of cash at his disposal. It was then that he decided to use his talents of persuasion for good. He decided he would dedicate his life to bringing the power of modern advertising to the political challenge of changing the world.

The first step for any left-winger, he understood, was to write a manifesto. Thus, in 1994, he published a booklet 'How to Change the World One Ad at a Time', which was now unfortunately out of print.

In his manifesto, Bertrand called for change based around popular slogans rather than taking up unpopular issues which, Bertrand argued, would take up too much time and effort.[19]

Recently, Bertrand had taken the next step and founded AdBack, a non-profit organization 'dedicated to changing the world one ad at a time'. To do this, of course, all he had to do was top the Google rankings. And luckily, if you google Bertrand Newton it turns out that he is the most famous Bertrand Newton in the world – he takes both first and second place. The first, of course, is the link to his Wikipedia entry, which some selfless and no doubt extremely good-looking person has written as their contribution to the collation of all the world's knowledge.

Since I'd already shown Bertrand his own entry on Wikipedia, and since he'd read it several times, he decided to see what the other entry, over at Answers.com, had to say about him.

---

[19] I would quote directly from his manifesto, but as I say, it's out of print. The whole 'out of print' trick is a brilliant one, and I recommend it to anyone wanting to round out their CV. Essentially the 'out of print' system means that Bertrand gets all the kudos of being a published author without having to go to the onerous task of actually writing anything.

Bertrand Newton is founder of the 527 <u>Political Action Committee</u> (PAC) AdBack. Newton is author of the influential booklet on political advertising 'How to Change the World One Ad at a Time' (2004).

AdBack is one of a raft of non-profit companies that were formed to support the <u>Democratic Party</u> in the <u>2004</u> Presidential elections. The non-profit company designed advertisements for several niche markets in the 2004 Presidential elections, including the award-winning 'GayBack' TVC that aired in the crucial swing state of Ohio.

Newton's philosophies on political advertising and organizing methods have their roots in organizations like MoveOn.org and have been closely connected to <u>George Soros</u>'s Open Society Foundation project.

Born in 1972, Newton started out as a student activist in the early 1990s, during which time he got involved in the 'No Blood For Oil' coalition at Berkeley Campus of UCLA which split the movement and ultimately led to his expulsion from the Californian Peace Coalition. He later studied at Oxford University in England.

This was eerily similar to what I had written about him on Wikipedia. Actually, identical. Without doing anything, or actually existing, Bertrand Newton's mildly impressive back story was beginning to spread around the Internet. After a brief survey of the site, Bertrand realized it wasn't perhaps as impressive as it first seemed. Answers.com's entire business model seemed to be premised on simply lifting Wikipedia's gapingly open content and placing context-sensitive advertising down the side of the page. Indeed, it even had entries for lots of stuff that didn't exist, from Edward McGuire to the *Reaganomics Review*. By combining the accuracy of Wikipedia with the integrity of a dot com business model, Bertrand's existence, and indeed much of the content of this book, had become magically cross-referenced, all without ever actually having existed! Bertrand tapped on his BlackBerry in admiration – the Answers.com model was exactly the sort of thing he wished he could think of – but for politics.

Bertrand's intention with AdBack was to raise large amounts of money from 'ordinary people' and foundations, and then use it to run advertisements telling people what to think. But before he did that, Bertrand had to connect with the existing left in America.

And so, as he sat alone with his laptop in the made-for-six booth of Drop Off Service, Bertrand surfed every left-wing website he could find. Almost immediately he noticed a stark difference between left-wing websites and conservative ones. To Bertrand's approval, progressive websites placed enormous emphasis on doing stuff. For every issue Bertrand could think of, there were at least half-a-dozen devoted websites. Not only that, but all of them had links to pages with titles like 'Get Active!' or 'Get Involved!' or 'What YOU can do!'

When Bertrand googled 'environmentalism' he was immediately directed to a site called Earthjustice. The site itself was very elegant with a photo of a rainforest as the banner graphic. Superimposed across the wildness was Earthjustice's logo and slogan 'Because the earth needs a good lawyer'.

Intrigued, Bertrand clicked on the 'Take Action' link, where he was presented with a list of five campaigns that Earthjustice was currently running. Each campaign had its own separate page, which briefly described its aims and methods.

> *Anti-environmentalists in Congress are trying to gerrymander the Ninth Circuit US Court of Appeals . . . We can't let partisan politics get in the way of enforcing the environmental laws that protect us. Please email your senators today!*

Beneath the text was an online form that allowed Bertrand to fill in his name and email and with one button click, Bertrand had 'taken action'. Next was a campaign to keep SUVs out of national parks. For this, Bertrand was asked to email his senator using the pre-written form provided. Which Bertrand obediently did, again.

Moving on, he clicked on a picture of a big polar bear. The instructions read:

Tell your Senator to oppose legislation that would gut the Endangered Species Act.

And so on. In each case, the campaign methods were exactly the same. Bertrand was asked to type in his name and email address, and an email would be sent out.

Frankly, 'getting involved' had not been as much fun as Bertrand had envisioned. He'd had images of joining hundreds of thousands of people converging on the White House, and making free love under the Washington Memorial, perhaps while sharing a peace pipe of high-grade marijuana. But perhaps he was just looking in the wrong place.

So Bertrand continued his search. He signed up to become an online activist with Greenpeace and joined the 'Campaign for America's Future'. He even went on a 'Virtual March' with 376 000 other people at StopGlobalWarming.Org. This march, in case you hadn't guessed already, involved giving them his name and email address.

Several hours later, Bertrand had visited 70 websites and signed over 200 online petitions. He must really be having an impact, he thought to himself. Unfortunately, the impact he was having was hard to gauge, beyond overwhelming his inbox with an enormous number of automatically generated emails. But, Bertrand thought, at least it was a start.

There was one thing that was bugging Bertrand. He couldn't work out how to actually get involved in helping run a campaign. It felt almost as if the websites were treating him like a consumer of their campaigns. Indeed, when he registered with Act for Change, Bertrand had received an auto-email from customerservice@workingforchange.com.

It was certainly true that sending off email petitions was a relief to Bertrand's middle-class guilt, but it was starting to seem as if all those worthy organizations were more concerned with getting his email address than treating him like the uniquely talented individual he was. Which was ultimately what led him to DailyKos, the largest left-leaning blogsite in America, with over 6 trillion unique visitors a week[20], where the flow of opinion was at least in both directions. Somewhat.

Bertrand's CV was on Wikipedia for all to see, and yet it took 65 comments from people putting Bertrand down for no good reason before someone bothered to find a reason and do some research on Bertrand to find out who this upstart was.

- Elmo: *Hmmm. Someone who designs political ads suggests that what the Democrats must do right now is plow a buncha money into . . . political ads? If this guy sold shampoo, would he be suggesting we all go wash our hair right now? I'm thinking yeah.*

Tipped off, Dataguy also did a background check (I wonder whether he used Answers or Wiki?).

- Dataguy: *If we get roped into a gay rights agenda in 2006 or 2008, we will lose big-time. Your history writing ads backing gay marriage suggests that you are not a person of very clear vision, anyway (of course, you got paid, which is a logic in and of itself).*

The kill was winding down. The big bloggers with their incredibly profound views at DailyKos had managed to quell Bertrand's spirit

---

[20] This is not true, although being a web-based statistic it is impossible to find out the exact number. One conservative website says the DailyKos only gets 60 000 a day, but the *New York Times* recently said they got 500 000 a week. Meanwhile, the DailyKos claims they get 240 000 a day, and some lunatic Australian author has recently claimed that they get over 6 trillion visitors a week.

and see off another potential supporter. Bertrand would think twice before venturing an opinion again. That was not an open marketplace of ideas, but what Bertrand rather indignantly dubbed a 'bear pit of righteousness'.

Initially I[21] thought this was quite a funny thing to happen. For all the proclaimed openness of the Left, it was amusing that getting involved in the conservative community had been far easier than getting involved in anything meaningful on the Left. But after a while I became quite concerned. If Bertrand was not going to be able to infiltrate the Left, then where did that leave America and, more importantly, my rigorous scientific hypothesis?

But more pressingly, Bertrand had started to see all sorts of dark conspiracies in his lack of progress. 'It's not funny, you know,' he whined. 'People are going to read this book, and hear all about Edward, and everyone's going to think you're some sort of horrible conservative.' This was true and a real concern – I had been hoping for the book to become Greenpeace's Book of the Month (even though deep down I've always hated whales).

For Bertrand it was too much of an injustice for the left to be judged by their actions – 'What about their intentions? They mean well,' he said as he pleaded for my help. Like a true big-government liberal that his opponents accused him of being, Bertrand was demanding a leg-up.

At first I was hesitant – after all, giving Bertrand a leg-up would unfairly advantage him, even if he didn't quite see it this way. 'You're only focused on equality of opportunity,' he yelled in a fit of left-liberal passion. 'What about equality of outcome? What about those of us who don't have the opportunities laid out in front of us?' said the Manhattan advertising executive.

Eventually, after days of Bertrand whining like this, I yielded. At least it would shut him up.

---

[21] I'm referring to me, Charles Firth, here.

I decided to help Bertrand link up with Eli Pariser, the head of MoveOn.org, the largest non-profit political organization on the Left, with over 3 million members. MoveOn started in the late 1990s and grew rapidly as the main online group agitating against the war in Iraq. During the 2004 elections they raised over $12 million mainly to spend on television advertisements. Two years later and MoveOn was still sending me emails boasting about how good their ads were. Nowadays, MoveOn's central mission was to raise money to make ads and generate emails which changed the world. Judging by their emails, MoveOn was clearly the most significant development in politics since the French Revolution.

I'd become a member of MoveOn as soon as I'd moved to the US and Eli had been personally emailing me every few weeks since then, asking me to click this button or donate that amount of money, or even just give him some feedback about how he was going. The warm, conversational style of all his emails had made me think we had a really good rapport going. In fact, I counted Eli as one of my closest American friends, and I was certain that Eli would have some contacts and might even be able to help Bertrand score a blogging gig. So I wrote him a quick note:

> Dear Eli,
> Since you seem to email me all the time, I thought I might take some time out and email you back. It's only polite. I hope your petition is going well. I've always thought Internet petitions are a great way to change the world. I was wondering whether it would be possible to get an interview with you at some point. I'm an Australian based in New York, and I'm writing a book about the American Empire, and there's one guy who I've been profiling that is doing work very similar to you – his name is Bertrand Newton (do you know him?). Since you seem to be the guy who pioneered this whole Internet organizing, I thought I should go to the source and interview you.
> Charles Firth
> Author
> 'Empire'

Within minutes Eli had written back to me! I couldn't believe how efficient he was:

> *Thanks for contacting us. We get a ton of email, but we really want to hear from folks so please bear with us! If you want to unsubscribe, go here: http://www.moveon.org/subscrip/i.html?id=-6600856D5lZ 24rhz4wYlBNz.Nsakw*
> *If you're trying to change your email address . . .*

I won't bore you with the rest of the email, but let's just say I'm not even sure Eli had even read the email. And to add insult to automation, the email wasn't even signed, which seemed a little impersonal. My favorite word in the whole email was this one:

but

Actually, I should put it in context:

> *We get a ton of email, **but** we really want to hear from folks so please bear with us!*

I don't know, call me paranoid, but do you get the sense that Eli didn't really want to receive email from me? In fact, I was beginning to suspect that Eli and I weren't such close friends after all. Angry, I wrote back to him, hoping that if I treated him a little meaner he'd start paying attention.

> *Everyone at MoveOn,*
> *Great, thanks for such a personalized response. I really appreciate it. It makes me appreciate Internet organizing for all it's worth. I'm assuming that you'll follow this up with an automated phone call? I gave you my number in the last email, but just in case you've misplaced it, here it is again: (646) 763-5100. If I don't answer, just leave a message on my machine and I'll get straight back to you.*

And guess what happened after that? I never heard from MoveOn.org ever again. I don't know whether they have some sort of automatic cut-off system for people who employ too much sarcasm in their emails, but I was cut off, out of the loop. Eli – who'd personally sent me half-a-dozen emails over the previous 6 months – never sent me an email again.

That was it. Bertrand and I had had enough. If we couldn't even get emails from MoveOn – whose sole purpose is to send out emails – then how was Bertrand going to become a gun commentator of the Left? I felt genuinely sorry for the man.

It was as if the only way he was going to break through was to know someone and be someone. It was time for Bertrand to set his sights higher. He might still write the occasional article at DailyKos, but he wouldn't pin all his hopes on it. Bertrand needed to become a player and he needed a project that wasn't so open to attack. In fact what Bertrand needed to do was what everyone else seemed to be doing: set up his own organization and start collecting email addresses.

But how? To me it seemed hopeless – I was all out of ideas. But Bertrand was defiant. Instead of just writing manifestos about changing the world one ad at a time, he decided that it was time to step up to the plate and make at least one part of his Answers.com entry true.

'I'm going to make AdBack a reality. I'm going to take on MoveOn and win,' he said. He went over to the bar and ordered us pink champagne to celebrate.

7
MISSING IDENTITIES

Walker

Iraq – being stabbed in the jaw
Iran – won't give in to our law
Arabs – prostrate on the floor.

Waking on the banks of the Euphrates, I listen,
but there is no noise
Not today. Not any day.

The noise will begin when the last nail is driven
From the coffin of within
From the wooden bin of history.

Why oh great Walker? What did we do? Wrong place?
Wrong time for a hungry predator and limp prey?
We can't turn back time, or can we? The Walker never rests

But must collapse.
Oh he must collapse.
Or it all will.

It was early morning and I was getting feedback from Khorin al-Ghrant – a poet I'd met at an anti-war recital – about the first few chapters of the book. Her main point was that for a book purporting to represent a diverse cross-section of the American population there were a few gaps that I had to fill with my last character.

As Khorin read and scribbled on a pad, I was enjoying the 'Extreme Creme Taste' that can only come from a packet of

Oreo O's, the marshmallow-based breakfast cereal that contains a full 24 grams of sugar per 54 grams of serving. Khorin noted sternly that none of my characters so far were women. I had created four white males.

I had bought the Oreo O's partly for the creme taste but also because it promised 'Outrageous fun for everyone™' on the back of the pack. I explained to Khorin that the absence of non-white males was itself a kind of powerful meta-absence designed to actually *draw attention* to the marginalization of marginal identities in mainstream discourse over the past decade.

I was almost halfway through the bowl and I still wasn't having 'outrageous fun'. I looked at the side of the box. Apparently the sweeter-than-sugar chocolate pellets I was eating were an 'excellent source of Six B Vitamins, Iron and Zinc for Growth'. In very small type down the bottom was information from the American Diabetes Association explaining that diabetic kids could forego other meals in order to experience this high fructose corn syrup treat. (While at the same time presumably ensuring the long-term relevance of the ADA by literally promoting diabetes in America.)

There was nothing more to read on the packet, which meant I had to confront the issue at hand. Khorin was right. And so, as I finished the last bite of my fiber-free breakfast, I decided that in addition to being a woman, my new character might as well check off some of the minorities this book was missing. For example, it would be great to get in a Muslim – ideally from Iraq – and I had yet to cover the delicate issue of physical disability in America.

Thus my final – and in no way token – character became Khorin al-Ghrant herself – a poet in the traditional Iraqi sense of the word. Being a deaf mute Muslim woman, Khorin's story was an alluring if tragic one. Now 31, she was brought to America on a leaky boat at the end of the Iraq war in 1991. She and her family ended up first in Pakistan, then in Indonesia, where they were helped by a contact at the embassy in Jakarta who took pity on the strikingly beautiful deaf, mute Khorin (then 16), who had also been temporarily blinded by the sea spray.

Khorin was delighted to be included in the book, but almost immediately she became suspicious of my motives. 'Why do I have to be deaf and mute?' she scribbled on a piece of paper.

It's true that this was a little unfair, but I explained to her that she was the ultimate 'other'. Only by fully embracing the 'otherness' of her character was she going to be able to forge a philosophically meaningful neo-amalgam that truly embodied the anti-male.[22] Khorin nodded earnestly at this explanation. Clearly, Khorin was some sort of post-modernist too.

Khorin, in short, was the exact opposite of me. This, I figured, would make her extremely easy to write for, while at the same time comprehensively and sensitively taking care of my utter neglect of everyone in society who wasn't a white male.

There was, however, also a practical reason for making Khorin deaf and mute. I'd been doing a lot of practise accent-wise, but I wasn't sure I was cut out to impersonate too many Americans, and I was even less likely to be able to convincingly pull off impersonating a woman. Because Khorin was a deaf mute nobody would ever bother to call her, and her only contact with the outside world would be through email. Furthermore, if she was ever required to attend an event, the fact that she was Muslim would mean that I could, conceivably, dress up in full burqa so as to hide my non-Arabic, non-female features (actually, I look surprisingly feminine in a burqa).

Khorin, however, was not impressed. Quite unfairly, right from the start she had it in her mind that my commitment to equality and inclusion was 'convenient' and 'shoddy'.

---

[22] In case you're wondering what this means, don't worry – I don't understand either. 'Other' people will understand it.

I explained to Khorin that for her tale to succeed in the battle-field of opinion, it must also be a tale that Americans wanted to hear. As such, she would not argue against the Patriot Act, she would not complain about her treatment by airport security. Instead, her message was to be one of hope: that the United States was not yet the empire that those in power sought to make it. That it wasn't too late for the US to reverse its course and stand out as the honest broker of international politics. In fact, she believed it would also serve the best interests of her adopted country which she had grown to love. Khorin, therefore, was to be one of those rare beasts, the left liberal nationalist.

Of course, I didn't tell Khorin, but there was another upside in having a deaf, mute, Muslim poet amongst my cast of characters. Seventy-five percent of all books are bought by the top ten percent of book buyers – 'the literati'. This meant that if I could write a book that scandalized the literati, I'd almost certainly end up with a best-seller on my hands. And the thing that those types really get stuck into is a good literary hoax. Look at James Frey and JT Leroy. Admit-tedly I'd never heard of these people before Bertrand Newton was invented and he started reading the *New Yorker* in small wine bars that had only flea-ridden couches for furniture – but apparently these hoaxers had sold millions of copies, mostly on the back of the publicity about how they are utter frauds, or probably utter frauds.[23] Don't get me wrong, I find the whole idea of making stuff up and then passing it off as real to a gullible reading public absolutely reprehensible.[24]

---

[23] Apparently the secretive, transsexual, transgender novelist JT Leroy hasn't yet been exposed as a hoax, which in no way undermines my argument. In his/her case it is the mounting anticipation of a literary hoax that is driving the top 10% of book buyers crazy for his/her stuff. If JT Leroy is genuine, then all it makes him/her is a marketing genius, from whom we should all learn.

[24] Khorin al-Ghrant was already shopping a long essay around various literary journals on James Frey and what a disgrace he was.

Khorin al-Ghrant offered the marketplace of ideas something that Bertrand could not. She was authentic.[25] Whereas Bertrand had the slick professionalism of someone who wanted to be a mover and shaker, Khorin adopted none of the sound-bite language and demographic demagoguery of Bertrand. She was just an earnest, angry young woman, metaphorically screaming to be heard. She was, in short, something that Americans (or at least book-buying Americans) desperately wanted to hear: she was the Arundhati Roy of America (without the endless rants about dams).

Khorin stumbled across her first project by accident. She was looking for Iraqi poetry on the web, and the first result in every Google search she did returned the website PoetsAgainstWar.org. That was a description of Khorin herself. She was a poet and she was against war. She clicked on it. 'Poets Against War continues the tradition of socially engaged poetry by creating venues for poetry as a voice against war, tyranny and oppression.' Perfect. Khorin, controversially enough, was also against tyranny and oppression.

Instantly Khorin fell in love with the organization. PoetsAgainst-War had been set up in the wake of the Iraq war, and had gathered anti-war poems from all around the world and presented them to the US Congress in September 2004. Since then, the site had become the top anti-war poetry site in the world. Their latest newsletter had a commentary by Walt Whitman, and various poets, including Nobel prize winners, had donated anti-war poems to the site's collection. It featured poems by dozens of 'prominent poets' none of whom I'd ever heard of, but who Khorin assured me were all very impressive. Their current campaign was – and I'm not making this up – a petition against hypocrisy, which they were planning to submit to the 62nd annual UN conference on human rights.

Initially Khorin had thought she wouldn't write poems for the web. That would be too mainstream. Instead, she was only going to

---

[25] -ish.

place her poems on the back of toilet walls so that their success could be measured not by objectivist notions of 'number of people who like them' and 'whether they're any good' but by the impact they had on individuals. But this website seemed too perfect to resist.

And so Khorin wrote her first poem, relying very much on the personal experience that she had undergone being a deaf and dumb Muslim living in America and watching commercial television.

Dumb not stupid

TV is on again.
Blaring with silence.

The more I want, the less I need
Longing for the false hope
Of commercial dreams

Hear it scream red and yellow
Blue and red. Just give me
Green. All for green.

I wait for a feeling that will feed my eyes
And nourish my skin. That will give me
A lack of silence.

I turn it off and the silence ends.
I can hear once more.

Personally, I'd never written poems before, and I certainly can't tell a good poem from a bad one, but I'm pretty sure the way it works is that nobody else knows whether poems are any good either. It all depends on how sexy your bio sounds. And luckily Khorin had the best bio of any poet ever to be shopped around America. So before she submitted the poems, it was very important to get her bio straight. And not only that, it was important that her bio come from a humanist angle that would flatter the sort of people who would organize a petition against hypocrisy, and at the same time demonstrate her patriotic credentials by distinguishing between the American people and their evil imperialist government.

Khorin al-Ghrant

31 years old. I'm an Iraqi woman who grew up in Baghdad and recently settled in Brooklyn. (I moved to Jakarta in 1991, and then to Los Angeles in 1994 – luckily, my father is an engineer.) Before I left Iraq, my poetry was published quite frequently in my school journal. Unfortunately I was born deaf – which informs many of my poems.

This poem is about my personal experiences as an Iraqi woman in America. Although these are anti-war, I should say outright that I don't blame the US for what they have done to my country. I hate the war, but understand that it is not Americans but their government that is driving the imperial ambitions of the United States.

To that end, Khorin then wrote 'Walker' (which starts this chapter) – in case you're some sort of non-literary idiot, I should point out that Walker is, of course, an allusion to George W Bush's middle name, something Khorin hoped the literary types would find both 'witty' and 'powerful'. And since she was having so much fun (and they're actually very easy to write, you just have to put on a silly accent and they dribble out of your brain), here's one more poem – to solidify Khorin's body of work and cement her status as one of America's foremost deaf, mute Muslim poets. This one is again a very personal, very authentic piece about the experience of going through security at the airport.

Airport Security

I assume she's saying let me feel you.
But she's saying so much more.

67

Actually I might just cut that one short. You get the point, though. Khorin's poems were turning out to be even more earnest than she was, something I had not thought possible.

Khorin submitted these poems to the Poets Against War website, but as the days passed, she heard nothing. Indeed, she actually received a Mail Delivery Subsystem notice saying her emails had not been delivered. Oh well, she thought, perhaps she should go back to submitting her ideas on the backs of toilet doors. At least the rejection was less automatic. Over the coming weeks she submitted her poems to various literary journals and websites, but without any real enthusiasm. If a deaf mute Muslim woman couldn't make it onto the biggest anti-war poetry site, what was the point of it all?

A few weeks later Khorin checked back at the PoetsAgainstWar website, jealously wondering what the site was up to, and certainly not expecting to see her own work on display, and yet there, by some sort of miracle, were all of Khorin's poems. Clearly the auto-rejection email was just a way of warding off shallow imposters. One of the project's volunteers had trawled through the mass of submissions and seen Khorin's irresistible bio, which was prominently displayed above the poems. After weeks of torment, Khorin al-Ghrant was now a fully qualified contender in the marketplace of ideas.

But Khorin was unimpressed. The positioning of her CV above the poems just confirmed to her everything she'd suspected: that the world valued her the same way I did: for her CV. She was being judged by the quality of her CV, not by the content of her character.

That afternoon, she and I went for a stroll along the boardwalk at Coney Island Beach. 'This is stopping right now,' she scribbled.

'But Khorin,' I said, 'you succeeded. You got your poems published. This is just the beginning of a massive literary hoax!' I was excited by her potential and had already thought about some ways we could flesh out her back story to be even more tragic. I wondered whether she might also be one quarter Jewish.

But Khorin had had enough. She threw down her paper and pen and jumped into a small inflatable motorboat that was moored on the jetty. She sped out into the Atlantic Ocean and disappeared over the horizon. I think she was going home to Iraq.

I kept walking. I hadn't expected it to end this way. It was so abrupt. It was also a real pity. She'd had almost instant success with her poems and I had great ambitions for her as a grand hoax in the making. Now her contribution to this book would have to be through her absence. This 'meta-absence' she hoped[26] would serve as a constant, damning reminder that this book was run by white men for white men. It was almost as if by removing herself from the book's narrative she was serving as some sort of allegory about America in general. Or perhaps it was just an allegory about this book in particular. I never really understood allegories anyway, but I was hoping this meta-absence thing would impress someone – hopefully the literati.

Perhaps Khorin's disappearance was simply her form of poetic justice. If it was, it was better than any of her other poems.

---

[26] Or would have hoped had she still existed.

8

MASS MOVEMENTS 3.0

From a brief survey of existing institutions it seemed to Bertrand that the first thing you do when you're setting up a large left-wing activist organization is to set up a website. Luckily, the domain name AdBack.org was available, so Bertrand quickly registered it and wrote some copy for it:

AdBack *is a boutique non-profit organization dedicated to changing the world one advertisement at a time. We specialize in helping the* **community sector** *and* **progressive lobbying organizations** *to 'think outside the square' when it comes to messaging with Middle America.*

In today's world, simply **doing good is not good enough**. *You need a strategy to sell yourself and the work you do to the broader public. Only then will your impact be broad, and* **your effort will be worth it**.

If your organization needs help communicating its message to the wider public, contact **<u>Bertrand Newton</u>** *and see how AdBack can help you win back the initiative. Whether it's a one-day brainstorm or a fully fledged TVC campaign, AdBack can give your organization the power and profile you deserve.*

The People Behind AdBack

Bertrand Newton is founder and head of AdBack. Newton first became involved in politics over fifteen years ago, when he joined the 'No Blood For Oil' coalition at the Berkeley Campus of UCLA, a key member of the California Peace Coalition. In 1992 he briefly transferred to Oxford in England where he read economics. Dissatisfied at the lack of salesmanship shown by progressive forces on both sides of the Atlantic, Newton quit college and went into advertising. Over the next decade, Newton traveled the world gaining expertise at marketing everything from shampoo to cell phones in Brazil, Japan, Australia, Malaysia and the Netherlands.

During the 2004 Presidential Election, Newton re-entered politics, but this time armed with invaluable marketing experience which prompted the Toledo Leader *to dub Newton 'the future . . . Karl Rove of the Democrats'.*

Newton caught the attention of many Democrats after he put together a team and ran the successful 'GayBack 2004' campaign which targeted gay and lesbian voters in the crucial swing state of Ohio using narrowcasting marketing techniques such as text messaging, truck-side advertising and targeted display advertisements in restrooms.

In helping your organization, Newton brings with him fifteen years of campaign experience in both the political and corporate world.

AdBack didn't really do much except collect email addresses, but Bertrand figured that was the perfect setup for someone who wanted to change the world without getting his hands too dirty. After all, one of the main reasons Bertrand had set up AdBack was so that he could speak as the head of an important-sounding organization to whomever he liked.

But what should AdBack's first big campaign be? Bertrand was astute enough to know that there was no use in just talking to his friends, all of whom were white and well educated. His interest lay in the 'unconverted', the 'contestables', the 'swingers' and the 'waverers'. Although everyone he knew thought the world was collapsing – the war in Iraq, corrosion of civil liberties, the rise of R and B music as the predominant pop music form – Bertrand thought that most people didn't think at all. Somewhere 'out there' was a mass of extremely malleable people, who at the moment thought the world was fine, but with the right television commercials, and a follow-up email campaign, would realize how bad the world really was. It was these people that Bertrand had his sights on. The question was: how did he get their all-important email address?

Bertrand went back to his trendy East Village apartment, sat down on his futon and thought really hard. What did ordinary people like? Bertrand really didn't know. What would connect ordinary people? Bertrand's tiny apartment didn't have anywhere for me to sit with him while he thought. Indeed, the two-room place was so cramped that the kitchen had an illegally installed bathroom in it, with the consequence that the fridge sat directly next to the toilet. Bertrand could, of course, afford a bigger apartment, but as far as I could work out he actually seemed to think that having an apartment fit for a trendy NYU student gave him the philosophical outlook of a trendy NYU student.

Bertrand noticed me standing awkwardly next to his Jasper Johns poster of the American flag ('It's not unpatriotic to be liberal,' he had told me when I first noticed it). Since he didn't have a spare chair, he suggested we go for a walk through Alphabet City, around a small park on Avenue B.

As we trudged through the sludge that accompanies the boom-bust cycle of hot and cold during a New York winter, we noticed a group of people milling around. Bertrand's nose twitched. I smelt something too. It was a faint whiff of marijuana. Almost immediately Bertrand's face betrayed his jealousy. Was this some sort of trendy smoke-in that Bertrand, yet again, hadn't been invited to even though he ran his own 527? Even though he came up with an advertisement in the 2004 elections that even George Soros had said was 'quite good'? No, it was just a small dog park, where people brought their pets to poo and sniff each other's bottoms while the owners looked on proudly and the local drug dealers plied their wares. I was intrigued by this scene, and even suggested to Bertrand that perhaps we should go and strike up a conversation with a dog owner or two.

'No. I hate dogs,' Bertrand said abruptly. He had been mauled by one when he was five. He seemed to be almost proud of his hatred, as if he thought it gave him personality.

We passed the dog enclosure and continued along Avenue B – past a strip of cafes, all of which served burnt coffee during the day but became trendy bars at night. Bertrand reflected on other, simpler people's love of their animals. He told me that one day he would like to be like pet owners and lead a simple life, and gain simple pleasure from simple things. It would be so good not being so good.

I looked at Bertrand blankly – it seemed a rather, well, confident frame of mind for someone who had recently had a string of failures. I wondered whether Bertrand might do better if he dropped the bravado and listened to the 'simple' people for a change.

Amazingly, Bertrand agreed. 'Yes!' he said. 'I need to connect with the simple people!' It wasn't quite what I had meant but Bertrand increased his walking pace and I was struggling to keep up in my now freezing sludge-ridden shoes. 'That's how I'll get my message out against the Bush administration.'

Bertrand's epiphany was this: simple people enjoy themselves without a care in the world; 'There was not even one BlackBerry in sight in that park,' he told me excitedly. This presented him with an obvious idea, one that, as far as he was aware, had never been tried before.

And so Bertrand had his first stroke of genius: PetsAgainstBush. org – a website dedicated to bringing down the Bush administration one poodle at a time. By linking together the sort of simple folk he had seen in the park that day, Bertrand figured a community of people would emerge that numbered in the hundreds of thousands. And Bertrand would get their email addresses and send them out witty, touching and ultimately angry emails, and together, inspired by Bertrand's demagogic skills, and combined with the power of Internet petitions, PetsAgainstBush.org would be a player. The sheer simplicity of Internet organizing – the fact that you don't need to meet anyone, except for maybe a web designer, also appealed to Bertrand. He'd never been particularly fond of people, so being able to touch their lives without going through the boring task of meeting them was downright revolutionary.

MoveOn might appeal to the diehard activists, but Bertrand's email list would be even more powerful – these would be the simple folks, the hoi poloi who had normal concerns, such as what to feed their pets and ordinary stuff like that.

And so Bertrand launched PetsAgainstBush.org. It was surprisingly simple. Of course, Bertrand didn't actually have a pet, but he was able to find tons of photos on the Internet and fake them up so it looked like the pets were opposed to Bush. It's amazing how far Photoshop skills can go in massaging into existence a mass-based political movement.

The only place online for household pets to express their opposition to President Bush.

As many pet owners know, household pets are becoming increasingly vocal against President Bush. If your pet has been barking, meowing or squawking strong views against the present White House administration, please help them post their pictures here. Who knows, perhaps even Bush's own dogs, Spot and Barney, will get up the courage to bark out.

The day it launched, Bertrand submitted his website to dozens of search engines, hoping that he would become the number one pet site in America, if not the world. Within hours, he had posted notes in major chat rooms and on lists.

Yet when he googled PetsAgainstBush, to his absolute horror he saw that someone had not only done it already but had also created specific sites for cats and dogs. DogsHateBush.com and CatsHate-Bush.com were not only far higher than Bertrand's PetsAgainstBush. com on the Google results, but they even had their own merchandising range! And the websites were not parodies. They were genuine. Or were they? Perhaps they were conducting an elaborate hoax? Whatever, they were posing a massive problem for Bertrand. His months of virtual movement building had literally come to nothing.

I was exasperated too. The single dickiest idea, perfect for the most superficial character on the entire planet, and people were coding around cyberspace actually carrying these things out in earnest. They weren't even being satirical. Who were these people? How obscure did you have to be to own a bit of space on the Left? What possible combination of constituents could possibly not be accounted for? If people are willing to earnestly engage in a kind of ritualistic self-parody, then perhaps, I thought, I was out of my depth.

PHASE TWO
The Long War

9

FASHION WARS

Kaufman's Army and Navy Surplus was a long, thin shop over-loaded with, well, surplus gear. Boxes of newly arrived jackets, helmets, nettings and holsters lined the floor, while the latest equipment – from knife holders to various camouflage suits – hung from the ceiling. The effect was a dimly lit store that had the same messy feel as a teenage boy's bedroom: boys with toys don't tend to tidy up that much. Near the counter three or four uniformed soldiers, all with close-cropped hair, were hanging around. They didn't seem to be buying anything, but rather killing time, probably waiting to board a bus – the shop was opposite the large bus terminal on 42nd Street.

Andy and I were there to pick out an outfit for his Iraq trip. After sorting through box after box of XXXL sized equipment, he'd finally found a medium-sized khaki flak jacket with about 55 000 pockets on it (we still haven't finished counting), and a matching dark green cap. This would look good in the photos that accompanied his article, he explained. Having picked out some clothes, we pushed through the intimidatingly dressed soldiers to the messy counter at the front of the shop.

The news that Dr Andy wanted to go to Iraq had knocked me for six. Or to use an American sports analogy, it had struck me like a home run.[27] It's not that I didn't want to go to Iraq. I'd love to go to Iraq. After all, the original pitch for the book was that I would travel

---

[27] I really should look into how to use American sporting analogies. I don't know, but I'm beginning to suspect the baseball and cricket sporting analogies don't translate literally. Unfortunately Google doesn't have a function to translate between different sporting codes, so there's no way of finding out.

to all the major conflict zones in the world and hopefully find a mass grave or uncover some hidden nuclear-refinement plant. You know, something that would win me a Pulitzer. But now that I'd moved to the greatest consumer paradise on earth I had started to realize why military recruiters must be having such a hard time getting people to voluntarily leave the place. Iraq did seem an awfully long way away.

Let me explain something. When you're pitching to a publisher it's important to make the book sound as though it's going to be really dramatic. That usually involves lots of international travel.

So my pitch went like this: 'This book will be a satirical tour de force. As the Enfant Terrible of the New Media, I will travel to dangerous hotspots and investigate the chilling reality of the American Empire. Iraq, Iran – I will embed myself in the very fabric of the sharp end of American foreign policy, and through that write a bestseller in the 18–35 male category in the lead-up to Christmas.'

Of course, now that I had the book contract I had no intention of going anywhere near those places: it was far too dangerous. But Dr Andy was insistent. After a couple of days in Iraq, Dr Andrew O'Keefe would be more than qualified to market the war in any way he saw fit. He'd be able to shout down any opponent with the words, 'Well, have you been there, Mr Colmes? Have you actually seen with your own eyes what it's like? The Iraqis love Americans. Iraq is a good-news story that's been turned into a bad-news story by the media!'

But Dr Andy knew that wasn't the way to convince me: his pitch to me was even more seductive. 'The best thing about going to Iraq is that the book immediately becomes incredibly topical, and thus likely to go out of date within weeks.' At first, this hardly struck me as an advantage. But then I realized what this meant – I would be able to release endless different editions under the guise of 'New, Updated Edition' with 'Over 100 new pages of updated analysis'.[28]

---

[28] This is known as the 'Thomas Friedman Method of Publishing'. Friedman currently releases new, updated versions of his book on a daily basis.

As long as I made sure I included lots of figures that went out of date quickly but could easily be updated with a quick visit to the military's DefenseLink website, then I would be well and truly on board the topical-book gravy train. Dr Andy was a genius.

And the best thing was, going to Iraq would up the stakes dramatically. Until I returned safely from Iraq (assuming that I do), the question at the back of your mind (and, indeed, mine, dear reader) will be: what will happen in Iraq? Will he get taken hostage? I wonder what the service in the restaurants is like in the Green Zone? What's the appropriate tip to leave? Do they have room service there?

As we were buying the gear, I explained to a grumpy man behind the counter who wore matching shades of military gray (I think he must have been Kaufman, but I was too afraid to ask) that we were going to Iraq. He paused and stared at me. I felt very small (I think that was mainly because the ground behind the counter was raised six inches on a platform). Slowly he 'suggested' that we buy the genuine Iraq camouflage equipment. When I use the word 'suggested' I mean suggested in the 'or I'll break your neck' kind of way.

I didn't know what to do. We had looked at the Iraq camouflage but Dr Andy had thought it all looked a little ordinary. The colors were much lighter and more washed-out than the conventional equipment, and they didn't look very good against Andy's pale skin. To Andy, it didn't look soldierly enough: 'I just can't see Hawkeye or Radar wearing this.'

But in Kaufman's grumpy opinion, it was imperative that we buy the latest gear – 'It's designed for the conditions,' he told us. I tended to agree – you couldn't be too safe. But then I saw the price. A simple designed-for-Iraq flack jacket was at least three times as expensive as the conventional gear. I asked the owner why, and he explained that it was in high demand from stage and screen producers. Despite its macho image, much of Kaufman's clientele is Broadway shows and film studios. It is, after all, on 42nd Street.

Now I'm not one to skimp on safety, but in the back of my mind it struck me that it would be an enormous waste of money if I spent a whole load on the equipment and then for some unforeseen reason ended up not going to Iraq. I told Andy that this was his mission and he should buy whatever he liked, especially if it was the cheaper outfit. After all, if we did make it, we weren't going to be there very long, and Andy had agreed that we'd spend most of our time in the Green Zone. Perhaps the green camouflage would help us fit in there.

Angry at his failure to upsell us, Kaufman rang up our purchases in silence. He took my money, packed up our gear and then, as he was handing us our change, gave me a wooden coin. 'Here's a Kaufman dollar,' he said, suddenly friendly. 'One dollar discount next time you come back.' His mood had been trumped by his latest marketing gimmick to encourage return customers – if they survived, that is.

10

A REAL PERSON

Meanwhile, it was time for Bertrand to swallow his pride. After the debacle with PetsAgainstBush, he had been angry at his inability to think of anything original that hadn't already been done by the Left. But as the days went by and all he received were more bulk emails from all the organizations he'd joined in his initial flurry of 'activism', it became increasingly clear he was going to have to actually talk to a real person about how to get involved with the Left.

Finding out how to contact someone was more difficult than all the 'Get Involved!' buttons on the websites had led Bertrand to believe. Since I'd already burnt the Eli lead, Bertrand had decided to contact MoveOn himself by telephone. AdBack was now a fully functioning organization with its own website and so Bertrand assumed this would be relatively straightforward – he would be able to talk as the head of one organization to another. But MoveOn wasn't listed in Bertrand's BlackBerry. Not only that, the Yellow-pages module he'd downloaded onto his PDA had no listing for it, nor did a quick Google search on his other broadband Internet wireless phone and music player. He was out of luck. He later found out that MoveOn does not have a publicly listed phone number anywhere in the United States. Bertrand, however, was surprisingly understanding – if AdBack had 3.3 million members, he wouldn't want to talk to them either.

Indeed, there appeared to be only one way to make real human contact with MoveOn: to pretend he was a member of the press. Initially Bertrand was hesitant – he wanted to chat to the head of their organization, or at least their email list manager, not some PR spinner. But eventually he relented. As soon as MoveOn saw that Bertrand was the head of an important organization, they were sure to give him unfettered access to their own. And so he went to the press section of their website and sent this message, making sure to talk to them as an equal:

Hi, I run an organization called AdBack which aims to change the world one advertisement at a time – which seems fairly similar to the work your organization is doing.

He asked them to contact him, and then hit the submit button and got this instantaneous reply:

Thanks for your message! It will be reviewed by a real person very soon.

A real person? This was real progress. All Bertrand had to do was sit back and wait. And wait. And wait.

While Bertrand was waiting he decided to try to contact some of the other organizations he'd become a member of in recent weeks. As it happened, one of these organizations had started sending him increasingly excited emails about some sort of mass protest against George Bush. The first one had the subject line 'IF YOU BUILD IT, THEY WILL COME . . .'

You've read the site. You know about the crimes. You smell the scent of fascism in the air . . .

There is a moment that must, and can, be seized – NOW.

There are people who want to act – NOW.
Reach them. Change your routine, for a week, and reach them.

Change the direction of history. Before it's too late.

Bertrand was excited to say the least. The provocative copywriting reminded him of a deodorant commercial that had won a Silver Promax award a few years back; it had involved a man chatting up a beautiful woman while his wife waited in the car. The slogan had been 'Change your routine'. On the other hand, I was a little more wary.

'Don't you think it's a little melodramatic?' I asked.

'Doesn't matter – this is about connecting with ordinary people,' Bertrand told me earnestly. He explained that although he personally didn't have a routine to change, he could see how that message would connect with anyone who had a boring life. Bertrand couldn't quite work out what the email was asking him to do, but it appeared that they wanted everyone around the country to take to the streets to bang pots and pans during the President's State of the Union address, which they ultimately seemed to think would lead to his resignation.

> *World Can't Wait is calling for people to be in the streets, bring the noise, politically drown out Bush's lies, and drive out Bush's Regime.*
>
> *Is there really any question? Haven't we done enough sitting around, atomized, cursing and crying while fascism is put in place? Changing the course of history is NOT a spectator sport.*
>
> *Do something that matters. Be in the streets. The world, and the country, is ready for our demand and many are stepping forward to speak it: BUSH STEP DOWN.*

In recent days, I had noticed fluorescent green stickers advertising the 'action' popping up on telephone polls and on the subways – but excitable flyers from fringe groups were nothing new. 'How do you know this is from a respectable organization with enough resources behind them to organize a national rally?' I asked Bertrand. He didn't care, he was already sold – he was sick of being a spectator when it came to changing history.

The very next day, World Can't Wait ran a full page ad in the *New York Times*, calling for a national rally to converge on Washington DC the following month. The ad copy toned down the talk of fascism, and mentioned the names of numerous celebrities, including Gore Vidal, Sean Penn and Jessica Lange. Perhaps this was it. Perhaps this was the moment Bertrand had been waiting for all his life. Perhaps his dreams of smoking the peace pipe of free love under the Washington Memorial would come true after all.

Bertrand checked his email to see if there were any further instructions about how to get involved. Sure enough, World Can't Wait had sent Bertrand another email, although this one was more focused on practicalities.

If you're in the eastern part of the country, GET ON THE BUS! If you're in the west, send money now. Everyone can be part of demanding BUSH STEP DOWN in DC!

Bertrand was in the eastern part of the country! Before I could stop him, he had clicked a button and pledged to turn up in DC for the rally. In his enthusiasm he even booked a cheap hotel room right near the White House so he would be in the thick of the action. Fascism was not going to happen on Bertrand's watch.

11

CAN'T WAIT

A few days later I found myself sitting at the back of a press club room interviewing Travis Morales, a short man with large square glasses and a bushy, slightly graying goatee beard and moustache. Even indoors, Travis was wearing a baseball cap, perhaps to mask a bald patch. The cumulative effect, however, was that it was hard to work out exactly what he would look like without the glasses, beard and cap. The beard's thickness resembled Stalin's moustache, but the goatee conveyed a certain Leninist, or even Trotskyite, look.

Travis was one of the national organizers of the World Can't Wait rally, and I was having a chat with him to find out how Bertrand could get involved more directly. I'd seen Bertrand get enthusiastic before only to have his hopes dashed – especially with that whole PetsAgainstBush debacle – so I wanted to make this experience as positive as possible for him. More to the point, the World Can't Wait was the only organization that I'd had any luck in getting in contact with person to person.

Now in his fifties, Travis had lived his life in Houston, Texas, and had got involved in politics in the late 1960s 'as everyone else seemed to', he told me earnestly. Since dropping out of medical school he'd had various jobs, including working in a steel mill and various office jobs 'just to pay the bills'. Late last year, however, something had changed in his life and he had moved to San Francisco and started organizing against 'the Bush regime'. Recently he had moved to the East Coast to continue the fight at a national level.

Almost immediately it became apparent that Travis was treating our chat as if each answer was his last, and therefore he had to summarize all his opinions in a single sentence. I had a tape recorder but I had made it clear to him that our chat was not going to be broadcast anywhere. Yet no matter what I did to put him at ease, Travis kept speaking in very long, grammatically entangled sound bites that made it almost impossible to quote him, except in full. It made for a very weird conversation. Let me give you an example. The first thing I asked him was a simple enough question, 'How did you first get involved in this movement?'

Now before I tell you his reply, Travis's verbosity has led to a fairly ironic situation. Unfortunately, if I do quote him in full, one of the consequences is that this book will be several pages longer, thus contributing in a small but significant way to the deforestation of woodlands, and global warming.[29] And since a brief web search reveals that Travis has attached himself to both of these issues in the past few years, I'm sure he would be appalled if that happened. So instead – to give you a taste of Travis, while respecting his strongly held opinions on everything – I'm going to quote him in full, but in a very small font size. So this is how Travis, in a simple monotone replied to my first question:

Back in the late spring a number of us were looking at the whole trajectory, particularly of Bush's so-called re-election, the moves to eliminate filibustering in the Senate so they could pass any laws that they wanted, the whole Terry Schiavo[30] controversy that was basically a grab for power by the Christian fundamentalists led by

---

[29] Assuming, of course, that it sells a few million copies. But I think that's pretty safe to assume.

[30] In case anyone was sleeping through the Terry Schiavo case, it was a big political battle in 2005 that involved a woman who was brain dead but on life support. The thorny ethical question, as far as I can work out (and which went all the way to the US Supreme Court), was whether someone who is already dead has the right to die. I love America.

Bush. A number of the measures we saw accelerating this power-grab by these fascist forces and that it was necessary to bring forth the millions and tens of millions of people who were outraged, angered by the torture, by the indefinite detention, by the endless war, by these moves to suppress science that didn't fit the agenda political and economic of the Bush regime. That we had to very quickly bring forth the force of millions of people to actually stop this whole dangerous trajectory.

As you can see (if you've got good enough eyesight), Travis seemed to want to link his rally to pretty much every major news event of the past six months. I asked him what his background was, but Travis was committed to staying on message.

I'm one of the organizers at the Washington office and one of the things that we're doing is saying look, you millions and tens of millions of people out there, including people in the DC area who are outraged by the torture, the endless war, the holding people without charges, the move towards fascism, you yourselves can and must take responsibility for actually stopping this whole dangerous trajectory. That's what it's going to take. You're taking independent historical action. Not relying on some congressmen but relying on your own efforts.

This is what Bertrand was so enthusiastic about. The idea of taking independent historical action just sounded so ... cool. I asked him if he thought that this rally would be the pinnacle of the campaign.

No, it's a nodal point in bringing forth even more people and reaching out with this message to millions of more people and taking action right now toward driving out the Bush regime. When we gather at the grounds of the Washington Monument with thousands of people we will be representing the sentiments of millions and tens of millions of people who are outraged by the torture, the endless war, the secret detentions and all these moves towards a Christian fascist faith who are demanding Bush step down.

And so on. You get the point. But just as I was getting bored of the whole thing, Travis suddenly got interesting. I asked him whether his goal – to make the President resign – would succeed. Instead of staring at the tape recorder as he had been the whole time, he looked up at me and simply replied, in a kind of grumpy way, as if I was making fun of him: 'Yes.'

'This year?' I asked.

'Well . . . yes.'

'Wow. So when he's gone,' I said, 'what will you do then?'

He was getting really grumpy now. Surely he'd thought of an answer for that? 'What do you mean?' he asked.

'What's your utopian vision?'

'Well that's a bit beyond the scope of this interview, that's a whole other discussion.'

Surely this wasn't going to be the one question he evaded. Was it? . . . No.

'Okay but I think one thing: we'll have brought forth millions of people who for the first time will make the struggle two-sided. Then we'll be in a position to have a conversation of how we're going to have a better world because we will have lifted the terrible burden of what the Bush regime is doing off the back of the people here and around the world. And we can have a discussion about how to have a better world, a discussion that we can't have in the sense of where they're headed right now.'

So his utopian vision was about having a long discussion, which I suppose is unsurprising for someone who enjoyed talking at such length. By the end of our conversation I'd decided not to ask about how Bertrand could get involved in organizing the rally. I had realized that it would be better if Bertrand found his own way in the Left, without my help.

After I'd turned off the tape, I asked Travis what organization he really belonged to. The International Socialists? The Spartacus League? Travis stared at me for a second and, for the first time in the day, didn't say anything. I pushed. I told him that it wouldn't change anything. We were committed to coming to the rally no matter what.

'The Revolutionary Communist Party of America,' he said. 'Although,' he assured me, 'the World Can't Wait is an entirely separate organization, it's based on a broad coalition of celebrities, community organizations and activists who are seeking to drive out . . .'

And so on. I would tell you his whole explanation, but I'd already turned off the tape. I just wanted to leave. Indeed, like the rest of the world, I couldn't wait.

12

THE NAME GAME

Back in Ithaca, Edward's first piece of punditry in 15 years was going well. The morning after he'd posted it on Townhall.com, Edward had arisen early, eager to see how his piece was going. The answer was not bad at all. Overnight, he had received seven serious responses to his posting. It was not going to change any White House policies, but it was enough to make Edward excited. Frankly, it had surprised me that Edward had met with any success at all.

To write the piece, Edward had given his old friend Dr Andy a call to see if he had any interesting leads. As it turns out, Dr Andy did – he had been in the middle of an important research paper about the way the current administration was marketing the War on Terror. It hadn't been made public (and almost definitely never would – it was far too classified), but Dr Andy had gracefully given his acquaintance a glimpse, which Edward had gratefully written up.

Why We Should Rename The War on Terror

By eddiemcguire

The problem facing President Bush's second-term anti-terrorism agenda is this: he has no marketing strategy to sell America's foreign policy to the rest of the world, let alone to Americans. The War on Terror sounds great, but where does it take you? Bush faces a war on all fronts with no clear victory, and with domestic support being eroded by opportunistic politicians on both sides of politics. Every time a freedom-hater blows himself up in London or Bali or Iraq, the War on Terror implicitly faces another defeat.

There is a solution to this. The Lamarck Institute (www.the lamarck.org) has been conducting a study about the words and rhetoric used in the media about the War on Terror. Its conclusions won't be published in full until next March, but I can let you in on its initial findings, which is a rather novel solution to the problem that Bush faces. War on Terror should be renamed 'The Terror Wars'[31]. That way, each war can be enumerated as they come to their natural conclusion.

This will immediately provide a massive benefit – the ability to declare victory. Terror War I was Afghanistan, and we won it. Terror War II is Iraq, and that's going to be a bit more difficult, but it doesn't mean you can't start Terror War III and Terror IV against Iran and Syria – something that is going to have to happen sooner or later if America is going to make a clean exit from Iraq.

From a rhetorical perspective, renaming The Terror Wars provides what it calls 'an in-built self-justification' – implicitly providing justifica-tion for the more extreme measures used by allied troops. But The Terror Wars' in-built self-justification provides an easy answer to critics: the only way to fight Terror is with Terror. It's the only thing they know. It's not pleasant but these are The Terror Wars after all . . .

From day one, the 'War on Terror' has been mocked by liberals as being a war against tactics. That was easily dismissed in the aftermath of 9/11, but as the memory of it fades from the Attention Deficit-minded public, what is left is a tarnished brand that is not doing allied troops any good at all. The problem is the 'War on Terror' is an ill-conceived marketing device. It does nothing to advance America's interests against the rest of the world – in fact, it puts America on the back foot much of the time.

The Institute's study brings into broader question many of the administration's techniques used to promote the War on Terror. 9/11 gave enormous leverage to the White House to market its agenda domestically.

---

[31] I would like to point out that although Edward and Dr Andy first wrote up this concept, the term 'Terror Wars' is entirely my idea and if it catches on and there are any academics out there scouring this book to discover the etymology of the term, it really should be attributed to me, and not to my characters. I'm sure Winston (Churchill) felt the same way after he came up with the term 'Cold War'.

It was a once-in-a-century opportunity for America to reshape its foreign policy in whatever way it chose. But neither Bush, nor Cheney, nor Powell, nor Rumsfeld, nor even Karl Rove was prepared to commit to the marketing that it required. Instead, the administration comes across as defensive about the war in Iraq, even though it is defending America's national interests!

Everyone should be given a stake in the War on Terror. America needs to galvanize its citizens around the Terror Wars. We need Hollywood blockbusters that champion our guys and demolish the bad guys. A name like 'The Terror Wars' immediately sparks hundreds of great ideas for movies starring Bruce Willis; not so for the War on Terror which has to make do with painful sappy allegories such as War of the Worlds *starring Tom Cruise, which may do well at the box office but are so vapid in their attitude to the war they are about as useful to the administration as a Meg Ryan romantic comedy.*

The Government and the Pentagon should team up with industry to galvanize the American public. This is wartime – our big corporate leaders such as Microsoft should be made to publicly come on board. America needs a 'Patriot' version of Windows that includes an application allowing you to report the suspicious activities in your neighborhood. In short, Bush needs to learn a few lessons from Winston Churchill. He should be collecting the steel pots and pans from ordinary citizens for use in The Terror Wars. He doesn't have to use them but it's the marketing that counts.

America needs to get honest about its bread and circuses. The War on Terror isn't just about fighting terrorists. It's also about making this sort of war tenable to a notoriously fickle American public. The military campaign will prevail, but only if the White House lifts its marketing of it domestically. Throughout the Roman Empire its leaders consistently put on a good circus. Karl Rove and George Bush should take a leaf out of their book. [32]

---

[32] http://www.townhall.com/blogs/soapbox/eddiemcguire/story/2005/10/05/159558.html

Okay, so it was no William Saffire, but I was pretty pleased with it, and for a brief moment it spread across the web. Within a few days of its publication it became the number one result on the Google search 'Rename War on Terror' – and remained in the top five results for several months.[33]

Almost immediately other conservatives earnestly took on the challenge outlined in Edward's piece. MrHitt suggested his own name for the War on Terror – 'War for the Preservation of Freedom and Democracy'. In his 78-word tome, MrHitt improved upon Edward's original thesis by arguing that war-profiteering was part and parcel of the preservation of freedom:

> *Or the 'War for the Preservation of Freedom and Democracy'*
>   *By MrHitt*
>   *Really that's what it's about. Just because corporations benefit doesn't negate the reality that if we don't fight to protect our freedom from the current Islamofascist totalitarian threat, we will fall to it. It must drive some folks nuts that if we win, then 'big business wins', so we really lose either way. I disagree. If my remaining free means profits for Halliburton, then cha-ching, baby.*

Cha-ching, indeed. Edward was in business. People were taking note, were engaging with his ideas. Edward had taken his first step to becoming an agenda-setter and he liked the feeling. Indeed, he even ordered 500 business cards which read 'Edward McGuire –

---

[33] It should be noted that since Edward put out the piece, the Pentagon has genuinely rebranded the War on Terror. Unfortunately, the name they picked was not Edward's suggestion but the 'Long War', so unfortunately, the search results for 'rename war on terror' have been swamped by newer articles discussing this change. Still I personally think that Edward – and Dr Andy – deserve credit (and perhaps a Purple Medal of Honor?) for seeding the whole rebranding concept in the first place.

Pundit'. I pointed out that it was unlikely more than about 50 people had read his piece, but Edward's enthusiasm could not be dented. The immediacy of the feedback to his ideas – and the fact that people were engaging directly with them – gave Edward a small taste of what it must be like to be an op-ed columnist for the *New York Times* and he liked it. In particular, it reinforced his belief that his own opinions were just as valid as anyone else's – no matter how ill-researched they were.[34]

'The only difference between me and media elites,' Edward told me with a completely straight face after we'd read through the seventh (and final) comment on his Townhall.com piece, 'is that they've got a larger audience than I have. But just you wait.' The side of Edward's character that had made him such a good pundit during his days at *Reaganomics Review* – ie, his brashness – had, very unattractively, started to re-emerge.

Edward's apparent success had caught me off guard. I'd had some vague notion that online commentary was a popular hobby, but I had assumed that Edward's ideas (no matter how ingenious they were[35]) would simply be subsumed into the background noise of cyberspace. But instead, almost immediately, Edward had carved out his own slither of the infinitely large pie of online commentary. By being the first person (at that point at least) to seriously suggest renaming the War on Terror as a means to fixing America's woes, Edward, for the moment, essentially owned that idea in cyberspace.

I pointed out to Edward that, in fact, the number of people who had read his article was actually infinitesimal given the number of people on the Internet, but he shrugged off my analysis. The fact that the article had bubbled its way to the top of Google was

---

[34] Or indeed, non-researched.

[35] After all, let's not forget who the actual author was . . .

undeniable proof to him. In a world of infinite commentary, it only required a few people to engage directly with his idea to make him feel like he was the next Samuel Huntington.

Admittedly there was one comment that made even me a little bit proud of Edward's first piece. It suggested that, if nothing else, Edward had at least hit the right tone. It simply read:

You are a true American. I thank you.

13

BOWLING ALONE

'Did you know that the Los Angeles public transport system is the biggest in the world?' Darryl asked me as I lay in the motel bed. Darryl, it turned out, was into factoids.

'Great. Goodnight,' I said, holding my eyes shut to get to sleep.

'And it's also one of the best. I read that on one of the ads on a bus.'

So far the most notable aspect of Darryl's life was the waiting.[36] It had taken us what to me felt like an excruciating one-and-a-half hours of waiting to get the shuttle bus to the LAX–Inglewood Super 8, which advertised itself as 'only 2 miles' away. Darryl seemed resigned to the wait, if not particularly happy about it. Indeed, he reflected, it was lucky he had called ahead from the courtesy phone. In fact, Darryl had ended up calling from the courtesy phone five times, and each time an Asian man had lied to him about the bus being 'almost there'. At check-in the same man had informed us that we had the last room available, and that it was lucky we hadn't arrived any later.

The room itself didn't look too bad. The door into the room was moist and ridden with mould, with the result that it had to be jammed shut – but at least it could be locked. It was on the third story – the top floor, and the balcony looked out onto the wide but, at this late hour, largely deserted LA street. In the distance, Darryl noted a neon sign, with a silhouette of a buxom woman. The only word Darryl could make out between the palm trees that lined the street was 'CASINO'. He suggested that perhaps we should go and

---

[36] Indeed, even if the 'world can't wait' it seemed Darryl certainly could.

try our luck. I suggested that walking at least a half a mile in the deserted night streets of LA was perhaps testing our luck a bit too much. Darryl stared at me with a half-smile that gave me the impression he thought I was a bit of a coward.

'It's not that I'm afraid,' I explained completely truthfully. 'I'm just very tired.' I yawned to demonstrate just how tired I was.

Darryl switched on the television.

During an ad-break in a rerun of *America's Funniest Home Videos* ('I've seen this one,' he noted after a few minutes) Darryl assured me that as soon as he got back to Phoenix he was going to buy a car. He'd seen all the recent advertisements for GM's $500 deposit down, hardly any payments for the first six months, plus they guaranteed you were getting the same price as the people who worked at GM. Darryl liked the financing – it made the car cheaper than a second-hand one (in the short term, at least) – but he mainly liked the idea of getting an insider's price. His father had been in the Teamsters Union during Darryl's childhood so he understood the benefits that workers in union jobs got. He was glad that for once that everyone was able to get in on it – even if it was for a limited time only.

Darryl himself wasn't in a union. His wasn't the sort of job you could get union representation for nowadays. It was a standard bar job in downtown Phoenix: $20 for an 8 hour shift, plus tips which were usually $100-$200 bucks, as he told his mum. Actually, they were usually closer to $30, and he'd only once got $200 and that was last Super Bowl when a bunch of college students had crashed the bar. That night, though, the owner had insisted on taking a 40% cut of all the tips.

'Why don't you just join your union?' I muttered. 'They'd be able to protect you from that sort of thing.'

Darryl didn't really understand. 'It's not a union job.'

'But surely you can just join a union?'

'But it's not a union job.' Darryl said, and added that perhaps when he got a proper job he'd be able to join a union. He'd heard most of the defense-contract factories around Phoenix were union jobs but it was pretty hard to get a gig there – he'd been trying to edge his way in for the past eighteen months.

For the moment Darryl was more focused on getting a car that would allow him to get to those factories on the outskirts of Phoenix, should he strike it lucky. The ad break was over – Darryl fell silent as he re-watched the slapstick antics of Middle Americans. 'People are idiots!' was the last thing I heard him exclaim before I fell asleep.

Next morning Darryl and I sat on white plastic chairs in the motel's foyer/kitchen/cleaning-products-storage-area. Both of us were half-awake sipping the 'free coffee before 10 am' that had been one of the key attractions in choosing this particular 'airport area' motel. The coffee was hot and self-served from a large thermos, which had the word 'fresh' emblazoned across it. The creamer was powder.

Darryl was looking forward to going bowling. 'It's a great way to wake yourself up,' he told me. 'Something to get you out of bed at a decent hour.' As we boarded the shuttle bus to the LAX transit terminal, Darryl noticed the driver was the same one who had driven him the night before. 'You were here last night?' he asked. Slowly, as his brain started to wake up, Darryl realized that he wasn't speaking in an American accent, even though he'd had a conversation with the driver in an American accent only the night before.

'Yeah,' said the driver, a black guy with dreadlocks that were tied with transparent plastic beads. He hadn't noticed the change in accent in the intervening six hours.

Was it possible to shift Darryl back into an American accent without the driver noticing?

'Your shift goes till eight?' said Darryl, now in an American accent.

'What?' The driver looked at Darryl strangely.

'Your shift goes till eight?' Darryl said again, ploughing on with the accent.

'Oh. Er. Yeah.' The conversation died. It was, after all, a fairly inane question. But the midnight to 8 am shiftwork explained the redness in the driver's eyes. The previous night I had assumed he'd been stoned. Darryl had pointed out that it was possible he was both tired and stoned.

Worryingly, Darryl's accent was all over the place. There was only one solution this early in the morning. I – Charles – would have to intervene. The rest of this conversation would be conducted by me, in a normal Australian accent, and then Darryl could take over once I had a firmer handle on the day.

There was one other guy on the bus. A surfer from Sacramento. He and the bus driver were chatting away, pulling off their own American accents with enviable ease.

'Three dollars twenty a gallon! Unbelievable!' said the bus driver.

'It must be cheaper further out,' said the surfie man.

'No. I was in Indio last weekend and it was $4! Four dollars a gallon. Can you believe that?'

The surfer couldn't.

'The US has got too much going on at the moment!' said the driver, shaking his head and laughing. 'Gotta pay for all these wars.'

It was weird hearing the word war used in the plural, but it was true. It was not just war any more, it was wars.

We chatted a bit more about politics and sport. A friend of the driver, a guy called Andre, used to play for the Clippers, and with some pride the driver boasted that he knew several of the guys on the team. Later, after we'd gotten out of the van, Darryl explained to me that black guys always claimed to have friends on sports teams. He sounded as if he didn't believe the bus driver.

'But, Darryl, why would he bother lying about that?'

'I don't know, but they always do.' This was a side to Darryl I hadn't expected. But over the coming days his observation turned out to be true. Many of the black people we met ended up talking about some sports star or other that they knew. To me the impressiveness of knowing the quarterback for the Los Angeles Raiders was somewhat muted since I knew nothing about basketball.[37] But I came to realize that Darryl's comments weren't borne so much out of distrust as jealousy – which struck me as a weird emotion for a white man to be having about a black man, in what remains very much a white man's world. But then I realized that sport in America is very much the black man's world.

Although the LAX public transit center has the 'LAX' designation that would suggest it shares some proximity to LAX airport, like the Super 8 motel, it was miles away. The inconvenience of Darryl's lifestyle was really starting to annoy me. To Darryl, it seemed perfectly normal.

By the time we had got dropped off, the free coffee had kicked in, so Darryl took the lead as we arrived at the transport hub.

It was now time, Darryl explained, for us to wait. And wait. The seven or eight people who were also waiting for the same bus stood far apart from each other, something that was made possible by the sprawling concrete concourse boarded by a fence lined with newspaper-vending machines, most of them in Spanish.

One older guy kept looking around restlessly. He had a three-day beard and was wearing a blue baseball cap. I pointed out to Darryl that everyone was wearing blue. Or rather, the occasional person had a blue sweater, or a blue cap, but nobody was wearing anything red. This worried me – I was carrying a bright red backpack. I asked Darryl whether he thought this was one of those colors gang areas, where we'd be stabbed to death just for wearing the wrong color. Darryl looked around and paused. His face dropped in fear. My heart jumped. Then he smiled. 'I don't think so. Besides, what are they going to do? Steal my credit cards? They can have them.'

---

[37] That's a joke by the way. I know that quarterbacks don't play basketball. They play baseball.

There was a reason I was so uncharacteristically jumpy. I had been to the South Central LA train station about a decade ago with an Australian friend of mine, Andrew. Back then the place had seemed a whole lot scarier. We had been standing on the crowded platform for only a few minutes before we were approached. 'Have you got a gun?' a stranger asked us as we stood around talking loudly about how weird it was to be the only white people in sight.

'No,' I replied.

'Oh man, you better get yourself a gun – unless you want to be killed. This is South Central LA.' Andrew and I stared at him blankly. He pointed to a block of apartments, 'Over there are the developments. This is where the LA Riots started.'

The color drained from Andrew's face, something that made him, unfortunately, look even more white than ever (I, on the other hand, distinctly remember remaining stoically calm).

Overhearing the conversation, a large black woman came over and told us, 'Look forward, avoid eye contact, and then when the train comes just get in and you'll be alright. Nobody can shoot you on the train – there's no getaway.'

Andrew and I stood there in silence for the next ten minutes, keenly aware of race politics and the practical problems associated with economic disenfranchisement. It was around this point that I realized I was still wearing a Mickey Mouse tie.[38] Eventually the train arrived, and that first stranger proceeded to board the crowded train, sit down with some friends who were already on board and, in a loud voice, so the entire carriage could hear, tell his friends that Andrew and I had been walking around on the station *without a gun*. About four black men in their mid-forties then proceeded to

---

[38] We had been at the airport trying to get stand-by seats, and we had been told that we had a better chance of scoring business class seats if we were dressed respectably. Unfortunately, the only tie at the airport store had been a Mickey Mouse one.

laugh themselves silly at the foolish tourists and their recklessly unarmed state.

This, it turned out, was not Darryl's experience. Since those days, the police had set up a base underneath the bridge of an elevated train track. As I stood there worrying, Darryl pointed out there were four marked police cars and plenty of officers standing around chatting with each other. 'Not that they'd help you anyway,' Darryl derided. His previous run-ins with the police when he was a teenager in St Louis had not been positive. 'Crims in a different uniform,' had been the prevailing attitude in his town.[39]

Our bus, when it finally arrived, had ads along the top of both sides above the seats. There was only one advertiser for this particular route, with the consequence that the same ad was repeated half-a-dozen times. 'ACCIDENTES' it screamed in large yellow lettering, 'Juan J Dominguez – Abogado'. The face of the workers' compensation lawyer, in his mid-thirties with a very thin handlebar moustache, beamed out at anyone who bothered to look up. Darryl explained that workers' compensation was a lottery system for people who couldn't afford lottery tickets. It certainly employed similar advertising techniques.

By the time we arrived at our stop, it was after 9 am and we were starving. We got off at a junction between two eight-lane roads – the normal size of non-highway thoroughfares in LA. We decided to grab something to eat before we had a bowl, but looking around at the vast expanse of empty land between each building, it was apparent that there were only two choices for breakfast for those

---

[39] Darryl's attitude towards the police comes from his status as a Statistically Generated Character. In a rigorous survey I undertook for this book during a dinner party, I discovered that six out of six people from the Midwest believe that all police are corrupt. Mind you, the main complaint was that during their adolescence, the police would take their stash of marijuana without charge so that they could smoke it themselves. I'm sure that this sort of behavior is limited to police from the Midwest.

without a car. Burger King or Del Taco. Darryl decided to go for the local chain. The place was bright; the color scheme was shades of green, yellow, red and purple, carefully arranged so that each table of four had one of each color. It was as coordinated as possible, with the consequence that it looked completely uncoordinated. After surveying the extensive menu, Darryl selected from the 'traditional breakfast' menu a bacon and egg quesadilla deal, with a small drink and five small lumps of deep fried hash browns. After he'd ordered, the Latino assistant excitedly handed Darryl a flyer with a coupon which would bring the cost down from $1.89 to $0.99. Darryl duly handed the coupon back, along with a one-dollar note, and the assistant then meticulously ripped the coupon out of the flyer and rang it up on the register: '$1.08' which is how much a $0.99 meal costs in LA.

'They screw you on taxes everywhere,' Darryl explained as he fumbled in his pocket for a spare dime. It was the main reason he'd voted for Bush in 2004 – at least Bush was against tax. The assistant behind the counter then said to Darryl in a fast monotone voice, 'Do you want to make it macho?' The assistant had already pressed some button on the register before Darryl had a chance to respond. Darryl looked up at the board above the counter. Macho was Del Taco's authentic Mexican version of the Supersize – it was the largest size for all their authentic Mexican fare: burgers, fries and thick shakes, oh, and burritos.

We sat down at a purple table. I was unable to stomach the quesadilla, which was filled with a tasteless, tepid, orange gooey substance, which Darryl said was cheese. Darryl was unperturbed. 'I love Mexican food,' he explained as he tucked into his hash browns and Coke.

Back in the 1980s, when Darryl was living in Arkansas, he was in a league team called 'The Strike Backs' that came third in the district competition two years in a row. However, with the onset of the recession in the early 1990s, Darryl had been forced to leave

Arkansas, and with it his league team. Nowadays he worked shift hours so he was unable to be a reliable member of a team. But he had started getting back into bowls. He just tended to do it on his own.

Southwest Lanes was fairly large – 24 lanes – but intimate enough that you could make eye contact with pretty much everyone bowling – even the ones up the other end. The computer scoring system looked as though it was from the mid-1980s. The monitor for each aisle was an eight-inch green monochrome deal with worn buttons that had to be pressed hard to make them work. The 20-inch monitor overhead was white monochrome, with jagged graphics that, Darryl reflected, a Commodore 64 would have done a better job producing. Still, it served its purpose, which I didn't understand at that point.

We bought two games at $2.50 each, plus $2 for the shoe hire. The friendly guy behind the counter offered Darryl a discount coupon for a soft drink , but Darryl declined – he'd already received 11% of his daily sugar requirements from the 300 ml of Coke at Del Taco. 'Well, just yell out if you need anything. I'll be around,' the man behind the counter assured him.

There was a pile of *Western Bowling News* on the counter, and as he went down to his alley, Darryl took one. He told me he enjoyed catching up on how the various leagues were going – they always told you about who got perfect scores around your area. Darryl had got his name in the paper quite a bit back in his league days. While he was setting up his stuff – putting on his shoes and selecting the right bowl – I browsed through the newspaper which was packed with lists of people's names and their scores in various competitions, as well as gossip, and ads run by bowling alleys touting their unique selling points. 'Where Locals Bring Their Friends!™' boasted one.

By the time Darryl had set up there were already two people bowling. A Latino boy and girl – teenagers – who kept taking time out from their bowling to kiss. Darryl nodded to the boy as he put on his shoes. The boy nodded back. Darryl was on lane 6, the couple were on lane 3. Already, I realized, Darryl was feeling far less alone.

By his fourth bowl, Darryl had gotten his first spare. As he turned and walked back to the computer scorer, he nodded again to the Latino couple in acknowledgement of this small triumph.

At this point a black guy with a shiny bald head arrived, carrying a small sports bag. His black T-Shirt depicted the white silhouette of a person mid-bowl, with the word 'FABULOUS!' emblazoned across the top. He immediately headed over to a center lane and got out his ball. Slowly, meticulously, he shined it with a towel, and then placed it on the bowl belt. Then he got some shoes out of his bag and put them on. Finally he went up to the counter. It was unmanned, so he ducked behind the counter and grabbed a bottle of Coke. I looked at the time. It was three minutes to ten. Darryl explained that he was probably a shift worker who needed a non-alcohol-based pastime during the day.

The man in the center aisle bowled a clean, powerful strike. It was an impressive bowl and included a large amount of spin that was awkwardly obtained by an inelegant contortion of his body. As he walked back to his seat, the man looked around to see who else saw the achievement. Darryl nodded back in acknowledgement. Satisfied, the man returned to his bowl.

This comforting ritual continued. Eventually Darryl managed his first strike; he looked around, got the nods and then headed back to his base. It was at that point I understood the role of the overhead monitors when bowling alone. In large letters at the top of the monitor now appeared the name 'Darryl Summers' and underneath it a large X flashed off and on. Darryl looked around and saw a couple of old people sitting up near the counter who had noticed the flashing X. Darryl nodded at them and they nodded back.

After the games, Darryl wanted to have a quick look at the club noticeboard before he left, to see if he recognized any names. An old black woman was already standing there. She was paying particular interest to one notice. It was printed out from a cheap color ink-jet printer. In bold red lettering it read 'MISSING'. Underneath that there were color school photos of two black kids, one 12 years old, the other 11. Scrawled in pen across the top of the notice was: 'Found: accidental drowning in lagoon' and a date which was less than two weeks earlier. 'Oh dear,' she muttered, pointing at the message, 'terrible thing.'

Darryl, however, was more interested in the notice that got pride of place on the board. It was a local newspaper article about a bowling star, Fero Williams, who, the article noted, 'bowls primarily out of Southwest Lanes' – this very hall. There was a photo of Fero – a tall, bald black man who was wearing a traditional bowling shirt, a baseball cap, and was holding a bowling ball. He beamed. 'My number one goal is to get better,' the article quoted him. 'Number two is to give back to bowlers who never had coaching, and number three is to open a pro shop.' Then, in a rather disappointing turn of events, the upbeat article noted that Fero planned to do just that when he moved to Dayton, Ohio in January. 'I'm moving to Ohio because the money is not here. The cost of living is cheaper there and in the Midwest the bowling is bigger.'

It was now April, three months after the date Fero had decided he was leaving. 'He's still around – he usually comes down here on Wednesday and Thursday nights if you want to see him bowl,' the old woman boasted. Darryl rolled his eyes at yet another black person boasting about some sporting star they knew.

I asked if he was still moving to Ohio. 'Oh yeah – he's going to Ohio – as it says in the article. He's planning to move there some day.'

As we walked back to the bus stop, Darryl announced a change of plan. We'd originally planned to head straight back to Phoenix from LA – an eight-hour trip on the Greyhound – one of the shorter inter-city legs available. But now a more interesting route had presented itself. Darryl explained that the bus was traveling through Indio, CA, and had a 30 minute layover there. Perhaps, he thought, we should get out and make a quick trip to the casino there. After all, the whole town came highly recommended. The clincher was an ad I had just found in the *Western Bowling News* for the place – it was called the Fantasy Springs Casino and Bowling Alley. We could go bowling alone and gambling alone. Perhaps Darryl could even win the money for a deposit on that car! The perfect plan.

14

GENUINE IMITATION

I was standing in Vincent Fiore's small attic study in a leafy suburb of Long Island, New York, holding his most prized possession: a letter written to him by George W Bush. It was a short letter, which Fiore conceded was presumably drafted by a staffer. The letter acknowledged receipt of a letter Vincent wrote to the President, and thanked him for his comments.

Vincent had other Republican memorabilia up on the wall, including no less than five pictures of Ronald Reagan – one of which was also personally signed. But the thing that gave it pride of place was that Vincent was almost certain the letter had been personally signed by Bush himself. 'They're pretty sophisticated, with those signing machines, but this one, if you look at it closely, it's not a machine. He signed that himself,' Vincent told me proudly.

I had a lot of questions I wanted to ask Vincent. After all the effort I had gone to getting Edward's first piece published, I'd quickly realized I needed to get the word on how it was done from someone in the inner sanctum of conservative blogging. Sure, Edward had chalked up a couple of successes over the past few weeks with his piece about renaming the war on terror, but nothing like Vincent Fiore. His name – and face – kept popping up on every conservative site. How did he manage such a successful syndication? Was there some organization behind Vincent that facilitated the distribution of his pieces?

I had decided to visit Vincent on my own without Edward's 'help'. Whenever Edward spoke, the response he provoked ranged from people quietly furrowing their brow to angrily yelling, 'WHAT!?'. Edward was pretty disappointed by his exclusion, but it was early on in my investigations and I explained to him there would be plenty of time for him to come along once his accent had been smoothed out. Instead I left him in Ithaca, brooding grumpily, curled up on the couch with a copy of his favorite book – *Reagan, In His Own Hand: The Writings of Ronald Reagan That Reveal His Revolutionary Vision for America.*[40]

For months I had been continually astounded at Vincent's ability to write columns that contained no primary research. Every column he wrote was quoting other commentators on other websites. I was keen to get tips on how Edward could become a commentator without actually doing any work. Getting in contact with Vincent had been easier than I expected. I had emailed him, asking for a chat, and he'd phoned me back almost immediately, kindly inviting me to his suburban home in Long Island.

I had pictured Vincent as a conservative whose desire to maintain the status quo arose out of his own comfortable surroundings. I had the image of a comfortable middle-class white male, sitting at home typing away at his computer, with his wife and two kids by his side in a McMansion on Long Island. I had pegged Vincent Fiore as a willing proponent of the interests of the rich and powerful because he was one of them. From race relations to economics to the war, his politics wreaked of the attitude, 'I made it without any help, so why should I help others?'. He was a classic small-government conservative, supporting the privatization of, as far as I could work out, pretty much everything. A few months earlier he had written a piece essentially denying the existence of racism:

> Blacks and all other minority groups that cover themselves with the cloak of 'victimhood' may have had real concerns once upon a time, but today suffer the same transgressions that everyone else in society from time to time deals with.

---

[40] I know. Unbelievable as it sounds, this book actually exists.

I imagined that the relative racelessness of his own suburb probably led him to extend that belief to the rest of his country. Combine that with his angry 'Go Home, Cindy' tirade against anti-war protestors, and I had imagined, frankly, he must be pretty rich and comfortable, and fed up with people less lucky than himself.

And my expectations were confirmed the moment I reached his suburb. Or so I thought. As I drove into Princeton Street, Williston, I passed house after house of beautiful wood and brick. Stupidly brilliant sunset-colored leaves fell from the impeccably spaced trees. This suburb was a whole level of consciousness away from the hustle and bustle of Manhattan. The suggested speed signs were 10 miles per hour. A notice underneath a stop sign informed me that 'unmarked and marked cars patrol this area' – an indication that private security guards were part of this idyllic streetscape. I know it's a cliché, but on that brisk afternoon, the birds twittered in the mellow fruitfulness – literally. Stunned at the sound-studio surroundings I pulled up outside a house with a flowerbed full of bright red impatiens, a basketball hoop adjoining the driveway and a lone basketball dead in the middle of the front yard. A sign on the picket fence read 'Beware of the Dog'. It was 4.20 pm and the occasional car passed, perhaps one every ten minutes. Office workers who'd knocked off early. Perhaps this was not the real upper class, but it *was* an authentic imitation of the upper class. Even the street name – Princeton – had an Ivy League ring to it that was a complete fabrication. This was Middle America, straight out of a Tom Hanks movie. The occasional American flag adorned a front porch. The people of Williston, I thought, don't need to go on suicide-bombing missions to enter paradise – they've made it right here on earth.

It was late October, and garden after garden had Halloween displays erected – pumpkins and witches' hats and goblins. Some were just plonked on the front lawn no assembly required, while others were elaborate decorations that covered the whole house.

Oddly, not one of the fifty houses I passed featured real pumpkins in their display – they were all store-bought. Growing up as a kid, I had lived in the US for a year, and one of the fondest memories of Halloween I have (besides putting ketchup on my stomach to pretend I had been stabbed) was trying to carve a face out of a pumpkin, then handing it over to Dad who produced something that – at the age of seven – looked pretty scary, especially if you put a candle in the middle.

I wondered why this ritual had passed away. Where did the dream go so wrong that people were too busy even to share the essentially American ritual of watching Dad cut his hands to shreds as he carved a face out of a pumpkin? It dawned on me that this type of nostalgic yearning was quite familiar – all of a sudden, I could see where Vincent's conservatism was coming from. Mass-produced pumpkins represented exactly the sort of decay of American values that Vincent was so incensed about.

I got out of the car and looked for the number of his house. It didn't seem to exist. Where it should've been was just an empty path between two houses. Had I been given the run-around? Was Vincent Fiore himself a made-up character in someone else's wild imaginings? I knocked on the house next door to where Vincent's house should've been. A young mother with blonde hair and pyjamas falling off her shoulder answered the door. She looked like someone Meg Ryan would play. I asked her where the missing house was. 'Oh, which suburb are you looking for?' she asked.

'Williston.' I said.

'Oh. This is Roslyn Estates. That's one town away. There are two Princeton Streets within a mile of each other.'

Williston, it turned out, might only be a mile down the street, but it was a socio-economic world away. I drove down the other Princeton Street and noticed that instead of brick mansions, most of the houses were smaller, thinner and made of clapboard. The thing that really caught my eye was that the elaborate Halloween decorations had been replaced with American flags. More than half the houses had donned large bright tributes to the Star-Spangled Banner.

Vincent's house was easy to find. It was a small step up from those around it – a combination of brick and weatherboard, with a massive American flag obscuring the front steps. But this was not the plush comfort that I'd imagined Vincent would live in. This was still Middle America – although in many ways Vincent's house was an imitation of those in Princeton Street, Rosyln Estates. It was as if Vincent was imitating the imitators.

As we sat at the dining room table, wrapped in plastic, I realized that pretty much everything I had expected Vincent Fiore to be was wrong. Vincent Fiore, it turned out, was a gentle, cheerful guy – not the conservative firebrand his articles would lead you to believe. A plumber by trade, Vincent was attached to the New York Fire Department, and he was even a member of a union – the Plumbers Local 1. A few years ago, as he was approaching his fortieth birthday, he suddenly developed a passion for politics. 'I cannot put my finger on it. I started to become interested in politics in 1999,' he told me. 'I believe it was the late summer, and I started to develop a real hunger. That's all I can say.'

In May 2002 Vincent sat down and wrote his first political opinion piece. 'It was for a website that's now gone – Bushcountry.org – and they were the first site to post one of my articles. I remember how excited I was. I was thrilled. And I was so grammatically challenged. I didn't know a colon from a semicolon.'

I nodded understandingly and gave a 'we've all been through that' look: underneath I desperately tried to remember the difference between a semicolon and a colon; I knew that I should know that: why couldn't I; you know: remember?

Over the following eighteen months Vincent – who was very conscious of the fact he never went to college – would sit down at his computer for three hours every night, researching and writing. On the weekends he would stay up to the early hours of the morning. At the end of each fortnight, his effort would reward him with a single article of no more than 1000 words of his own opinion about an issue that had grabbed him. He would then send it to conservative sites all around the web.

For all this effort, Vincent got no monetary reward, but he wasn't in it for the money. He had his plumbing business for that. What he got was something far more meaningful. 'It's so important that I get my thoughts out there. And it's not just my thoughts any more. My email tells me that it's a lot of people's thoughts.'

What Vincent was describing was exactly what Edward had gone through after he'd posted his first article on Townhall.com. It seems obvious, but the effect of receiving just a few comments of positive reinforcement is as good a motivation as any.

Then in late 2003, Vincent got an email from a guy named Marv Essary. Essary was eighty years old and a former newspaper editor. At the time, Essary was the editor for ChronWatch, a conservative website set up to keep tabs on the liberal bias in the *San Francisco Chronicle*. Essary offered to take Vincent under his wing and develop his writing skills. Vincent was at first hesitant. 'Naturally, since I'm an American, I was instantly suspicious and wanted to know "what's in it for you, what are you really after here?"'

I was curious too. 'So what *was* in it for Marv?' I asked.

'He wrote back. He said, "Look, I only offer this to two or three people ever."' This struck me as a somewhat perplexing answer, but Vincent seemed satisfied with it, and from then on Vincent sent his column to Marv, who would suggest corrections and send it back.

'I have to make the corrections, but he puts everything in blue and he wants me to understand and this is why I love him for this. He wants me to understand what he's doing. And I do. I didn't before he started with me. I didn't know a colon from a hyphen from a dash to a whatever, but now I do. I know that, for instance, you never capitalize the word presidential. Did you know that?'

I didn't, but wanting to maintain the air of a well-seasoned professional author, I nodded, using my 'of course I'd know something as obvious as that' look.

Above all, Marv gave Vincent confidence in his writing. 'I didn't have the money or the worthwhile to go to college. I would like to go, I think, now. That might be in the future for me. But my writing has really improved because of Marv.'

What I really wanted to know, though, was how Vincent got published on so many sites. Luckily, he was more than happy to share the secret. Unfortunately, the secret sounded like an awful lot of work. Vincent simply emailed his column to the sixty or so sites he got syndicated on every fortnight – each one individually personalized. A laborious job.

'Certain websites, like OpinionEditorial, you go right to their site and they have a page where you can load up your piece, you can post it up. Most of the time, though, I have an email address for each website's editor or owner and I write a little note: ". . . Dear Tom, Here's my latest piece. See what you think. Send appropriate corrections back to me, any ideas blah blah blah."'

But ultimately the lesson that I would take back to Edward was that it was all in the marketing. 'I try and promote myself as much as possible.' In fact, in doing so, Vincent explained that recently he had landed his first paid gig with NewsBusters.org, a media-based website dedicated to 'Exposing and Combating Liberal Media Bias'. For a weekly column reviewing the *New York Times* and *Washington Post*, they pay Vincent $100 a month.

Having watched *All the President's Men* as preparation for writing this book, I knew to follow the money. Skillfully, like a latter-day Robert Redford, I prodded Vincent to reveal more. Aside from the mysterious Marv, wasn't there a puppet-master steering the debate? The NewsBusters site was run by the Media Research Center, run by William F Buckley's brother-in-law. But at $100 a month, it was hardly the global conspiracy that would bring down a Presidency,

I mean, presidency. Hadn't Vincent been approached by some secretive White House insider who told him the message of the month? Didn't he get approached to write dirt pieces on conservative enemies?

'I had an editor from an up-and-coming website called People Political.org,' Vincent recalled casually. 'She wants me to write articles that pertain to all the good news that's not being reported from Iraq. And while that's true, it's not something that grabs me.'

I asked Vincent about his column 'Go Home, Cindy', in which he lashed out at Cindy Sheehan, the mother of a dead war hero, who was protesting outside George W Bush's holiday ranch in Texas. Edward had particularly loved Vincent's fiery rhetoric in the piece.

No, Mrs Sheehan, you have not opened up anything resembling debate. You have only continued the anti-war left's maniacal behavior and many outrages since this war began. You have brought nothing new to America's table of debate. You have instead used your son's death to try to politically assassinate a war-time president.

As sympathetic and endearing as you may think you look to your leftist cohorts and a small minority of the country, know this: You are a tool, Ms Sheehan, in a grand game of political chess, and like most pawns, you will be discarded, and forgotten.

Edward shared Vincent's fury at the inability of conservatives to argue against the anti-war opinions held by the relatives of dead war heroes. But according to Edward, Vincent's piece was a stroke of genius because he had found a loophole. Instead of attacking her ideas head-on, he attacked her by attacking the puppet-masters behind her. This had the simultaneous effect of creating the punditry equivalent of a proxy war, as well as subtly suggesting Cindy's opinions were not her own passionately held beliefs.

I'd told Edward that Vincent was probably put up to writing the article by someone higher up in the conservative movement. But

Edward had reeled at this suggestion.[41] And when I asked Vincent, he, too, said I was wrong. 'Her actions infuriated me. To me she was a phony from day one.' He leant in and poked at the table. 'I knew there was something more behind this – not that the mainstream media told you about it, which also led me to write such a fiery piece against her. And I admit it was fiery. I called her a disgrace, which is a tough thing for me to say to a mother who buried her son. I didn't want to say it. There was a point where I regretted it.'

But in the world of Internet commentary, Vincent had hit the jackpot. He received over 3000 emails, 'And most of them were hate mail,' Vincent said.

'It was purposely shopped around, that article, I know it was. In other words an organization got hold of it. An organization in Texas.' I was sensing that Vincent didn't know whether to feel proud or bitter. 'The Crawford Peace House, which was one of the organizations that was sponsoring Mrs Sheehan when she was in Texas. They are a thoroughly communistic and, um, very leftist organization. They posted my picture up at a very big democratic website called Democratic Underground, urging their readership to write to me.'

From there, MoveOn.org – the 3 million member left-wing email organizing site that Bertrand had been trying to get in contact with – also picked it up, and within hours Vincent's inbox was swamped with abusive emails. Vincent Fiore had broken through. Admittedly it was by criticising the mother of a dead war hero. But hell, that was clearly what worked best in the marketplace of ideas.

Up in the attic, 'where it all happens', Vincent's shelves were lined with books on conservative politics, including, many of William F Buckley's, books by George F Will, biographies on

---

[41] You would think, seeing as Edward is a character created by me, I would not be constantly astounded by him, but I am. Edward seems to be pathologically unable to spot any form of irony.

Reagan, and numerous other books with titles like *The Conservative Question* and *On Being a Conservative*. Vincent showed me his favorite – the *New York Times Style Guide*. It seemed odd that he would like anything from the notoriously liberal (in his eyes) *New York Times*. 'It's the only thing published by the *New York Times* worth reading,' he joked.

On his walls he had photos of Reagan, Bush I and II. I asked him whether he'd ever met any of them. Vincent said no, but confided what he really wanted to do was save up enough money to go to one of those Republican fundraisers in DC, where you pay $500 and for an extra $500 you get a photo with a Republican bigwig like Donald Rumsfeld or Dick Cheney. That would be something special for his wall.

It was becoming clear that even if the conservative Internet media was coordinated by a cabal of disciplined spinners – what some people called the Republican 'noise machine' – Vincent was not in a position to tell me about it. Perhaps if he were more mercenary he would be further up the chain, but as it was Vincent didn't need a party whip to tell him what to write – he already believed in America. 'There is no other country on the face of the earth remotely like it. I mean, as a matter of fact, if we ever built a fence around our country it would be to keep people out, as opposed to East Germany, who built a fence to keep people in.'

His inspiration didn't need a puppet-master – it came from the conservative institutions that were already out there: conservative radio – 'Rush[42] is my hero' – television – 'Fox News, of course, and *Meet the Press*' – and the right-wing Internet commentary he immersed himself in.

---

[42] Rush Limbaugh is a conservative radio shock-jock who is syndicated throughout the country. He uses a mixture of humor and hokey commonsense to spread an affable message of hatred towards any idea that would have majority support in San Francisco.

By the end of my visit I sensed Vincent felt he still hadn't broken through to me – as if I wasn't hearing him well enough. 'Spirited confrontation is the best thing to have,' he told me as he led me to his front door. He admitted that one day he'd like to be a guest commentator on Fox News. 'I don't want to sit there and say "F- you", that's not what I'm talking about. I'm talking about spirited confrontation and you're banging away at each other like two ideal-istic gladiators. Going after one another. There's nothing wrong with that. It's what America needs.'

Vincent's version of robust debate might not be as dialectical as the forefathers had perhaps envisioned, but by taking up blogging, Vincent was being heard in places he'd never dreamed of. 'I've got hate mail from professors at Berkeley. I mean, I was flattered that I could affect a professor in Berkeley and I could actually talk with him in his own language.' Vincent sensed the professor in question was using language to bully him. But Vincent – with his new-found confidence – said he stood up to the professor. Thanks to the conservative blogging community, Vincent Fiore, a plumber with no college education, was living the American dream.

As I left the suburb of Williston, I decided to go via the upscale streets of Roslyn Estates to see the Halloween displays now that night had fallen. As I drove past each display, I realized there was a far easier explanation for the disappearance of the home-made pumpkins. In the suburban darkness of the Princeton Street and Cherrytree Lane, it quickly became apparent that the store-bought pumpkins were infinitely superior to home-made ones I remember from my childhood. They were larger and bright orange, not small and dark green. In the darkness of night, the orange glow of their built-in electric bulbs contrasted brilliantly with the mass-printed black lines of their eyes and grin. They were bigger, scarier, and required less band-aids. And they wouldn't even smell rancid if you left them out too long.

Clearly, it's entirely rational – in fact, excruciatingly rational – for a family to invest in a pre-produced pumpkin for their Halloween display. It is not the failure of the American dream, but the runaway *success* of America's consumer market that has driven out the ritual I so fondly remember. And though I had blindly ignored it on my way in, staring me in the face was a whole new ritual that had emerged in its place: a low-level Halloween Decoration arms race between neighbors, fueled by cheap imports of orange plastic from China. No wonder Vincent blogged.

15

MR FIRTH GOES TO WASHINGTON

'Lower', said Grant, a friend of a friend, who came from Georgia. 'You've got to speak from your balls.'

Inevitably, there would come a time when all my characters would begin interacting with real people, not just by email, but by phone and in person. This posed a large-ish problem. As an Australian who had lived in America for only a few months, it had become quite clear that my fake American accent wouldn't cut the mustard.

Already my experiments to perfect the accent had proved less than successful. I thought it was impeccable, but every time I tried it out on an American – say, in a bar – they would howl with laughter and get their friends to come over and listen to my feeble attempts. This did not inspire the confidence I needed to pull off my mission. My trial runs talking to bus drivers, fast-food employees and people in bars were fairly low pressure because I didn't have to build a relationship of trust with any of them.

But if any of my characters were going to infiltrate the movements they were part of, then pulling off a convincing American accent over an extended period of time was going to be vital.

Thus I found myself being voice-coached by a former star college quarterback who had dropped the jockstrap and was now training to become a teacher. He and his former-cheerleader fiancée, Liz, and I had found ourselves at the Thanksgiving dinner of a mutual friend, and for some reason the table of Americans had decided to turn their attention to how bad my accent was.

Grant was bringing to bear all his teaching skills on my voice. 'You've got to speak lower, and slower, and it's got to be in one tone. Instead of going up and down, just speak with one note.' As he spoke, he did everything he said with the impossible perfection of a native speaker.

'Now say "cider",' he said.

'Si-da,' I said.

'No. Ciderrr. Rrrr.'

'Ciderrr.'

'Good. If you practice that for a few months, you should be able to pull it off.' The truth was I didn't have a couple of months, but I decided to politely steer the conversation onto something else.

'I reckon I'll be fine,' I said.

'And don't say "reckon". You sound like a hillbilly.'

* * *

It was time to head to Washington DC for the World Can't Wait rally. The original plan I had envisaged had involved me being Bertrand for pretty much the entire time I was there. However, after the Thanksgiving lesson, I decided that Charles Firth was a safer cover. Bertrand could come with me, but he wouldn't be doing much talking.

At first, Dr Andy objected. He wanted to go to Iraq as soon as possible. And so did I – of course. But I told Dr Andy Iraq wasn't going anywhere so I could afford to spend a bit of time helping out Bertrand.

Right from the start I got the feeling that I wasn't ready for DC, or perhaps DC wasn't ready for me. In his enthusiasm, Bertrand had insisted I book a hotel right near the White House. I had agreed this was prudent. It was important to be close by in case I scored an interview with the President or the Secretary of State or someone. (I had put in some phone calls, and was hoping for the thumbs-up –

I even dropped names: 'You know Thomas Friedman – I'm sort of like him,' I'd told the White House receptionist.) Bertrand had in mind the Watergate Hotel, and although I agreed in principle, it turned out that despite all the free publicity it has received from its notorious past there was no special discount rate for 'potential Pulitzer prize nominees'.

Booking the absolutely cheapest hotel near the White House turned out to be somewhat of a mistake. The website described it as 'a welcome sight to the eyes of the budget conscious traveler' but I should probably have looked up a more independent-minded site where I would have discovered seven out of seven people agreed with the review entitled 'Stay Away', and seven out of nine agreed with the review headlined 'You gotta be kidding'. Indeed, it not only had received exclusively bad reviews (the most positive review had the rather defensive title 'Not As Bad As People Say') but I later discovered it was ranked 107th in Trip Advisor's popularity index of downtown Washington hotels (out of 116 hotels).

But after a long drive I was glad just to be there. I let myself into my room only to find it was full of cigarette smoke, so I spent an hour at reception changing rooms. Finally, I got to my new room, exhausted. Sure, the bathroom sink had several pubic hairs in it, but at least it had a bed. As I lay down on the old spring mattress, my head hitting the pillow, it slowly dawned on me the pillow was damp. Really quite damp. Indeed, the entire left corner of the bed was both damp and smelt of mould. Too exhausted to do anything, I just put down a towel and slept on the damp, mouldy, smelly bed that was really close to the White House.

Mr Firth had arrived in Washington.

The next day I was woken by a call from someone at the Leadership Institute, a right-wing think tank that offered internships and training sessions. They claimed to have trained 48 000 conservatives since 1979. I had been vaguely thinking that Edward should do an internship there. They had some great courses such as 'Grassroots

Activism' and 'Public Speaking Workshop', but the one that really interested me was a forum on 'The Roots of the Ultra-Left: What they Really think'. Unfortunately, Michelle Miller, a spokesperson from the Institute, was angry.

'You can't fool us, Mr Firth,' she curtly informed me.

'I'm sorry, what?' I said.

'You're a comedian,' she said, and hung up.

What a strange town, I thought to myself, as the rest of my brain scrambled to wake up. The whole conversation had left me torn – I was, of course, flattered that she thought I was funny, but at the same time I had been looking forward to finding out about the Leadership Institute's 'Effective Voter Mail' program, where you learnt to 'acquire quality voter lists'. It sounded slightly illegal.

Of course, this was the risk of coming to Washington DC as 'Charles Firth'. Back then, if you googled my name – something which I rarely, if ever, would do, of course – many of the entries were about a character I had played in a television series a few years ago, called *CNNNN*. The series was a send-up of cable news channels, and I had played 'Firth' a right-wing shock-jock investigative reporter – sort of Geraldo meets Bill O'Reilly. If Michelle had been so slapdash as to only read my first entry on Google, this is what she would have found:

For Charles Firth journalism is about telling other people's stories. From innocent children in Rwanda being sold defective GI Joe dolls to the thousands of starving men and women of Los Angeles, Firth is fond of saying he's 'seen it all and covered it all'.

Firth's career started in 1969 when he scored a scoop interview for his school newspaper with astronaut Louis Armstrong.

Ever since this contentious start, Firth's reports have provoked more than his fair share of lawsuits, Senate oversight committees and Royal Commissions. But as Firth is also fond of saying, 'that's just part of the job'.

During his career, Firth has prided himself on never shying away from reporting the facts, no matter how ugly. Of particular note is Firth's pivotal role in the Iran-Contra affair during the 1980s as a media advisor to Oliver North.

Firth joined CNNNN in October 1987 after his 1976 prediction of a stock market collapse was finally vindicated.

In 1991, Firth was appointed CNNNN's first permanent War Correspondent at Large. During the Gulf War, he pioneered the possession of handguns by journalists in the battlefield. For this and his many contributions to the war effort, the British Army awarded him the special Royal Patriot Badge for positive reporting above and beyond the call of duty.

Firth's award-winning coverage of US humanitarian intervention in Somalia ended just hours before the famous 'Black Hawk Down' incident in October 1993.

Firth is a fervent supporter of many human rights. His fearless campaigning for the death penalty on behalf of auto-theft victims has seen him deported from Norway on three separate occasions. Even so, Firth vows he'll fight on. As he's fond of saying, 'where there's injustice, there's Firth'.

He lives with his son and two wives in Sydney.

In hindsight, I probably should have asked for the bio to be taken down, but I had been lulled into a false sense of security only days earlier by Vincent Fiore. 'Let me guess – you're 40 years old,' he had said as we stood in his living room making small talk while his wife got the camera ready to take a snapshot of us.

'Um, no, I'm closer to 30.'

'Oh, but on the web, it said you had been over in Iran in '79 and . . .' Vincent trailed off, confused.

'Oh that. No, um. That's a send-up. That's not really me, that's a character I played,' I explained.

'Oh I see. I thought you were older . . . I couldn't pick it . . . cos I looked you up on the web and saw the stuff about Iran and it's one of the reasons I thought I should talk to you.'

In contrast to Vincent's touching naivety, the Leadership Institute was run with hard-nosed realism and was denying me any access. I couldn't imagine why – the only reason I could think of was that they must have been deeply involved in some sort of horrific cover-up. Later on, I contacted the Institute again with no luck. Eventually I ended up asking them whether it was true they were actually just a front for a massive pedophile ring. They did not respond – so clearly they've got something to hide.

Later that morning I met Bertrand at the Starbucks on DuPont circle – the closest place downtown DC has to a café strip. Bertrand was well rested, having spent the night in the Watergate Hotel. 'If you're going to change the world, why not do it in style?' he had decided the night before.

The day was cold and rainy but Bertrand was still excited. Eager to make a move, he insisted we get our coffee 'to go', which didn't make any difference since it was all served in the same paper cups anyway. Bertrand had hired an SUV to drive the 20 blocks or so to the rally and was eager for me to see it. In my morning daze I couldn't work out why Bertrand was so proud of it – indeed, I couldn't work out why a committed lefty would be so excited by an SUV at all.

'It's hybrid,' he beamed. 'Completely guilt free – gets almost as good mileage as a small car.'

I asked him why he didn't just hire a small car then. He looked at me blankly.

After three loops, Bertrand finally navigated his way off the roundabout at DuPont circle and towards the White House. Now all he needed was somewhere to park his large vehicle. In the back were half-a-dozen signs Bertrand had hand-painted 'in case the organizers run out of placards'.

I still hadn't told Bertrand that the rally was being organized, at least in part, by the Revolutionary Communist Party of America, and as such I wasn't expecting it to be very big. I didn't have the heart. Even so, Bertrand's expectations that it would be 'the next moratorium' seemed a little overblown. And I couldn't work out why he kept talking about tipping points. It seemed pretty clear to me that the language the organizers had employed in their advertisements had been too shrill to reach a mass audience. There were, however, a few things that intrigued me about it.

For a start, the organizers had spent over $500 000 promoting the rally nationally, and in recent days its website had said there were bus loads of activists coming from as far away as Texas to join the campaign. Perhaps, I thought, this really might be the start of a campaign that would gradually grow bigger and bigger, much like the anti-Vietnam War movement. Perhaps Bertrand's naïve optimism was rubbing off on me, but it is true that every movement has to start somewhere.

Bertrand had even read hints on discussion boards that if the feeling in the crowd was right, organizers would ask people to stick around and essentially sit-in over the coming days and weeks. Travis himself had been quoted in the press hinting at such a possibility. Presumably his thinking was if they sat there long enough the Bush regime would collapse under the sheer weight of moral pressure that can only come from a long discussion.

Thus the optimism of Travis and the rest of the organizers in the days leading up to the rally had ill prepared everyone, even the most cynical observer, for its grim reality.

The rally was scheduled to start at 11 am. Despite the rain, Bertrand decided to park his two-ton tribute to the environment about 10 blocks away to avoid the inevitable traffic jams – we were 10 minutes early so we could afford the time. As we walked along, it became clear that we'd parked too soon – the closer we got to the Washington Monument, the more parking spaces there were. As we walked down 17th Street, past the White House, we passed van after van of Mr Softees who'd eagerly staked their spots along the side of the street. Their windows were open for business – anticipating brisk trade over the next few hours. At Constitution Avenue, right next to the park where the rally was being held, the police were directing traffic – manual override to cope with the expected crowds. At the intersection there were two activists handing out flyers – one about the rally and another about an organization called the Free People's Movement. And nobody else. On that corner you could see more Mr Softee vans than people. We stood there for a while, hesitant to cross the road and go into the seemingly empty park. Bertrand got out his map of downtown DC. 'No, this is it. That is the field.'

I didn't believe Bertrand. His blind optimism was starting to turn into plain old blindness. No longer willing to trust him, I asked the woman handing out flyers, 'Is this the rally? Where's the rally?' The woman pointed to the park across the road and said that if we just walked up the footpath we'd see it. Bertrand gave me an 'I told you so' smirk and walked ahead.

In complete synchronization with the traffic lights, the police officer redundantly hand-signaled to stop an oncoming Mr Softee van arriving late, and allowed Bertrand to trudge across the street on his own. Reluctantly, I hurried after him.

The rally was being held in the same field as the Washington Monument, a tall obelisk that soars 555 feet[43] in the air. Organizers had chosen to place the stage and logistics tents at the other end of the field – in the north-western corner, perhaps 200 meters from the imposing tower. Bertrand understood their thinking. They thought the crowds would stretch back across the lolling field, and

---

[43] Which, I believe, represents the number of wooden teeth Washington had made into dentures during his lifetime. Or am I getting two American History factoids confused?

the monument would act as a natural backstop, to keep the crowds contained in the one space. At capacity, the park could probably fit several hundred thousand people.

The first thing we noticed as we walked in through the entrance to the park was the row of portable toilets lining the northern border. Stretching into the distance, I counted 75 dark green doors before my eyesight gave out. There must have been at least 100. Bertrand said that it demonstrated how well the rally had been organized. I pointed out that there seemed to be more toilets than actual people. But Bertrand was unfazed – he said that as we were approaching from behind the main stage, it was impossible for us to see how many people were gathered in front of it. It was possible that as we passed around the front of the stage we would see tens of thousands of people sprawled across the field. The speakers had already begun and the huge PA system could conceivably be drowning out the noise of crowds.

We walked past a tall pile of green 'Bush Step Down' placards that had been strategically placed next to the footpath so that people could pick one up as they arrived. There were several thousand placards waiting to be taken; inside one of the logistics tents, five volunteers stapled posters to poles, adding more placards to the pile. I suggested to Bertrand he add his to the pile, just in case they ran out. Bertrand was not amused, but for lack of anything else to do with them, he timidly added them to the growing numbers.

The stage itself was huge, but as we turned the corner it was the backdrop that really caught Bertrand's eye. A massive billboard-sized banner stretched across the entire back wall of the stage with the words 'Bush Step Down . . . And Take Your Program With You!' Marketing genius, Bertrand told me. With the banner there, the news cameras had no choice but to include the catchy slogan when they broadcast sound bites from the speakers. If any news cameras turned up, that is.

In front of the stage, about 30 meters back, the organizers had built a tiered communications platform, with three separate levels to allow television cameras an uninterrupted view of the stage. There was room for 10 cameras on each level – 30 television cameras in total. A lone man with a long beard sat on the second level of the platform and recorded the proceedings with a hand-held video camera.

To make the whole thing more telegenic for the absent television cameras, in front of the stage, to the left side, was a huge 10 meter high effigy of George Bush that towered over the assembled crowds-to-be.

In front of the stage, gathered on the field stretching back all the way to the Washington Monument, were no more than 300 people. Many of them held two of the green placards each in a vain attempt to bolster morale.

The footprint of the stage, and the logistics tent behind it, was bigger than the crowd in front of it. There was one portable toilet for every three participants. Or to put it in perspective – the money the organizers had spent promoting the rally equated to $1500 per participant.

Needless to say, Bertrand's enthusiasm was beginning to wane. Instead of letting on just how disappointed he was, he suggested we walk around the tiny crowd. The first woman we approached was standing next to a tent with a sign saying 'Guilty of War Crimes – ImpeachBush.org'. A well-educated woman in her mid-forties with a hand-knitted woolen shawl around her shoulders, she explained to Bertrand and me that she'd been to every single rally since 2002.

'How many is that?' Bertrand asked as I watched on, anxious to make sure he rolled his r's and minimized his use of the word 'reckon'. Anyway, I assured myself, it didn't really matter that Bertrand's American accent was barely passable. In the cold, miserable, muddy field, nobody was taking much notice of anything.

'You lose count, it's like keeping track of the day you stopped smoking, you just keep not smoking, you just keep showing up for the rallies. I think it's been at least eight.'

Bertrand pondered this answer. 'What else can people do?' he wondered out loud.

The woman was very definite about what needed to be done: 'We all need to find each other, and join hands and not stop until it's over.' A perfect plan, of course. Three hundred people walking around holding hands – that always brings down governments.

Bertrand next approached a few young twenty-something white men who were wearing bandanas on their heads and holding their own home-painted placards: 'No To Imperialists Out Of Iraq Now' read one, 'Out To George Bush – Down With Capitalism' read another. A man in his fifties walked by with a fishing line and a small effigy of Bush attached to it, with Bush hanging by the neck from a noose.

One of the twenty-somethings was wearing about 20 badges with witty slogans. One depicted a head shot of Bush looking confused and the words 'Got Oil?'. Another simply said: 'Support Our Troops: Impeach Bush'.

Before Bertrand could stop me, I asked the be-badged man how he was going to bring down the American Empire. The man was even more confident about his answer than the woman had been. 'I think people have to have a change of heart. I think the biggest problem that we have here is not a political problem, it's a spiritual problem around the world. People have to want to be fair and honest.'

It seemed that the rally was full of people who wanted to be fair and honest – and yet, to me, it didn't seem to be having much effect.

Next Bertrand sidled over to a middle-aged blonde woman with elegant makeup and jewelry. She was in a purple suit jacket straight out of the 1980s, complete with shoulder pads. As if to ruin the effect, on her jacket were two large green fluorescent stickers. Bertrand asked her how she thought the Left would achieve its aims. 'Stand together as a united people and stand up for what we believe is the best thing . . . rallies, protests, writing to our senators and congressmen. Sticker campaigns . . . everywhere you can put them. And the media.'

Bertrand thanked the woman for her thoughts and walked away. I started to joke to him about the awesome power of sticker campaigns but trailed off. Bertrand was not in the mood. Perhaps my cynicism was starting to rub off on him, but even a true believer could see that it would take more than 300 people, 1000 placards and a sticker campaign to unseat the government of the greatest superpower on earth. And yet the people standing in the muddy field next to the Washington Monument were touchingly hopeful about their gesture.

Silently Bertrand led the way as we walked out of the park, past the still massive pile of placards. It was just before midday and the crowd was beginning to thin out even though the organizers had scheduled the speakers and music to last until 5 pm. Most of the Mr Softee vans had already left.

Bertrand had no idea what to do – but then, neither did these people.

As we got into the SUV, Bertrand told me he wanted some time to himself, presumably to wallow. I told him I was happy to oblige. The fact that Bertrand was taking the rally's failure so personally seemed a little self-indulgent to me.

* * *

I arrived back from Washington exhausted. Partly it was the drive back, but mostly it was having slept, or rather, not slept for several nights in that damp bed. The trip had hardly been the triumph I'd hoped. I hadn't scored that all-important quote from the White House insider that I needed for page 221.

But as luck would have it, while my left-liberal character was floundering, my conservative economist was about to chalk up another success. As I was typing up my notes my cell phone rang. The number was withheld.

'Hello,' I said cautiously.

It was Neal, the mysterious editor of AmericanDaily.us and the head of the conservative organization MoveOff.[44]

'Edward? Is this Edward?'

My heart leapt and then started pounding in my throat. I put on my best American accent.

'Yes it is.' I sounded like some sort of high-pitched happy customer-service representative.

'This is Neal, from AmericanDaily.'

'Oh great. Nice too hearrr from you-ah Nealrrr,' I said. The words were far too labored. By this point, my fake American accent had caught the ear of my partner, Amanda, who had walked into the room and had almost immediately started pointing down. I had no idea what she was on about.

'I love your column,' said Neal. 'I'm going to put it up on AmericanDaily and NewsByUs, and we've got other sites. We've got lots of sites.'

'That's grrreat.' I said, trying to limit the amount I talked. Perhaps I could just pretend that I wasn't much of a talker. There was a pause. 'Well I reckon I've got plenty morrre arrrticles in me if you want some.' Amanda winced at my use of the word 'reckon'. There was another pause.

'I run MoveOff, we took it over recently, and we just want to encourage people like you. We can set you up as a columnist on

---

[44] In case you're confused that's because it's confusing. MoveOff is a conservative network of websites set up in reaction to the liberal website MoveOn. Initially its name was ironic, but nowadays its considerable size and influence makes it anything but ironic. But then, this is America – hardly the greatest place on earth for irony to thrive.

AmericanDaily and NewsByUs, and we'll give you an email address to send your stuff to, but you'll have to send it to both, okay, because I'm just helping out with NewsByUs – there's another guy who runs it. Okay?'

'Grrreat,' I said.

'I've had a few drinks, Ed. I'm pretty drunk.'

'Well it is the end of the day.' By this point I was under a lot of strain. Amanda was glaring at me, pointing down vigorously. My voice seemed unable to break out of its Australian roots – I was getting the r's right, but that was about it. My whole throat constricted every time I spoke. Not that Neal seemed to notice.

'They're after me. There's a lot of people after me. They could get me, you know. They want to foreclose on me I think, but that's why I don't tell people my last name any more. I used to but I don't any more.' Neal wasn't really making a whole lot of sense, and he seemed to be telling me more than I thought I should know. 'Do you have a web hoster? How much do you pay?'

'Umm, I don't know, it's part of a package,' I said. Again Amanda pointed to the ground. I looked down but I couldn't work out what she was pointing to.

'We can host it for you if you want. We can put Edward-McGuire.com on our servers. Anything to help out. We can make your numbers go through the roof.'

'Thanks, mate. That'd be fantastic,' Amanda looked at the ceiling in pure frustration.

He paused for a moment, and then went on. 'I can help with design if you need. I haven't looked at your site, I only know HTML, but we can help out.' Neal was clearly an enthusiast. He was offering to be to Edward what Marv was to Vincent – a mentor to help him work his way into the conservative movement.

'Anything you-ah can do to help, I rreckon that would be brilliyant.' Amanda winced. 'I've got to go, but I'd-ah be really interresterrd in you hosting EdwardMcGuire.com.'

'Sure. Thanks Ed. Bye.'

I hung up. After only a few weeks of punditing, Edward McGuire was going to become part of the MoveOff network. Edward was starting to receive material help for being a conservative: he was now an official member of the conservative cabal! Only one mystery remained: why had Amanda been pointing down the whole time?

'You weren't speaking through your balls,' she said in disgust.

PHASE THREE
Hearts and Minds

16

LET'S ROLL

Bertrand was incredibly busy. Stupidly so. The power button on his laptop had broken during the week, which meant that he couldn't turn his computer off. As a result he had found himself being contacted on email and through various instant messenger programs 24 hours a day. A lot of Bertrand's contacts came from overseas, and the rolling time zones were killing him. It was hard work trying to please everyone all day and all night.

You might wonder why he didn't just turn off the volume so that the *cha-tring* of arriving emails didn't wake him. The truth was, Bertrand secretly loved the grind. 'This must be what it's like to be President,' he thought as he dozed between emails (also, he couldn't work out how to turn down the volume on his laptop, but he didn't really want to own up to that).

Bertrand and I were sharing coffee and cake at Bertrand's favorite independent café in Park Slope. It was his fifth coffee of the day and he still looked tired. He'd decided to sit in one of the uncomfortable cane chairs, in a vain attempt to keep himself awake.

Like many liberals searching for the answer to the Left's woes, Bertrand was obsessed with conservative methods of organizing, and he was holding forth about it. 'Have you noticed,' asked Bertrand as he bit into an almond friand, 'that both sides of politics seem to be able to produce an endless supply of opinion pieces that are 600–800 words in length and draw a fairly broad conclusion out of the specifics of one recent topical event?'

This was very true. Obviously the message from each side was the opposite, but the form was fairly identical. 'It's almost a waste,' I joked. As I looked around the café, I realized that I was the only person not wearing sunglasses.

'What do you mean?'

'Well, you could just take a right-wing article, change a few nouns, sprinkle the word not in front of a few verbs, and you'd have a left-wing article on the same topic.' I decided to try a bite of Bertrand's friand. I instantly spat it out. The 'diet' snack was covered in lumpy (but organic) green wheatgrass – it tasted like dirt. The people with sunglasses stared at me. I felt very foreign.

Bertrand looked at me with a smile. To him, what I'd said was a stroke of genius. To make it as a left-wing blogger, he now realized he wouldn't have to come up with ideas for his own blogs and then laboriously write them up, researching all the tedious details. Instead he could just find a right-wing blog that he disagreed with and change it around to his own point of view.

It was the perfect cyber-crime. Vincent Fiore had already told me that the audience cross-over between progressive and conservative blogs was minimal. Perhaps, I pointed out to Bertrand, he could now even get some sleep. Tiredness truly was the mother of plagiarism.

'But there are differences,' I cautioned Bertrand. 'The left-wing bloggers tend to be more negative than right-wingers.' Given the dominance of the Republican Party it was unsurprising. Nevertheless, I had a solution. All Bertrand had to do was find the most negative conservative column on a particular topic and use that as his template.

And where better to start than Vincent himself? As always, Bertrand's computer was on – I left Bertrand to his friand while I went to work on his tiny laptop. First stop was VincentFiore.com where I found Vincent's most negative article – 'Is the Conservative Movement Dead?' – which he had written around the time that the first real divisions between George Bush and the rest of the conservative movement had started to open up. Amid plummeting popularity, Bush was in trouble with the conservative movement for appointing one of his mates – Harriet Myers – to the position of attorney-general rather than one of their mates. Although this seemed to me to be a fairly esoteric and even technical detail to get hung up on, it seemed every conservative cyber-pundit had become outraged by it. Indeed, even Edward had been getting angry about it.

Vincent had taken a particularly strong stance on this issue, openly asking whether it sounded the death knell of the conservative movement.

That may be what the New York Times *is lavishing its ink upon, and what George Stephanopoulos and Chris Matthews are politically – who knows, maybe literally – salivating over, but bedrock conservatives are concerned about something else entirely.*

Principally – and that is the optimum word here – conservatives wonder what has happened to the bedrock principles of conservatism that were founded and nurtured during the 1950s through the 1990s, have gone?[45]

Has the pioneering work of such conservative icons as Buckley, Reagan, and Gingrich gone for naught, in this, the beginning of what was supposed to be GOP dominance for decades to come? Right now, the political reality would seem to say exactly that.

Reinforcing this belief – or head-shaking disbelief – among conservatives and Republicans in general recently were two of its most astute and prolific members, Robert Bork and Bruce Bartlett.

And so on. While Bertrand pretended to enjoy the last few bites of the friand, together we surveyed the rest of the piece, and then, using the Find and Replace function in Microsoft Word, Bertrand made the following changes to Vincent's article. He:

- Replaced conservative with progressive
- Replaced conservatism with progressive philosophy
- Replaced *Wall Street Journal* with *New York Times*

---

[45] Yes, it would seem that this sentence is not grammatically correct. Obviously Vincent's mentor and editor, Marv, was having a bit of a bad day.

- Replaced Republican with Democrat
- Changed the proper nouns

This was the result:

That may be what the Wall Street Journal *is lavishing its ink upon, and what Bill O'Reilly and Rush Limbaugh are politically – who knows, maybe literally – salivating over, but bedrock progressives are concerned about something else entirely.*

Principally – and that is the optimum word here – progressives wonder what has happened to the bedrock principles of progressive philosophy that were founded and nurtured during the 1950s through the 1990s, have gone?[46]

Has the pioneering work of such progressive icons as Keynes, Kennedy, and King gone for naught, in this, the beginning of what was supposed to be GOP dominance for decades to come? Right now, the political reality would seem to say exactly that.

Reinforcing this belief – or head-shaking disbelief – among progressives and Democrats in general recently were two of its most astute and prolific members, Robert Smythe and Bruce Jones.

And so on. Within minutes – rather than the hours it usually took him – the piece was up on DailyKos for all to read.

Almost instantaneously, dozens of comments started rolling in. As Bertrand had come to expect, most of them were fairly negative. But nevertheless, many engaged earnestly and thoughtfully with an essay that Bertrand had created entirely using Find and Replace. Indeed, the article had provoked more intelligent talk of strategy than Bertrand had seen for a while on DailyKos:

---

[46] Though it pained Bertrand to deliver such grammatically challenged copy, I insisted that Bertrand follow the exact (albeit just-invented) methodology of the experiment. Otherwise – as any scientist would tell you – our results would be worthless.

I don't think that staying home and not voting is a very good strategy. To me the best strategy is to support the DNC which can if supported energize the grassroots and lead to a party that is more in tune with the people of the area.

I was delighted. 'You're in business!' I told Bertrand. 'Now go home and get some sleep. Here – I'll show you how to turn off the volume.' I pressed the mute button. He reddened with embarrassment.

* * *

'Frankly,' I told Edward, 'don't point the finger at Thomas. While Thomas Friedman is sucking down the mojitos, you're the one slaving away coming up with five times the content for about a three-millionth of the reward.' The relentless need for content in the marketplace of ideas had been taking its toll on Edward and me, and we had been growing increasingly snappy in recent days. The effort-to-reward ratio was off the chart and we were both exhausted.

Edward had found himself on a bit of a fast track within the conservative movement. After the phone chat with Neal, Edward had arranged to have EdwardMcGuire.com hosted on Neal's servers, and was given columnist status at AmericanDaily and NewsByUs. He was also invited to participate in a blog called TymelyTopics – another MoveOff site dedicated to fast-response conservative analysis of current events. But by far the most exciting development for Edward had been the internship he had received from his mentor, and growing friend, Neal.

A few weeks after Edward had been placed on the MoveOff list, he noticed this email, entitled 'Help Wanted . . .'

Intern position with great opportunity for serious Internet exposure. Maintain and populate:

http://behindourbacks.us/

http://behindourbacks.americandaily.com/

I know most of you are terribly busy, but maybe one of you can suggest a candidate. Both sites are seriously outdated at this point in time due to my personal neglect.

The intern would get big time promotion and serious credit for work. — Maybe 1 or 2 hours per day at most, the content potential is huge :=)

Neal

This was exactly the sort of thing Edward wanted – 'big time promotion' and 'serious credit for work'. He had a browse of BehindOurBacks, and found it to his liking. It billed itself as a website dedicated to exposing 'a variety of schemes, mostly from the Left, but also supported by the "elitists" operating behind our backs to take away the rights of we the folks'.

And so Edward, making very sure that he had signed his own name, sent off an email volunteering for the position.

Almost immediately he received a reply from Neal, informing him that he'd get 'full credit' as the editor, including links to Edward's own site to improve exposure. He also, frighteningly enough, left Edward a phone number at which he could be contacted.

Summoning up the courage, Edward phoned Neal, making sure he spoke through his balls. As the editor of BehindOurBacks, Neal explained, Edward was expected to spend one hour of his day, every day, trawling the web and finding links to stories that people of a conservative persuasion would be outraged by. Neal would also send Edward the occasional tip to help. Within a few days, Neal had prepared the site and handed it over. Edward was in business: the editor of a proper MoveOff website.

This, you would think, would be cause for major celebration. All the other characters were quite jealous of Edward's quickly rising star. 'What is it about a conservative economist that makes him so appealing?' whispered Bertrand to me one night as he was walking home from his bi-weekly yoga class. Andy was more scathing: 'Edward hasn't even left his desk and yet he's got further than everyone else. What about people with real ideas? I spent five years doing my PhD. Does no one value rigor any more?'

I told the characters to calm down. I pointed out to the rest of them that although Edward was clearly the best looking – and on the surface the most successful so far – he wasn't the 'brightest cookie in the jar'.[47]

And for Edward, almost immediately, the novelty of his job wore off. He was not used to having to do an hour of work *every single day*. Of course, with a history of laziness, and dropping out of things, it was lucky if Edward bothered to do his job more than a few times a week – but still, the expectation was there. A couple of times a week, Neal would send Edward a short email; a typical one read like this:

End federally funded textbooks
—> http://tymelytopics.com/index.php?id=P569
Neal

Edward would then be expected to go and read the article, then paste the link on BehindOurBacks.us with a short personal take on the topic. The one above, for example, led to an article by a strange long-faced old man called Henry Lamb who was questioning the wisdom of the federal government spending $110 million over the past eight years funding an organization called the Center for Civic Education for the preparation of textbooks for civic studies:

Of the many questions that surround this program, the first to be addressed must be the appropriateness of government funding of any

---

[47] Actually I told Bertrand that Edward wasn't the most 'wheat-grassy friand in the organic food section'.

textbook. Public education is not among the enumerated powers of the federal government.

Having raised doubt on the whole constitutionality of textbook funding, Lamb implied that the funding of these textbooks was a globalist conspiracy:

CCE's educational materials strive to transform American students into 'global citizens.' American principles of government, such as the Bill of Rights, are minimized, and global values are promoted.

The theme of the federal government overstepping their powers was common in Neal's tips, such as this one Edward received one evening:

The USDA plans to make every owner of even one horse, cow, pig, goat, sheep, chicken, or pigeon register in a government database and subject their property and animals to constant federal and state government surveillance, and the animal owner will have to PAY for the privilege of owning animals!

For the first time in my life, even I started feeling some sympathy for the plight of the average animal owner, wanting to avoid the bureaucratic red-tape created by government surveillance of pigeons. But recently, the email tips had become slightly more disturbing. Neal had started sending through some pretty hardcore anti-immigration stuff, trying to whip up anti-Mexican sentiment:

OUTRAGE! ARMED MEXICAN SOLDIERS CAUGHT INVADING TEXAS YESTERDAY

—> http://newsbyus.com/more.php?id=1712_0_1_0_M

For me, these postings were becoming a little too much to stomach. It was even a test for Edward. Although he considered himself a conservative, as an economist his views on free trade made him one of the 'globalists' that Henry Lamb so detested. It was a bit like the religious stuff on many conservative websites – it was clearly very popular, but as a rationalist, Edward had never been able to reconcile the existence of God with the laws of supply and demand. It became a choice of putting up with the more populist messages in order to maintain his popularity, or sticking to his principles. After a while Edward found it was much easier if he went with the flow.

The task seemed a little pointless: it was to post articles that were already on the web to another part of the web so that people who already agreed with everything they said could reinforce their own pre-existing opinions. The whole thing seemed so meaningless. I started to wonder who was hoaxing who here?

To be honest, if it hadn't been the entire premise of the book, I'd have ditched Edward the moment the internship's workload became apparent.

It struck me that all of Edward's conservative heroes had gotten into print because they had some sort of academic background that gave their conservative rhetoric a certain gravitas, that Edward was strugggling to replicate.

But when I suggested to Edward that he needed extra training, he looked hurt. He wouldn't have to know much about economics, I assured him, just enough to sound like a Thomas Friedman think piece. Something that would allow him to cloak his anecdotes with the legitimacy of an academic theory.

Edward, however, was too busy and too tired to listen to me. He had to update BehindOurBacks with a piece about how some idiotic left-liberal called Bertrand Newton was attacking Education Incentive Reform, an idea that Edward had invented which would allow the best and brightest students to be traded between schools, much like football professionals are. It was the obvious next step to Bush's No Child Left Behind Act.

The next morning, Edward woke to find himself slumped over the keyboard. The website he'd spent hours updating the night before had only received a handful of responses for all his effort. It was at that point he agreed: the only way out of this absurd cycle was for Edward and me to get a proper training in economics.

There were two criteria for the economics course that Edward was to undertake. First of all, it would have to be easy. What he needed was the confidence to be able to go out there and sell the ideas – not something that would get him bogged down in boring details. One of Edward's own sayings is that if you can't explain something in one line, then it's not worth knowing. So an easy one-day course would suffice. The other criteria was that the course would have to be free. Edward and I had spent the last of my book advance during the initial 'deep background' research phase which involved long and highly tax-deductible discussion sessions in East Village bars.

With those criteria in mind, I googled the words 'Economics Teaching' and the first link led me to the Foundation for Teaching Economics.

A click through led to a professionally designed website which boasted as its mission 'introducing young individuals to an economic way of thinking'. Edward loved the sound of that. According to its website, it was a privately funded non-profit organization dedicated to teaching economics to teachers and students. Eagerly, Edward downloaded the FTE's 88-page annual assessment report, and a random click on the PDF's side bar displayed a table which showed that by doing an FTE course, 75% of teachers reported 'increased confidence' in their knowledge of economics. Not only that but the foundation ran courses all year, all around the country. And most importantly, the course was completely free. In fact, it was better than free. The website said that if I went along to one of their courses they would pay Edward a stipend of $150 – just for turning up!

It was exactly what Edward was looking for. Best of all, all the materials from the courses were provided on the website which contained document after document of information, diagrams and handouts, all of which they encouraged you to copy – Edward would never have to write an article again.

The question for Edward now was: which course to do? There seemed to be two main courses available: (1) The Environment and the Economy or (2) Is Capitalism Good for the Poor? Since Edward had always hated the environment, the choice was obvious. It all seemed too good to be true. Edward, the drop-out cyber-pundit, was about to become a qualified economics teacher.[48]

I had questions too. Who was this strange foundation that would pay you to study and then encourage you to plagiarize? It sounded like a very unlikely sort of organization. And who would fund something like that? And why? It felt as though, through a combination of laziness, lack of money, and of course, Google, we had stumbled upon something quite strange.

According to the FTE's website, their benevolence was all thanks to their major sponsors, which included Citigroup, GE Foundation, HSBC, Bank of America Foundation and the Gillette Group.

As we sat back and read the list of corporations that had donated more than $100 000 to the FTE in the past year, Edward reflected what an excellent system corporate philanthropy was.

After all, what possible interest could a corporation have in funding a school course other than selfless generosity?

---

[48] -ish.

17

SERMONS, FLORIDA-STYLE

'How do you raise a million dollars?' I asked Jim.

'Well you go out to someone who's got a lot of money to give away,' he laughed.

'And . . . ?'

'And say "give us the money".' Jim laughed again, but I didn't laugh with him. I really wanted to know how. 'It's a long process, it probably takes a year to do the courting, and do the explanation and develop the proposal and give them the opportunity to provide feedback; and answer the questions they have about what we want to do and why we want to do it, so that it makes sense for them to fund it.'

Finally I was getting information Edward could use. Not about the money but about the flexibility of the message Jim crafted in order to raise that money.

I had come down to Ferdinanda Beach, Florida, to meet Jim Klauder, the brains behind the Foundation for Teaching Economics. Besides, coming to Florida would be an opportunity to recharge my batteries before heading into the war zone with Dr Andy.

I met Jim at the Seattle Coffee House. I had already sat down with a mug of burnt-to-order Americano coffee when the slim 60 year old with short-cropped gray hair walked in. His polo shirt was tucked tightly into his slacks, and he was impeccably clean-shaven save for a neatly trimmed but full-bodied gray moustache. As he introduced himself I couldn't help but stare at the hands-free mobile phone device attached to his left ear. It created an immediate impression. 'How important is this man,' it made you think, 'that he has to be physically attached to his phone?' Perhaps, I thought, Edward should get one.

Without even sitting down, Jim suggested in an authoritative in-the-know way that we decamp to a place down by the water. Gratefully, I abandoned my half-drunk mug of charcoal water, and as we walked down to the jetty we chatted about Jim. After spending his life on the West Coast, first as a Republican county commissioner in Washington State and, more recently, at the FTE in California, Jim had finally done what every single white person in America seems to do between the age of 60 and 70. He had taken retirement in Florida. And judging by the way he dressed, it was clearly within Jim's means to avoid the hundreds of miles of over-developed medium-density urban ticky-tacky, and instead find a quiet place in the out of the way, restrained olde-worlde town of Ferdinanda Beach, complete with a five mile per hour, speed-humped commercial strip, and olde-style wooden features on all the antique shops and delicatessens that smelt of potpourri and ripened cheese respectively. So much money from retired professionals had flowed into this town in recent years that in this small seaside paradise even the bookshops could afford to be independent.

Jim had become involved with the FTE by chance. Years ago, he went to an intimate dinner party at a friend's house where he met millionaire industrialist Jacqueline Hume. 'You know, just a table of eight of us, sitting around, and in the little bit of social conversation that can happen in that setting.' For Jim it was the kind of lucky break that could have happened to any Ivy League Republican county commissioner. Somehow I doubted that Edward, with his first semester lessons from Ithaca College, was going to get the same sort of break.

At the jetty, as we we sat in the winter breeze and looked out into the Caribbean Sea, Jim outlined the string of successful and impor-tant management jobs he'd had brokering relationships between corporate donors and political campaigns (on the Republican side of the fence) at all levels of government. Jim's work with the FTE was now more of a hobby. Having relieved himself of the day-to-day running of the organization, he was free to concentrate on the fun part: raising millions of dollars from corporations to design corporate-friendly curriculums for America's schoolchildren.

* * *

Still inspired by his spurt of self-improvement, Dr Andy was toying with the idea of also becoming a bit more religious. He'd picked up a copy of Norman Vincent Peale's classic *The Power of Positive Thinking*, the bible (so to speak) of Christian pop philosophy, and he couldn't stop reading it. So, the day before I met up with Jim, Dr Andy had insisted we travel to Orlando in central Florida to visit the Holy Land Experience, a $US16 million dollar theme park for Christians. Although he'd never really believed in God before, ever since he'd decided to go to Iraq Dr Andy had been thinking a lot about religion. It wasn't that he was afraid; indeed, it seemed to be almost the opposite. He was coming to see his crusade in somewhat overblown terms that included increasingly religious overtones.

Dr Andy had not lost sight of why he was going to Iraq in the first place: to rebrand the War on Terror. He seemed to remember that there were some pretty catchy slogans in the Bible. And if his catch-phrase had religious overtones, Dr Andy hoped it might gain more traction amongst Middle America.

But like the rest of his fellow conservative friends in Washington DC, his overwhelming reason for wanting to recommit to God was entirely for personal, heartfelt reasons, and not for anything to do with America's large and well-organized constituency of conserva-tive Christians.

I was happy to indulge him. It would mean that I could get what I thought was a pretty good scoop for the book: an interview with Jesus.

Holy Land is a replica of Jerusalem as it would have looked in biblical times[49] but it is also a replica of theme parks in general. In an attempt to give the whole experience a more familiar feel, the operators[50] have gone out of their way to give you the same experiences you would have at one of the bigger theme parks. The entrance to the place – a Roman city gate – leads into the Jerusalem Street Market, where, authentically enough, you can buy stuff, in much the same way as you can at Disney. But instead of Mickey Mouse T-shirts there are Holy Land sweaters, and instead of Daffy Duck key rings, there are wooden camels and flute pipes. Dr Andy's favorite was the Ten Commandments polyester tie – perfect for the local church formal.

I was already starting to have misgivings. Being an Australian, I had largely missed the entertainment revolution that had swept America's Christianity in the past two decades. I'd heard about it of course, but I'd never realized how, well, showbiz it was. To me church has always been about cold buildings and ponderous sermons. Not Holy Land action figures and Roman-themed car parks. It all seemed a bit cheesy – a little too familiar to be religious.

'I'm a bit scared,' I whispered to Dr Andy so that the Roman guard – dressed in a bright red uniform with a gold breastplate and one of those helmets that have a brush sticking out of it – wouldn't overhear.

'No no. Don't worry, they're not going to convert you – unless you want to be converted.' Dr Andy looked at me with just a little too

---

[49] Biblical times loosely means around the time of Jesus, but it's also more generally used to mean anything from about 6500 BC onwards – near the entrance, for example, there is an impressive recreation of the two tablets Moses brought down from the mountain, complete with the Ten Commandments written on them – although unlike the originals, they are in English, and they are made out of a material that's shiny.

[50] An organization called Zion's Hope, which proclaims the slightly unsettling mission of wanting to convert the world's Jews to Christianity, presumably one theme park at a time.

much sincerity for me to know which side he was on – mine or theirs. 'Besides, there must be something going for this place – one million visitors in the past four years,' he said as he scanned the park's pamphlet for any catchy liturgical epigrams.

Dr Andy bought me a holy hotdog from the Roman pretzel stand and we walked on. The next attraction was the Coliseum – a magnificent, shiny white replica of King Herod's palace that was exactly half the size of the original and therefore exactly half as imposing. With the bright white walls contrasting with the deep blue sky of the clear winter day, standing in the middle of the empty courtyard, I actually felt like I was on the top deck of a cruise liner. To complete the look, there were hundreds of fold-away chairs put out in rows, presumably to allow visitors to watch the condemning of Christ on the steps of the Coliseum without getting sore feet.

Dr Andy was keen to stick around and see the show. As it went on, however, his enthusiasm began to waver. For all the commitment to authenticity, the Holy Land's version was not quite as accurate as, say, Mel Gibson's. The Jews didn't repeatedly bash up Jesus like they did in the movie – and, oddly, they spoke in posh pseudo-English accents rather than Aramaic. A real disappointment, Dr Andy thought. Not only that, the crowd was not as huge as the hype had suggested – perhaps a dozen people, mostly over 60 – hardly a crowd able to make or break the rebranding of American foreign policy. Dr Andy's enthusiasm for a mid-book religious epiphany had seriously started to wane.

In order to keep his spirits up, I decided we should head directly to the heavily signposted star attraction of the Holy Land Experience and the only exhibit to get its own registered trademark: the Scriptorium™. And without wanting to give myself too much credit for what is essentially a fictional realization, it was here that Dr Andy finally understood what all the fuss was about Christianity. No matter how many bells and whistles modern American Christianity covered itself in, it was the underlying message that made it the perfect ally for conservatives like Dr Andy.

The Scriptorium™ is home to the Van Kampen collection – $18 million worth of old Bibles collected 'from Egypt to Babylon', including one printed entirely in gold. Needless to say, such a valuable collection needs to be kept in a secure place even if the meek are eventually going to inherit it all. Thus the Scriptorium™ is a large rectangular museum purpose-built with security in mind. Security cameras are visible in the corners of every room, and alarms arm every exit. Not only that, but the entire building is a monument to high-tech automation. Each room is dimly lit to preserve the million-dollar documents locked behind glass cabinets. This dim, mysterious atmosphere felt appropriately reverential at first, but after a while, frankly, got a little boring.

Luckily the people at Holy Land keep a close eye on the consumer preferences of ordinary people like me and had come up with an ingenious solution that made the Scriptorium™ more interesting without having to hire any more staff: the whole building was operated by an all-powerful computer that guided us through, opening the automatic doors when it was time to move on to the next room, and then closing them behind us to prevent us from going back. Not only that, but as we moved through the building, the computer's deep booming voice informed us of what each room held and which area of the Middle East it had been taken from. It would then light up each artefact briefly so that we knew exactly where to look and when. At peak times the computer could simultaneously speak to groups of 20 in each of the Scriptorium™'s dozen or so rooms – a truly omniscient, omnipresent authority. Everything about the experience was moderated and paced by a faceless force that commanded all, but this one was man-made by a religious organization in order to keep their audience distracted and entertained. Completely unlike God.

Towards the end of the tour, Dr Andy and I entered a dim room lined with red curtains, interrupted only by faux-Roman columns. There was no apparent exit to this room. The doors behind us closed automatically, and then a sound system started playing a haunting tune from a single clarinet with a very faint strings accompaniment. We were about to experience the Scriptorium™'s coup de grâce: a 7-minute sound and light show.

As we stood there the lights dimmed and a deep American male voice filled the room. I grabbed onto Dr Andy's shoulder – just in case he was scared of the dark. 'Devotion, courage, sacrifice . . . these are the qualities of those God used to transmit and preserve his word,' boomed the voice. 'Against overwhelming barriers this book has prevailed as the revered and inspired word of God. Moses.' Suddenly a spotlight lit up a red curtain, and we heard the clicks and whirring of the electric motor which lifted up the fabric to reveal an oil painting of an old man holding a shepherd's stick and standing in a field, his long white beard blowing in the wind. At that point Moses spoke in an old man's voice, complete with pseudo-English accent: 'The Lord will again rejoice over you for good if you turn to the Lord your God with all your heart and soul.' I let go of Dr Andy's shoulder. The posh accent made Moses come across as a bit camp.

Another curtain ascended with the mechanical whir and a young-looking Joshua appeared dressed as a soldier in a rippling metal breastplate. He, too, said a few words with a posh mid-Atlantic accent. Next Samuel appeared across the other side of the room. 'Behold!' boomed his completely American voice. 'To obey is better than sacrifice and to heed than a fat of rams[51]; for rebellion is as the sin of divination and insubordination is as inequity and idolatry.'

Now, Dr Andy had never been a particularly religious man, but at that moment something inside him stirred. Not because of the effects, which to me seemed too mechanical to be anything but

---

[51] I have no idea what a 'fat of rams' is, either. Please send your suggestions to: fatoframsmystery@americanhoax.com.

comical, but because of the message that was being handed down. Part of the whole problem with America at the moment was the level of rebelliousness and insubordination. If only people were prepared to make more sacrifices then perhaps the world wouldn't seem as though it was spinning out of control.

At this point the whole show became increasingly camp.

Peter was holding a basket of fish, half naked with rippling pecks. Storm clouds gathered behind him. His blond hair was accompanied by a rather gorgeous thick blond beard. 'Know this first of all – that no prophecy of scripture is a matter of one's own permutations.' He had a deep, raspy movie-trailer voice, and in the background the music neared its climax. 'No prophesy was ever made by an act of human will, but men moved by the holy spirits spoke from God!' If he hadn't been so blond, Edward would have sworn Peter was Darth Vader without the headgear. As it was, Peter represented all that Dr Andy thought America's military supremacy was based on – the hard, honest soldiering by the common folk – something that Dr Andy could appreciate, even if he'd never been fishing in his life.

The disciples were now lit up as the choir belted out notes that were getting higher and higher. As the room descended into total darkness, a thunderbolt cracked above our heads. Automatically we looked up, even though we were in pitch darkness, and then suddenly a voice, louder and even more booming than Peter's, spoke[52] down from above. 'I am the Lord your God, who brought you out of Egypt, out of the land of slavery!' I felt a momentary stirring in my chest, then realized it was just the vibrations from the speaker system. And next more thunderbolts as the Ten Command-ments – written in Hebrew – lit up in the sky above our heads, and God read them out to us – in American-English, of course.

---

[52] Or should that be 'spake'?

Finally, as the narrator explained how Jesus fitted into this scheme '[he] became the savior of mankind by his perfect life', a large white cross descended from the roof, tastefully lit up with a speckled white light. 'All who placed their faith in Him receive the gift of eternal life. This is the only hope of mankind,' said the narrator. In the reflected light of the cross, I could see Dr Andy nodding vigorously, utterly taken by the message's power and, above all, its simplicity.

Abruptly the music ended. The lights went up and the automatic doors opened into the next room – which, appropriately enough, led directly into a book shop.[53] Uplifted, Dr Andy bought a Scriptorium™ notepad in order to remember the Experience.

As we exited the Scriptorium™, Dr Andy was elated. We walked back around a large man-made lake, with a large hedge on the embankment opposite. The hedge was cut into the words 'He is Risen'. Even though Dr Andy was still wavering about whether he actually believed in God, he had certainly been impressed by His awesome power of persuasion.

Dr Andy and I were famished, so we decided to go to the Oasis Palms Café – possibly the only biblically themed, semi-authentic Arabia-American fusion cafeteria in the world. Dr Andy decided to have the Holy Land Fatoush with a side of Eden's Garden Salad, while I decided to go with the Goliath Burger[54] – with fries and Pepsi.

As we ate, Dr Andy held forth on the presentation we'd just seen. 'Obedience and sacrifice are going to be necessary if America is going to win the battle against Islamic fundamentalist terrorists over the next fifty years, right?'

---

[53] Actually, to be perfectly accurate, it was a 'book shoppe'.

[54] Which I particularly liked because Goliath, though large, is actually an anti-hero. Mind you, I don't think I would have ordered a 'David Burger'.

'I suppose so,' I said. The Goliath Burger was disappointingly dry. It didn't have enough Heavenly Ketchup on it.

Dr Andy said he admired how openly the church preached a message of self-sacrifice. 'For too long politicians have been promising the American population prosperity and decadence, allowing individuals to do as they please,' he preached. 'Hell, it's reached such a level that even conscription is out of the question even though we're at war!' He threw down his Holy Land Fatoush in disgust. I didn't know whether he was sickened by America's decadence, or whether the hummus was off.

Dr Andy could see it now, one of the central themes in the rebranding of the War on Terror had to be about obedience and sacrifice. And as a result the Christian Church was going to need to be a key ally.

And so as Dr Andy picked at the apple bits in his Eden's Garden Salad, he made a life-changing decision. If believing a commitment to God was what would swing the balance in the War on Terror and ultimately lead to America's salvation, then Dr Andy decided he too must appear to believe in God. He must put aside whatever personal skepticism he had about His existence – this was for the greater good.

Dr Andy looked up into the sky and held his hands together in a quick recommittal to God. 'Where's the gift store?' he asked.

Even though he was still looking skywards, after a moment I realized he was talking to me. 'Oh, er, there's one over there.'

'Come on. I need to go and buy a crucifix necklace.'

Finally, as we walked out of the Oasis Palms Café, we passed Jesus's tomb, where he was laid to rest, complete with the stone that sealed it rolled to one side. Hanging around outside his tomb was Jesus. And it was there that I managed to get an exclusive interview with the man himself. It was the first time that either Dr Andy or I had ever met Jesus. He was, unsurprisingly I suppose, the park's star character.

Jesus – who was played by a guy named Steve – had adopted the hippie look. He had a dense brown beard, and long-flowing hair. As it turned out, Jesus was a very humble guy. I asked him what it was like to play Jesus, and he said, 'The first word that comes to my mind is humbling.' I asked him how he got into character, and he replied, 'It's humbling when you dig into the scriptures and you think about Christ.' I asked him whether he thought it was blasphemous playing Jesus, and he replied that the process was very humbling – 'I believe it's the grace of God that he allows us to do this.' I asked him whether he enjoyed his job, and he responded – amazingly, that the process was very humbling.

It was clear that Jesus had been media-trained to within an inch of his life. In fact, it was as if he'd been nailed to the pre-written script in a modern-day PR crucifixion. I suppose that's understandable – as the Son of God, he would get an enormous number of media enquiries. It's important to stay on message – especially when you're Jesus.

Mind you, even through the media spin, you could see that the guy playing Jesus was actually a sincere Christian. The words that were coming out of his mouth sounded like a press release but there was a happy earnestness in his eyes that gave the game away. He was a true believer, and he wasn't ashamed of it. There was something very humbling about seeing that, because to show your belief like that always comes across as a little nerdy.

I presumed that one of the reasons Steve was the one chosen to be the Son of God was that his sincerity was quite infectious. I got the impression that although he was humble in this life, Steve was pretty sure that when his time came he'd be heading to heaven. He may not have delivered the most dynamic sound bites, but he had the 'it' factor that comes from being a true believer.

* * *

Jim Klauder, on the other hand, did not come across as a true believer, but that's not to say his manner wasn't equally infectious.

Like Jesus, one of Jim's roles was to spin the company line. His answers were far more dynamic than Jesus's but Jim still picked his words carefully. At first this sounded like he was sharing something special with you, but eventually Edward and I worked out that he was just making sure he didn't overplay his hand. 'I think a lot of teachers may be . . . how would I put it . . . skeptical about the benefits of capitalism versus the harm that capitalism does.

But the FTE understood that no matter what their opinion on capitalism, the average teacher was so overworked that they are open to receiving assistance in the form of pre-packaged curriculums. And that's where the FTE came in.

And the way they taught it made it seem economics wasn't so far from religion at all. Before I came down to Florida I had obtained the promotional DVD and CD-ROM which the FTE handed out to teachers – and I'd been impressed. The DVD itself was professionally produced, featuring a stern woman called Kathy Ratte speaking down the barrel of the camera in a slow school-teachery way.

'In 1980,' she said, 'by China's own measure, the number of people living in China who were extremely impoverished was 245 million. By 1999 that number had dropped to 33 million and it has continued to fall into the 21st century. What happened in China? Was it a miracle?' My heart jumped – was FTE a group of *Christian* economists? Not quite. 'Well I guess you could say it was a miracle.' She smiled. 'The miracle of markets.' In the background a photo of a Chinese street market flashed up, replete with baskets of fresh bok choy.

In recent times the FTE's ambitions had outgrown America. A couple of years ago Jim had found out that the Gillette company and Citigroup banking conglomerate were particularly interested in the rapidly growing Central European bloc. He approached them and they stumped up the cash for five programs conducted in Bulgaria, Czech Republic, Hungary, Romania and Slovakia. Like Christianity, the economics the FTE preached knew no borders.

But there was one profound difference in the FTE's method compared to those at the Holy Land. The FTE was, proudly, a fee-for-service organization that systematically gained an understanding of the exact needs of its customers – anyone with enough money to buy a curriculum – and then they tailored the package to suit those exact needs. This level of flexibility was something Jim took great pride in.

'We can change directions on a dime. We have an annual evaluation of our program. And we take this evaluation very, very seriously because all of the comments and criticisms are grist for the mill for how we improve the programs.' Thus, the FTE was not hindered by a fixed moral framework that existed in the Holy Land Experience, or indeed in the government mandates for curriculums. 'Once something starts going on in the public sector – you start a program – it's impossible to ever stop it. It just gets bigger and bigger and bigger . . . The people working in it have an incentive to keep it going and in fact to make themselves bigger and to make themselves more important, because of job security and power and all kinds of different things.'

There were no Ten Commandments at the FTE. Beyond a general commitment to market economics, the organization had enormous flexibility to deliver whatever message Jim's donors wanted.

It was a lesson I thought Dr Andy should take to heart. For all the excitement he now had for organized religion, I told him that in marketing the War on Terror it might be wise to come up with a catchphrase a little more morally flexible than one straight out of the Ten Commandments. After all, he'd seen up close that Jesus had his limitations.

It seemed clear to me that Jim Klauder was doing a lot better out of America than Jesus was. On the day I'd visited the Holy Land experience, the place was scattered with visitors in their sixties and seventies – they were talking to yesterday's generation. By contrast, the FTE was systematically directing its message at the school children – tomorrow's leaders.

Dr Andy might be more respectful of Christianity – but Edward was the one truly inspired. It was certainly prudent for Dr Andy to have invested in a Bible, but it was clear that Edward would be guided by an even more powerful force when he got his lesson in economics from the FTE.

18

FANTASY SPRINGS

Darryl's idea to go the Fantasy Springs Casino and Bowling Alley during our layover in Indio, California, was turning into something of a nightmare. For a start, we were running out of water. This was a bit of a worry because we were walking across a sandy Californian desert. We'd been walking for an hour and seemed no closer to the casino, which rose like a mirage out of the flat ground up ahead. I calculated that we must be about halfway – an hour to go. I was carrying a heavy backpack in the afternoon sun and my shirt was wet with sweat. To our left, in the far distance, Darryl noticed a sand storm was approaching. The first wisps of sand blew behind my sunglasses and into my eyes.

We had already missed our layover – the last Greyhound bus out of Indio had left half an hour ago – but I told Darryl that wouldn't matter because the advertisement I had found in the *Western Bowling News* included a coupon that would allow us to stay the night at the casino for only $69. After four hours on the Greyhound I just wanted to stop and rest.

One of the things you learn when you catch a Greyhound bus is how to tell the difference between a professional tattoo and a prison tattoo. Prison tattoos are usually one color – the standard bluish-black – the lines are thicker and the design is usually poorly executed. For some reason a straight line seems beyond the average amateur tattoo artist. I know this because, without exception, in the time between when Darryl and I left the bowling alley in LA and arrived in Indio, I was the only white person I saw who did not have a tattoo – prison or professional – on his arms. Not only that, but once we arrived in Indio and hopped off the bus, I learnt a valuable lesson: don't get money-saving advice from a man whose arms are covered in prison tattoos.

Indio is a sprawling town on a flat desert plain, which, like much of California, has been built out not up. The urban planning – or lack of it – has created a low-density muddle of houses, warehouses, car dealerships and casinos, all with enough space in between to make walking anywhere difficult and, judging by its emptiness, probably a bit dangerous. It therefore has a bus service to ferry the poorer of the 8000 retirees, ex-prisoners and illegal immigrants who inhabit the town between the Westfield shopping center at one end and the 109 residential developments scattered around the other. There is one tall building in Indio, and it is the Fantasy Springs Casino, which is, of course, on an Indian reservation on the outskirts of this delightful town. I'm guessing it is the only reason why 500 000 tourists visit the place each year.

Unfortunately, having not particularly planned this side trip, we had quickly found ourselves stranded at an empty bus terminal, which was in the middle of a sprawling, deserted suburban street – no commerce, no cars, no passers-by. After 20 minutes of walking through empty streets, Darryl finally found a barber's shop – direct from the 1950s, complete with red, white and blue pole out the front. It was the lone remaining shop in a strip of abandoned stores. The staff was sitting around smoking and chatting – an oddity in the usually puritanically anti-smoking California – and they were more than happy to direct Darryl to the local bus service, which was a ten-minute walk down the street.

By the time we arrived at the bus depot, Darryl had already drunk half of our only bottle of water. There were perhaps a dozen people milling around waiting for their bus to arrive. Darryl asked in his deep American voice if the driver, also on a smoko, knew which bus to take to Fantasy Springs. 'The 91,' he replied.

'Excuse me,' I heard a voice behind us say. A lanky man in his thirties with a missing front tooth and a blue baseball cap tugged my arm. I turned around sharply. The man had on what I would call a blue singlet. In America, Darryl had informed me, the singlet was more commonly known as the 'wife beater'. Up and down the arms of this polite but slightly-too-close man were tattoos that had unmistakably been drawn in prison. One was what looked like a frame from a Charlie Brown cartoon. Another was just a long pair of crooked lines that extended up the man's right arm.

The man spoke in a broad, cheery southern accent that made me feel as if I was listening to another language, even though I could understand every word he said. 'You're wanting to go to Fantasy Springs?'

'Yeah,' Darryl replied while I gaped at the man's unusual body 'art'.

'Well it'll be much quicker to walk. It's just across the bridge over there, and then you just walk through a . . . a . . .' The man couldn't place the word.

'Field?' proffered Darryl.

'Yeah, field. Save your money on the bus fare – you can spend it once you get there.'

Darryl was skeptical. He was happy to wait for the bus – he was used to waiting, after all.

'But wouldn't it be rude not to accept the man's advice?' I whispered to Darryl. The whole point of my trip here was to fit in. What better way than to accept the advice of locals? Also, I suspected Darryl was just being lazy – a short walk would do his chubby physique good.

And so, trusting the judgment of the man with the prison tatts, I overrode Darryl's hesitation and we embarked on a walk across a small traffic bridge and across the field of sand and shrubs towards a building that got further away with every step.

19
FLYING TOASTERS

There was still something missing from Bertrand's strategy, but neither he nor I could work out what it was. With his new Find and Replace method of article writing, Bertrand had been going really well on DailyKos. But his inbox was still nothing more than mass emails that he'd signed up for from all the causes he thought he should join: the numerous anti-Wal-Mart campaigns, the National Labor Council's anti-sweatshop campaigns. He was still enjoying the 'virtual protest march' to Stop Global Warming (that is, receiving emails from them). He was even getting updates from Petlovers.com, which he signed up for while he was organizing PetsAgainstBush. While Edward was getting internships with the conservative movement and developing personal contacts, all Bertrand had achieved was an inbox of spam.

One advantage of having his email switched on 24 hours a day was that Bertrand had been able to diligently follow up on all these emails – clicking on links to petitions, joining virtual protests, writing to Congressmen and CEOs, and mostly just visiting progressive websites and giving away his email address to cause after cause. For a while the sheer amount of activity made Bertrand feel as if he was having a real effect.

Yet, after I'd shown him the mute button and he'd got a good night's sleep, Bertrand had woken up with a slightly different perspective on the busy work that his life revolved around. He was starting to feel used. It was as if these organizations thought Bertrand was endlessly altruistic with his time and had no interest in expressing his politics in any way except through petitions and donations.

Indeed, pretty much every email he'd received asked for a donation. This was, Bertrand supposed, unsurprising since many of the causes would have been fairly unpopular with rich corporations. Nevertheless, it was one of the most noticeable differences between conservative and progressive organizing on the web. The progressive sites were obsessed with raising money. Perhaps money was the 'something' that was missing from Bertrand's attempts so far to make it in the liberal marketplace of ideas. But how exactly could Bertrand use the Left's obsession with money to his advantage?

Bertrand's AdBack was getting respect from ordinary people on DailyKos, but for Bertrand AdBack had always just been a means to an end. Like any person trying to make their way up the ladder of a strict hierarchy, what Bertrand yearned for more than anything was the approval and support of his superiors. He wanted to be noticed by the major liberal players.

The reason he'd set up the AdBack was not to receive emails from the little people but to send them. In turn those emails were supposed to be a way of getting noticed by the big guns. But Bertrand had not received one word of support from anyone higher up the ladder since he'd begun. There was no Marv or Neal contacting Bertrand to point him in the right direction.

And yet, the more the Left disdained him, the more desperate he became for their approval. He started turning up to left-wing events dressed the way he thought a left-winger would dress, with badges on that read 'Bush sucks' and 'Billionaires for Bush'[55]. He even endured a two-hour lecture about Global Warming by Al Gore at the New York Town Hall. At the end, Al suggested everyone go out and buy fluorescent light bulbs[56], which Bertrand did, but to no avail.

---

[55] Initially, Bertrand didn't like that badge at all until I pointed out that it was sarcastic.

[56] This is true. The two key messages that Bertrand and I took away from Al Gore's public lecture on climate change were: (a) Buy more expensive light bulbs and (b) Take your clothes to the dry cleaners in your own coat bag so that they don't have to wrap your shirts in a plastic bag. Viva la eco-revolution!

Still nobody contacted him. Even when he wrote an earnest letter to Al outlining his own (advertising-based) theories on climate change, he was met with silence.

After several weeks of Bertrand's increasingly fever-pitched attempts I had lost my patience. There was only so much time I was willing to spend on this earth hanging out with a man who now dressed exclusively in black stove-pipe pants and T-shirts with pun-based slogans on them. I don't know whether Bertrand was aware of how annoying he was becoming, or whether it was just a brilliant piece of passive-aggressive manipulation on his part, but it was at this point that I decided to do Bertrand a favor I didn't extend to any other character during the whole six months. Bertrand really was not getting nearly as far as the others. And so, for the sake of the plot, I allowed Bertrand to cheat. Just a little. But it was a cheat. And this was it: I phoned a (real) friend from university, someone who had been pretty successful and would probably be able to help Bertrand out. By the end of the conversation I'd received the Golden Chalice of the Left – two functioning emails that lead back to the founders of MoveOn. Wes Boyd and Joan Blades.

'Let's roll,' I said to Bertrand. We were finally going to meet someone who could shed some light on how Bertrand could get ahead as a left-liberal in America. Immediately I emailed Wes and Joan, making sure to follow my successful friend's advice and put the pitch of my book into impressive-sounding language. I told them the book was about 'the ideological framework that underpins America', and said I wanted to chat about how MoveOn fitted into the 'national conversation'. And just to make sure they would immediately respond to my email, I decided to play all my cards at once:

> *If you're wondering whether it's worth your time, all I can say is that my book will almost certainly outsell Thomas Friedman's latest book, and be at least five times as influential.*
> *Regards*
> *Charles Firth*

Surely that would clinch it? Now all I had to do was sit back and wait. And in fairness to Bertrand, I could hardly leave for Iraq until I'd at least lined up an interview with Wes or Joan.

I'd already heard of Wes and Joan before I'd even started writing this book. The story of the two 'silicon valley entrepreneurs' (as the MoveOn website described them) who'd transformed the 2004 election by raising millions of dollars for pro-Democratic ads was legendary within liberal circles. Everywhere you went, when you discussed MoveOn with left-liberals they would inevitably end up being described as 'very smart guys' or 'great value' or 'extremely intelligent people' and most intriguingly 'not egomaniacs'.

'You know the flying toaster on the Mac?' one liberal had asked me while I was doing some 'deep background' research for Bertrand (drinking in a bar in the East Village). 'They invented that and sold it to Apple for, like, millions.' The guy I was talking to stared at me proudly and then walked away. As if that was all that needed to be said. This was a little strange. I vaguely remembered the flying toaster, but to me that put them in the same category as the person who invented the Dancing Baby animation, or the author of the 'Where's Waldo' books. Yet everyone I met spoke as if it put Wes and Joan in the same category as Gandhi. Later that night, another self-proclaimed progressive boasted that during the 2004 election, money was falling off trees for progressive organizations willing to campaign for the Democrats. Apparently most of the money was coming from billionaire 'liberal' George Soros, who had been doling out money to anyone who looked vaguely worthy.

Months later, while I was waiting for the inventors of the Flying Toaster to respond to my email, I reflected on my conversations that night, and it finally struck me how Bertrand could use the Left's obsession with money.

Rather than push ahead with useless punditry, or trying to steal a chunk of market share in the lucrative PetsAgainstBush segment, to get the attention of his fellow left-liberals, Bertrand had to do something that would appeal to people in a way they most appreciated. He had to appeal to the most fundamental desires of people like himself. And what motivated the busy little people who wanted to run the world? Something that enabled them to imagine – just for a moment – that they were getting a little closer to the ultimate goal of rule by themselves. When you're trying to make the empire a little more feel-good, there is one thing that's always in short supply. There is one thing that will bring you just a little bit closer to the ultimate goal of absolute power: money.

And so after several months of fairly boring bottom-feeding and working on ideas that seemed to go nowhere, Bertrand decided to make his boldest offer yet. The creation of the AdBack Foundation: a non-profit grants system that offered $250 000 for ten worthy organizations.[57] Here is the text of the announcement Bertrand put up on the front page of the AdBack website.

*I'm a former advertising executive who is appalled by the direction this country is heading in. As a result I'm setting up **The AdBack Foundation**. I am seeking proposals ahead of a plan to offer ten grants of up to $250 000 each for projects that seek to further progressive politics.*

The ideas must relate broadly to progressive politics in the United States: environmentalism, feminism, pacifism, unionism, anti-racism, anti-imperialism and social radicalism.

The emphasis will be on new and novel ideas, and as it is the intention for the schemes to work, it is important that they are creatively exciting.

---

[57] In case you are thinking all of this is highly illegal . . . umm . . . well. There are two reasons why I'm pretty sure it's legally all above board. Without actually having a law degree as such, it is my understanding (certainly my hope) that tort reform in the USA – led by the insurance companies – has resulted in the situation where nobody is actually responsible for their actions anymore. Also, if you actually read the text carefully you will realize that rather than offering $250 000 I'm merely 'seeking proposals ahead of a plan to offer' the money. Watertight.

Think of bringing the creativity and power of advertising to progressive politics. It can be a one-off event, or an idea that builds the progressive infrastructure of politics in this country.

I am particularly interested in projects that push the envelope in the tactics employed in social action. Anything that re-energizes progressives in one shot will be considered. I also am interested in helping new people with good ideas: a lack of experience will not count against you.

Please write a one page description of the project, including who the project will target and a timeline about how it can be implemented. Since $250 000 doesn't go that far nowadays, the grant can be used as seed funding for larger projects. Please do not submit proposals of more than one page. All great ideas are clear and concise – if you can't describe it in a few short paragraphs then it's probably not worth doing.

A brief budget outlining how the money will be spent should also be included. This need only break the spending down to 4–5 major line items.

Like George Soros, Bertrand didn't know any poor people, and he certainly didn't know anyone who was currently actually changing the world, but by God he'd like to meet these people, and maybe even steal some reflected glory from their projects.

Of course the new AdBack Foundation Grant Scheme wasn't aiming to actually solve any of the world's problems. But Bertrand believed that with a great advertising campaign and a couple of million dollars, he'd at least be able to get the message out there. He was not quite sure what the message was, or how he'd cope if the message turned out to be popular, but if there was one thing he had learnt from the Left, it was that a lack of knowledge needn't get in the way of action. And at least this plan of action guaranteed to get him noticed . . .

20

TEN-ROOM MINIMUM

Darryl and I were standing in the desert, gazing at Fantasy Springs shimmering in the distance. He swigged the remaining drops of moisture from his warm water bottle as I looked on with jealousy. Darryl was proving quite effective at making me shoulder the blame for this whole 'walk across the desert' fiasco – even though the whole idea of stopping over had been his in the first place!

We continued trudging. A full hour later we reached a dusty road which wound around a discount motel development and into the lush surroundings of the resort. I had a searing headache and my mouth was parched. Darryl's olive complexion had given him a nice even tan. By comparison, I was bright pink.

As we approached the gates of the complex, the ground abruptly turned from dusty brown to deep green – a manicured lawn with a watered garden. Instead of the occasional cactus or brown-green shrub, there were neatly lined rows of blossoming orchids above which soared large, well-watered palm trees. Darryl and I jealously looked on at the irrigated garden. We were very, very thirsty.

There was no footpath on the side of the road; when people come to Fantasy Springs they drive, or at least catch the bus – which, Darryl pointedly noted, dropped them right outside the door. Indeed, a 91 bus was just leaving, speeding down the road having dropped off half-a-dozen fresh, well-rested, fully hydrated passengers.

The entrance itself was plush, with plenty of flashing light bulbs and freshly cleaned glass with brass fittings. The bitumen was that dark, high-grade stuff, with neatly painted traffic lines. Darryl's shoes and jeans were filthy, as were mine. The dust had turned my shiny black leather shoes a whiter shade of pale, and the bottom of my jeans were covered in light-colored soot. I was leaving a trail of dusty footprints against the dark road, but nobody seemed too fussed. A Native American porter who was standing outside the valet parking section in a formal black and gray suit looked at us and smiled. The unwashed masses were welcome around here.

The first thing that hit us inside was a rush of cool airconditioned air, closely followed by the sound of coins clinking out winnings above the beeping and burping of the 10 000 or so electronic slot machines. There was no foyer at all, and not even a map or sign. I could see Darryl's heart was racing as he wandered ahead of me in a daze through rows and rows of machines, both the upright and table-level varieties. The nickel machines were arranged in long thin aisles so that if you started walking down one of these aisles you had to walk halfway across the main room before you could turn left or right.

Darryl led the way as we walked past the bar, which was packed with 20 stools around its L-shape. In front of each stool, recessed into the tabletop underneath clear glass, was a slot machine. Most of the seats were taken; the avid gamblers bet with one hand and sipped beer with the other. Complimentary bowls of salty nuts completed what for Darryl was a picture of paradise. 'We'll have to have a go there a bit later,' he said.

We walked past a room with a large all-you-can-eat buffet, and then past a row of ten ATM machines, with all the major banks represented. Finally we found ourselves in a comparatively non-descript lobby. The white and cream walls looked positively hospital-like in comparison to the flashing, bleeping gaming room from which we'd just emerged.

Darryl showed the attendant behind the desk the coupon from the *Western Bowling News* and asked for a $69 room for the night. 'I'm afraid, sir, this is only valid for group bookings,' said the crisply dressed Native American woman politely.

'What?'

'The best rate I can offer you is $129 plus tax.'

Darryl stared down at the ad. In small lettering at the bottom was the following disclaimer: 'Rates are per room per night, single or double occupancy. 10 room minimum.' I had not noticed that fairly important piece of information. Too thirsty to argue with the woman, Darryl walked away from the counter without saying another word.

He was furious with me. 'Why didn't you check the conditions?'

'I don't know.'

'Always check the conditions. There are always conditions. Haven't you ever used a coupon before?'

I was about to explain to Darryl that the whole world of coupons was actually fairly foreign to me, but now was not the time. Instead, I suggested perhaps this whole plan had been a mistake. 'How can you honestly think you're going to win anything at a casino?' I condescended. 'It's stacked against you!'

'Oh yeah, good point. Perhaps I just stick to serving drinks for the rest of my life,' he said, then stormed out of the foyer and back through the gaming room. He walked past the gaming bar and out into the sea of machines. Somehow it seemed both narrower and longer than he remembered. He marched angrily down an aisle, trying to get a glimpse of the exit over the rows of tall nickel slot machines, but to no avail. At the other end of the aisle he found himself in a cul-de-sac of 25 cent machines. He turned around and tried to get his bearings. The aisle had curved around slightly, with the effect that Darryl couldn't even work out how to get back to the gaming bar. He turned left. These slots were now 25 cent cardies – Darryl's favorite because they required a level of skill at blackjack that the simple tap-and-wait ones didn't. He had no idea which way was out, and there were no signs to direct him. He sat down at one of the cardies and put a dollar bill in.

'Excuse me, sir,' said a woman's voice.

Darryl turned around to see a cute young woman in a low-cut black top and elegant short black skirt holding a tray of drinks.

'Were you the one to ask for the club soda?' she asked, and then without skipping a beat, 'And if not, would you like a drink anyway?'

'What? Oh. Er. I'd love a club soda,' said Darryl. She handed him a disappointingly short glass of soda which was mostly ice. 'What I'd really like is a glass of water with no ice.'

'Are you sure you wouldn't like something stronger? I can get you anything you like from the bar.'

While Darryl was silently losing his money on the 25 cent cardies I decided to go and get the all-you-can eat $20 buffet meal, which included five types of roast meat: lamb, pork, beef, chicken and veal, and maple-syrup gravy.

As I ate, Darryl continued his losing spree on the roulette wheel, and then at the nickel slots. Finally he decided to use his last $10 to go bowling. After wandering right to the back of the main room he found a small white doorway which led around into a massive 24 lane alley. It was packed. Families and friends were eating hotdogs and drinking sports drinks while loudly cheering each other on. At the end a few lanes were still free.

Darryl walked over to the counter. 'One game please,' he said.

'Sorry, groups only at the moment,' the frizzy-haired woman dressed in a bright green and white uniform replied. She pointed to a sign that reinforced the strict policy.

'But over there lanes are free.'

'But they're only for people who are bowling in groups.'

Unable to even bowl alone, Darryl decided to try his last $10 on the one-penny slots, to make it go as slow as possible. Although he hadn't eaten all day, the nourishing sugary drinks were good enough sustenance. With a whirr the machine accepted his bill, and he clicked on what he thought was the 'one-line' button. It was the 'max-limit' button, which placed all of Darryl's $10 onto the next spin of the electronic wheels. He tried to reverse the click, but nothing would change the machine's mind. With a sense of terrible foreboding, Darryl hit the button to spin the wheels. Nothing, not one single matching line.

Meanwhile, I was sitting at the L-shaped bar with the tabletop pokies and was $50 up on a strange game involving a whole lot of numbers which I didn't understand but seemed to be quite good at.

Out of the corner of my eye I noticed Darryl getting up from the one-penny machines right across the floor near the exit. It suddenly became all too apparent why the one-penny machines were there. With nothing left, he was walking out of the hotel. I cashed in and raced over to catch up to him. With my winnings we bought a room for a night at the discount motel down the road. Darryl went to bed tired, drunk and hungry.

Next morning, he woke up with a very large hangover, and I woke up with a mouth full of ulcers. The ulcers had been growing ever since I had boarded the plane two days beforehand. In Los Angeles I had stopped off at a drug store, where the pharmacist had told me that my ulcers were stress related.

'Is there anything that could be making you stressed?' she had asked.

'No. Nothing at all,' I had lied, trying to focus on Darryl's American accent – he was buying some Mega Millions lottery tickets at the counter next to me.

But now the ulcers were seriously getting in the way of me speaking like an American. Every word that Darryl uttered was painful because, ironically enough, the ulcers mainly affected the open-vowel sounds that are uncommon in the nasal Australian tongue but ubiquitous in most American words.

This was proving a real problem. As was the Greyhound bus. Months ago Darryl had bought special tickets to an event in Phoenix that afternoon – the Miss Hooters Arizona Pageant – but he now discovered, in a mouth-achingly painful conversation with the motel reception, that the next bus out of Indio was not for four hours – he would miss most of the show. But there was nothing Darryl could do. He shrugged and sat down on the new-but-uncomfortable motel couch in the foyer. He picked up a copy of *USA Today* and prepared himself for the long wait.

Perhaps I'm too middle class to fully understand what Darryl was thinking. After all, he earned $20 a night plus tips, had a $12 000 credit card debt and had lost the $240 that was in his wallet the night before – a month's worth of discretionary spending.

But I was sick of it. I simply wasn't prepared to wait four hours just to make Darryl's experience authentic. I had been looking forward to the Miss Hooters Pageant. If I rented a car, we would be in Phoenix in plenty of time. Darryl could go to the bikini competition instead of spending another day on a cramped, smelly Greyhound with the banging toilet door and with the antiseptic smell that you just knew was masking human poo. I wouldn't have to listen to a man on his cell phone talking to friends about nothing, and then every time the call dropped out in the middle of the Californian desert ringing them back and saying, 'Yeah, I don't know why it dropped out.' Frankly, I had gotten a glimpse of how Darryl and the unwashed masses lived, and all I need to tell you is this: everyone is pretty much the same, but the places you hang out in are a bit dirtier. And you have to wait forever for everything. Oh, and most importantly, you have to take extra care to read the conditions on the bottom of coupons.

But the thing that most infuriated me was Darryl's total acceptance of all those facts. He didn't even try to put up an argument when he was hit with the small print in the coupon ad, and here he was again just sitting there accepting the bus delay. At the risk of sounding condescending, it seemed to me that Darryl was behaving like a sucker.

Not that his understanding was any less sophisticated than anyone else's: he assumed that the war in Iraq was about oil, and he knew too well that the casinos had an edge and so it was a bit of a sucker's game. But he still supported Bush and played the pokies.

As he sat on that uncomfortable couch, reading the worst newspaper in America, I was getting mad at him for lacking hope that he could do anything about his lot in life. But I was doing it while I was using an empty credit card that he didn't have and a laptop that he couldn't afford.

He was channeling his hope into things that were tangible – a lucky win at the casino or the possibility of picking up at the Hooters gig, while I was getting frustrated at him for not being more hopeful about some vague, intangible idea that the world could eventually be a better place for him if he only did something about it. I started to understand where he was coming from.

And so I logged on and looked up local car rentals, then I used my cell phone with its middle-class calling plan and dialed Hertz; next I arranged for the $20 taxi ride across town (the same price as Darryl's bus ticket to Phoenix), and within half an hour I was sitting in a shiny blue Mazda 3, driving at 75 miles per hour towards Phoenix. Darryl was neither jealous nor impressed. He was just pleased for the ride.

21
SOCRATIC GAMES

'Biggest decrease in extreme poverty. What do you say? Thailand or Vietnam?'

An excitable male teacher gave a whoop as he placed an orange dot on Vietnam. The move was a bold one: most of the dots were on China and India.

As I entered the hall at Hofstra University (Long Island's largest private university), there was already a din of activity, punctuated by laughter and the occasional yell. Everyone else had arrived and they were engaged in heated debate with each other as they looked at a couple of world maps pinned to the wall.

Today was Dianne Pari's big day. A petite woman in her late thirties, she bustled around dividing myself and 32 teachers into groups. After much back and forth between myself and Dianne I had managed to swing an invitation to today's Foundation for Teaching Economics course. Initially I had made my enquiries as 'high-school teacher Edward McGuire', but I had quickly abandoned that course of action. For a start, Edward was nervous about using his American accent for an entire day. This was totally unfounded, I told him – to me his accent sounded perfect. However, after Edward had had a brief conversation with Amanda, my partner, about whether his accent was 'ready', I had come round to her opinion that it wouldn't hurt to spend a little more time refining Edward's r's.

The other reason was logistical. It quickly became clear that Dianne knew every school and every teacher in the catchment area for this course. And while my commitment to Edward's character was limitless, inventing an entire school didn't seem worth the effort, especially as it was only going to get Edward my $150 stipend. Besides, I didn't want it to be on my NSA file that people had described me as a creepy foreign man who pretended to be an American teacher to gain access to schoolkids' curriculums.

And so I was here today as Charles Firth, writer. I had explained that I was interested in the course 'Is Capitalism Good for the Poor?' because I thought it went to the heart of what economics was about. Personally, I was pretty sure I could predict exactly what the course would say. It would take the standard economics line: 'Okay, poor people have it pretty bad and inequality is only increasing, but in the long term, the best way to deal with this is through conventional economic means – more free trade and more free investment.' We would all fall asleep by lunchtime, and then in the afternoon I would have to eat my left arm off just to make it through to 3 pm (while keeping my right hand uneaten so I could write notes for Edward to crib off). As it turned out, the whole course was anything but boring.

It all started harmlessly enough. After Dianne had introduced the speakers – Dr Ken Leonard, a professor at Washington State University and a private consultant to the *Wall Street Journal* (Classroom Edition), and Kathy Ratte (the same woman who had been in the DVD). She was a former teacher who helped set the national mandated exams on economics – Dr Ken walked over to the maps on the walls, with all the stickers attached, and started asking people to identify which one they'd put up and why.

'Who put a blue one on Haiti?' asked Dr Ken. Blue represented the most poverty-stricken country; most had been placed on Africa.

Eric, a lanky man in his mid-thirties, unshaven and with an orange baseball cap on, replied that he did. He explained that they produced charcoal, which resulted in deforestation. 'And their main export, I think, is mangoes!'

Dr Ken was friendly but stern. 'How do you know this?'

Eric casually replied that he'd read some of the UN reports, 'plus I know someone from Haiti'.

Dr Ken smiled at this answer and went on. Over the next twenty minutes he fielded answers from many of the teachers in the room, quietly getting a sense of how much people knew, while always coming back to the question of *how* they knew.

Ken moved on to Sudan. Another teacher from across the other side of the room admitted to putting a blue sticker there.

'How did you know this?' asked Dr Ken again.

'I read an article in the *National Geographic* about it and I've had an interest in the worst countries in the world. I think it was listed in the CIA world fact book.'

Dr Ken liked this answer. He smiled without betraying why he was smiling.

To me they were all good answers, and the breadth of knowledge surprised me. It made me think that Edward should read more widely.

The table from Floral Park High had selected Bangladesh.

'Why?'

'I read somewhere that it was very poor,' said a slightly chubby teacher up the back.

After 20 minutes of back and forth, Dr Ken finally had the answer he had been waiting for. He leapt into action. 'Exactly!' he beamed. He stood in front of the maps and, one by one, made eye contact with everyone in the room. The gravitas of his voice was mixed with an ever-so-slight derision as he proceeded to impersonate the responses of the teachers. 'We all have the same kind of answer to where did I get it from . . . We all *read that somewhere . . . I know someone from there . . . I read an article in* National Geographic. We don't have a crisp understanding of world poverty. We have a more general impression.'

Everyone's best friend, Dr Ken, was suddenly turning their own answers against them. Having built up their trust, he was now attacking them – but in a magically non-confrontational way. Ken was bringing into question the beliefs of people who taught global studies for a living, not by questioning *them*, but by questioning their *sources*. He had turned the fact that they were widely read against them. Dr Ken's lesson was clear: the general knowledge that was valued in classrooms – such as information gleaned from shoddy publications like *National Geographic* – was not going to pass muster in this course. I silently wondered what Dr Ken did consider legitimate sources of knowledge.

Dr Ken then tried to move on to the next topic. But several teachers interrupted him. 'What's the answer? What are the poorest countries?' they asked.

'I'm not going to answer,' replied Dr Ken with reassuring objectivity. 'It changes, but the data says there are 7–10 countries in sub-Saharan Africa. It depends on which data you use, which indicators you use. Whether you use IMF figures or the World Bank.' Clearly, Dr Ken's wide reading habits extended to both IMF *and* World Bank reports.

'How do you define poor?' asked Dr Ken, ever the enthusiast for the Socratic method.

'Not being able to provide for your basic needs. Food, shelter and clothing,' replied a female teacher.

'Okay,' said Dr Ken, 'but how much food does that mean, what sort of shelter? A mud hut? A thatch roof? What sort of clothing are we talking about?'

One of the teachers from Elmont High interrupted Dr Ken. 'But to some extent has capitalism created poverty?'

Dr Ken didn't quite hear the question. Eric enthusiastically interpreted the question for him. 'I think what he means is that when an economy moves from subsistence agrarian-based economy to an industrialized economy you're necessarily creating rich and poor people because they can't feed themselves any more.' Eric reminded me of Edward, but with a better touch.

Dr Ken smiled and opened his hands to his audience: 'They're all good questions,' he said and moved on. The teachers in the room looked around at each other. Eric had raised what seemed a fairly fundamental – and sophisticated – question, and yet Dr Ken had ducked it.

Dr Ken was not there for long and complex debates about capitalism. His mission was to persuade teachers to abandon messy indicators such as access to 'shelter' and 'food' as measures of poverty, in favor of the measures that economists use: dollars and . . . well that was it actually.

It was becoming apparent from the disappointed expression on Eric's face that he had no idea that the Foundation for Teaching Economics was privately sponsored by some of the world's largest banks. Eric seemed to want a debate about the fundamental questions that capitalism posed, but Dr Ken had no time for that: he was trying to teach economics.

Dr Ken's lesson was becoming interesting not so much for its strict commitment to neo-liberal economic measures, but for the evangelical techniques he was using to convert people to an economist's understanding of the world.

He flicked a button on the laptop, which put a new graph up on the screen. 'The percentage of people that are poor has been decreasing decade on decade for the past century.'

People looked at each other and started to mutter. But Dr Ken was, for a change, in no mood for questions. He continued on with the next PowerPoint slide. 'This figure knocks you off your seat. For the first time ever in human history over the past two decades, the number of poor people is decreasing.'

Dr Ken let that figure sink in – the PowerPoint slide showed a graph in which a black line was declining over time. Thomas, who was at Eric's table, politely put up his hand. 'I don't understand how that could be.'

Ken explained that poverty was the equivalent of $US 1 a day (in 1985 figures), and the data came from the World Bank. Ken pressed the button for the next slide, but Thomas was not finished. He politely pointed out that this was impossible. 'How can the number of poor people be decreasing? We didn't even have 1.1 billion people a century ago.'

It was a great point – and so simply put. Thomas was only inches away from identifying the sleight of hand in Dr Ken's figures. That night, while I was going through my notes, I pulled out Edward's well-thumbed copy of *Freakonomics* and together he and I figured out where the trick lay. Thomas was right – the absolute number of poor people has soared over the past century – but Dr Ken changed the yardstick halfway through. His first graph measured the past century but the second one looked only at the past two decades.

Ken hurried the discussion along, with a new slide, this time a map, with the rich countries colored in green, the middle-income countries in orange and the poor countries in yellow. 'Why is the world colored that way?' he asked.

An earnest woman in her mid-twenties dressed in a striking orange top spoke up for the first time. Her voice wasn't very loud, but she felt this was a question she finally knew the answer to: 'Imperialism – the rich countries took all the raw materials from the poor countries. The US took them for themselves.'

Dr Ken wasn't expecting such a communistic answer from the young, meek teacher. He had been staring at the middle table – with Thomas and Eric. He smiled and gave off a small laugh, and then with mock politeness, his voice dripping with sarcasm, replied: 'But I thought America was independent. From memory we had a war where we got independence from Britain. So which is it: imperialism or independence?'

The earnest woman tried to find the words. 'Well . . . independence . . . but . . . well there are two different causes.'

Ken realized he had overstepped the mark. Public bullying only worked on the strong, and in a bizarre 'Good cop, bad cop' routine he smiled broadly, walked over to the woman in orange and addressed her comfortingly: 'I'm picking on you. I'm picking on you.'

He was trying to sound conciliatory. 'It's just that I don't want your students to get away with saying imperialism. I want them to say imperialism *because* . . .'

Eric, ever eager, jumped in with his own explanation for the divide between rich and poor. 'It's exploitation. Some countries are exploiting other countries. Some countries went into other countries and exploited opportunities there.'

Surprisingly, Ken welcomed the answer. 'Exploitation,' he repeated with apparent approval. 'But exploiting *opportunities* is different to exploiting *countries*.'

Dr Ken seemed to have a glib answer to every non-glib question he was asked. I say this with no disrespect – it's quite a skill. It was beginning to dawn on me that Dr Ken wasn't really that interested in teaching economics at all. What Dr Ken was doing was a demonstration in the rhetoric of economics. Dr Ken considered most of the questions outside the discipline he was teaching, but to dismiss them he had to master the art of the friendly put-down.

The lesson I was learning for Edward had stopped being about economics. This was a lesson in belittling anything that fell outside your definition of what mattered. I wished Edward could have been there to see it, because it was a rhetorical sight to behold, shunning intellectual engagement while mimicking the language and form of scholarly pursuit. It was a kind of anti-Socratic dialogue.

In fairness, the measures that Dr Ken was using were incredibly neat and measurable – it was about dollars the country produced divided by numbers of people involved. Unfortunately, it also made him completely unable to grapple with nebulous, morally confusing topics such as 'colonialism' and 'imperialism', which the teachers kept raising, only to be given a glib response.

Over the next couple of hours, 32 teachers from the New York education system were bombarded with graphs, maps and fact sheets proving beyond all doubt that as long as you keep changing the time-scale by which you measure it, and stick to the World

Bank's figures, capitalism can be made to look pretty good on a PowerPoint presentation.

I learnt a second lesson for Edward. First belittle then bamboozle. Like a preacher selling the Word, Dr Ken had destroyed the confidence of a classroom of teachers, and then bombarded them with new answers to the questions that until now, they thought they understood pretty well. And it wasn't even 11 am.

Eventually, the other instructor, Kathy Ratte, a tall, thin ex-teacher in her mid-fifties, took over. Her expertise was curriculum, and her job was to translate the information Dr Ken had presented into fun classroom activities. She handed out some factsheets specially designed for use in class. While everyone read, I pilfered a couple of the laminated handouts to show Edward, and perhaps to use as the basis for an article. After all, Kathy had said she encouraged us to copy them; 'The art of good teaching', she joked, half-serious, 'is plagiarism.' A few teachers bristled.

As the reading time came to an end, Thomas, by now red in the cheeks but still maintaining a polite demeanor, put up his hand. 'Can I ask: what is the source of this data?'

Bingo. This was the million-dollar question.

'The Heritage Foundation,' replied Kathy.

Around the room there was suppressed laughter. I was confused. I'd only vaguely heard of the Heritage Foundation and didn't know anything about it. It sounded respectable enough.

Kathy sensed the room was turning against her. But whereas Dr Ken might have shrugged and moved on, or even accepted the punch and made a tactical retreat, Kathy played defense.

'There is similar sort of data that also comes from the Fraser Institute in British Columbia,' she said casually. There was a tense silence. I started to feel like I was sitting in a classroom of students who have just done something incredibly naughty and are about to be found out.

Bruce, another teacher sitting with Eric and Thomas, burst out, 'What? All the information is from the far Right then, if not solidly on the Right. Is all of your information coming from these organizations?'

Without waiting for a response, Thomas chimed in, 'Yeah. In terms of how it's presented it would seem to be impartial, but then all your information is coming from the Right.'

Thomas had finally lost it. But like any natural teacher, his anger was white, and even in a fury he remained on top of his material. He picked up the laminated classroom handout and read from it, his tone thick with derision. '"Regulation of business in the US economy is low by comparison to world standards . . . However, regulation is increasing and in some areas – civil rights, disabilities, environment and safety – is becoming a significant burden that is impacting productivity and output."' Thomas looked up at Kathy. 'Regulation is a *burden* on productivity? Civil rights are a *burden*?'

Kathy tried to interrupt, but Thomas was in full flight.

'Is that a provable contention that those things are a burden? Maybe it is. That is something I would ask my kids to have a debate about, but to throw it out there like it's a proven assumption is really disturbing.' Thomas threw the handout onto the table and crossed his arms. It struck me how brave he was being – he still wasn't fully aware how far FTE's roots stretched.

The pitch of Kathy's voice had risen about an octave in the past five minutes. It had also begun to break-up, as if it were coming from a scratched LP. 'If you're choosing to take the word "burden" as negative, then that's your business – but I'm saying it's not. It's just a choice that we've made . . .' Her voice trailed off. This was a low point in the debate. It was a lesson for Edward, though: never try to engage directly with your opponent's point. She should have gone for the belittle.

At that moment, unexpectedly, amazingly, the room began to laugh openly at their instructor. Kathy's attempt to defend the materials was too absurd. She returned to the PowerPoint presentation and shuffled through some papers.

About half-an-hour beforehand, I had walked over and sat down at the Eric–Bruce–Thomas table to chat to them about the FTE, to see how much they knew about how it was funded. But now, sitting at that table, the room seemed to be closing in. I looked up to find Kathy and Dr Ken, who had taken time out from his break, standing over the table. Thomas looked defiant. I was a bit scared.

'Do you know whether the Brookings Institute has any information that might balance this?' asked Thomas.

'No I don't know,' replied Kathy.

Thomas launched into an impassioned argument about how he wouldn't want his class to be given such biased information. Being at their table, I had no choice but to be on Team Thomas. I nodded along defiantly with the rest of them, trying to hide how embarrassed I was. I was supposed to be an impartial observer but I had become mixed up with the bad kids.

'I think this is a perception issue. As a teacher, you're the one to engage the children in that discussion.' Kathy's voice had risen in pitch again. 'You have two options: one, not to make use of the research; or two, to research it yourself. We got a Nobel Laureate on the team. We even got Robert Ransom from the University of California, Riverside, to argue the other side.'

Kathy was playing the expertise card. It was a foolproof way to win an argument without engaging with the issue. If a Nobel Laureate agrees with you, you must be right!

Kathy was now standing right across the table from Thomas, while Dr Ken was standing directly behind him. Remember, Thomas was sitting down, looking up at these two tall experts. We all felt very small. 'We didn't come out here to sell you a bill of goods,' she said, saying the exact opposite of what everyone was thinking.

'Have you checked the Brookings Institute?' repeated Thomas.

'They don't have this type of information.'

'A moment ago you said you hadn't checked there.'

'Well it sounds like you're very familiar with the sources on the other side,' Kathy said with a thick coating of sarcasm. She was getting into the belittling. I noted down in my pad a reminder to brush up on Edward's sarcasm.

'You should never present your own opinion in class,' said Thomas.

'Well, give them the handout with no reading at all. That's another way.' A strange argument, but disarming. She was essentially saying, 'If you don't like what we're doing, that's fine, don't use it. But don't argue against it.' It was simple, anti-intellectual and extremely disingenuous.

Kathy and Ken weren't there to engage with the ideas. At the end of the day, the course was like a highly personalized version of spam email. They didn't care if some of the users ignored the message – they were playing the percentages. 'So what if you disagree?' she must have been thinking. 'You're just one teacher, and we're training thousands.'

At lunch I went over and talked to Dr Ken and Kathy about the heated debate. They explained that the reaction they were receiving only really happened in two states: New York and Massachusetts. 'In most of the rest of the country, they just completely agree with you.'

This, if anything, was the lesson of the day. To talk like a true economist all Edward had to do was treat his ideas like a game. As long as he stuck to his guns and belittled those who pointed out the flaws, it didn't matter how wrong his theories were. Hell, he could probably even claim the world was flat using this method. Or at the very least that it was created in seven days.

22

WONDERFUL AND SMART

Bertrand was on a roll. From languishing in last place for most of the book, he had taken the lead in the past two weeks. And all he'd needed was a cool $2.5 million to do it. If only he'd thought of it sooner.

He sat down and switched on his laptop. He had come to his local Starbucks in Astor Place – an unusually sprawling version, with fifty tables in the cavernous, high-roofed basement of a century-old skyscraper which rattled every time a subway train passed underneath. In this particular Starbucks the normally cozy feel gave way to a university-cafeteria lack-of-ambience. With three separate entrances, and right near the touristy end of East 8th Street, it was also the perfect place for beggars to ply their lack-of-trade without being noticed by the staff. Although some of his friends objected to the corporate chain, to Bertrand it was just a modern expression of bohemian culture. Besides, even in the East Village it was the only place to get reliable chai. Except, of course, for the other Starbucks on the opposite side of the square about 30 meters away.

Bertrand also liked the way Starbucks wore its politics on its sleeves. For a while now Starbucks had been printing on the side of every cup a little quote from celebrities – from sports stars to musicians to business leaders. And most of the quotes had the faint smell of progressive politics about them which appealed to Bertrand. 'Mother-love is not inevitable. The good mother is a great artist ever creating beauty out of chaos,' wrote novelist Alice Randall. Bertrand was pleased to drink from the paper cup of feminism.

I gazed at Bertrand's cup. Underneath the quotes, Starbucks always printed a disclaimer: 'Please note: The opinions put forth by contributors do not necessarily reflect the views of Starbucks.' Every time I saw this I wondered what it was about mother-love that was so controversial.

Bertrand opened his email. While Edward and Dr Andy were gathering 'research' in the 'real world' and getting 'knowledge' from 'real people', Bertrand was finally gaining respect from his left-liberal counterparts. A bit different to the bad old days when he didn't have $2.5 million to throw around. There were 16 new emails in his inbox. He opened the first one.

> *It was with great pleasure that I read of your AdBack effort, which sounds wonderful and smart.*

Yes, thought Bertrand, changing the world one advertisement at a time was a wonderful and smart idea. He browsed through the email. It was a proposal to create a viral email campaign entitled 'Medicare for All', which, the proposer said, would lead to the establishment of a universal healthcare system in America. It proposed establishing a website, an email petition and sign-on campaign for political candidates.

Perfect, thought Bertrand. It was exactly the sort of innovative thinking the Left was lacking. An email petition – why hadn't anyone thought of that before? Obviously he'd seen it for other campaigns, but not for universal healthcare. It seemed like the best idea since sliced wholemeal bread!

Bertrand hit the reply button.

'What are you doing?' I asked.

'I'm going to tell them they can have $250 000.'

'But you don't have $250 000. Remember – we made that part up.'

Bertrand clenched his teeth in frustration. With all the flattery he'd been receiving in recent weeks it was hard to remember that he was still, in their terms, a nobody. But it was also disappointing. Some of the ideas that his money was bringing out of the wood-work were pure genius. He opened another email. This one was asking for money to create an 'online TV station' which would 'develop and maintain a new multi-media paradigm in communications'. All they needed was $80 000. What a bargain! Not only that, but the gentleman who proposed the scheme was sincerely touched by Bertrand's selfless generosity towards the cause of progressive politics:

> *In all cases, I thank you personally for your generous offer to help promote progressive efforts which is my larger motivation. I hope you've found very worthy causes that will do so and wish you the best towards those goals.*

While Bertrand glowed with pride, I had begun to worry. Bertrand's offer had generated scores of responses, but a lot of them were sincere people who genuinely wanted Bertrand's money and had put in time and effort to get it.

I'd heard that America was a litigious society. These emails were wonderful, but I was unwilling to test the patience of these people by making fraudulent offers of large sums of money. I started feeling that the insurance companies maybe had a point – tort reform which massively restricts the ability for people to sue for massive breaches of trust – wasn't such a bad idea after all.

I started to understand why Starbucks had decided its coffee-cup quotes needed disclaimers.

Of course there were several silly proposals too, like one that suggested using $250 000 to link willing volunteers into political clubs at a local level that would then meet up off-line to organize campaigns around issues that their local communities thought were important.

How ridiculous, thought Bertrand, the whole process sounded completely unwieldy. And what if people came up with the wrong ideas to campaign on? There seemed to be no way Bertrand could share his personal wisdom with each club without going around and meeting people face to face. The Clubs for Progress sounded like something straight out of the 19th Century.

By now Wes from MoveOn had responded to my email on Bertrand's behalf. He replied by saying that he'd be delighted to 'hear about' my book, but that he was traveling. 'How about a phone call?' he'd said. But he left no phone number.

Unperturbed, I had hit the reply button and sent this email:

Wes,

Yep, that sounds great. I'm pretty flexible, so why don't you propose a time next week, and I'll call you then? (or you can call me on 646-763-5100).

Charles

I don't know whether he was insulted that I'd called him by his first name, or whether the novelty of me knowing somebody he knew had worn off, but I never received a reply from Wes ever again. I tried emailing him a few times, but to no avail.

But now that Bertrand was flying high, he felt he didn't need my help any more. 'I'll handle this,' he assured me. Bertrand knew that a bit of bluff and a large amount of money to throw around was all that he needed to get Wes's attention. It was 4:02 pm on a blustery spring afternoon when Bertrand sent this email to Wes:

Dear Mr Boyd,

I was talking to Senator Ted Kennedy the other day about an idea I have to seed $2.5 million into progressive projects – particularly innovative 'silver bullet' New Media ideas that can solve the movement's problems in a swift stroke. He suggested that I contact you before going any further.

A quick background: I made a lot of money in advertising in my twenties, and now I want to give something back to society. For the past few months I have been trying to attract interest in 'Proposals for a New

"New Deal"'. My plan was to seed ten projects at $250 000 each. Unfortunately, my staff have been unable to attract proposals of the caliber I was hoping for. I'm not interested in repeating old ideas that haven't worked before.

Senator Kennedy suggested to me that perhaps MoveOn or one of its associated entities could make better use of my money. I would be keen to set up a meeting at your convenience to discuss this.

Yours sincerely,

Bertrand Newton

'Now wait,' said Bertrand. 'I bet you he'll reply as soon as he gets it.'

23

INSIDER OUT

Meanwhile, Edward and I were sitting in fancy chairs in downtown Washington DC. If I knew my woods I might have been able to say they were mahogany, but I don't. All I know is that they weren't pine and they looked very expensive.

'This is my presidents' corner,' said Lee Edwards, pointing to the corner of his office behind his desk.

Four framed photos were hanging on the wall. The corner reminded me of Vincent Fiore's attic display. Except that instead of being the type of photos you could order over the Internet, these were personal snapshots of Lee with each of the presidents. From the moment we met him, Edward was jealous of Lee.

Lee was the in-house historian of the Heritage Foundation, the right-wing think tank that the Foundation for Teaching Economics used as the source for their fact sheets. We had come here to find out why their facts so enraged Thomas and a hall full of teachers. Lee took me through the photos in chronological order. 'Recognize who this handsome general is?' he asked in his thin voice.

I had no idea, but there was a message scrawled on the photo which read 'To Lee Edwards – a stalwart friend. Barry Goldwater.' I used my formidable powers of deduction. 'Wow,' I said with a little too much enthusiasm. 'That's Barry Goldwater!' Edward rolled his eyes, pretending not to be impressed by Lee's association with the man who many think of as one of the founding fathers of modern conservatism.[58]

---

[58] In case you don't know, Barry Goldwater ran against President Johnson in 1964, and he arguably pioneered the Republican's approach of Presidential

'Yes it is. As you can see he was a very handsome guy. And I was in his '64 presidential campaign.'

Next to Barry stood a young Lee, almost unrecognizable. Back then he had a full head of hair and dark eyebrows. Now in his late sixties, Lee was almost completely bald, save for a few gray hairs around the very edges of his round skull.

'Recognize this guy?' He was pointing to a photo of himself with Richard Nixon.

'Have you ever been in the Oval Office?' I asked.

'Yep – right here. This is '84, and I'm interviewing Mr Reagan in the Oval Office.'

'Oh wow,' I said. There was nothing disingenuous about that 'wow'. Edward, however, was determined to remain cool at Lee's close association with the executive branch, even though his initial jealousy was turning to amazement.

'This was '84 and I was editor of *Conservative Digest*. So this is when he was up for re-election. And of course, I'd known him going back to the 60s.'

Where did the right-wing machine that had taken me to Florida and Long Island lead? To an eight-storey building on Massachusetts Avenue, just a few minutes away from the US Congress. If Edward or I had had any doubts that the conservative movement was anything but a well-oiled machine, then walking into the Heritage Foundation's spacious lobby on Capitol Hill had ended them.

Lee's success (and Edward's jealousy) stemmed from the fact that he personally knew every single establishment conservative I asked about, and he'd been photographed or written biographies about most of them too. And this was no accident – Lee was

---

candidate selection whereby an affable, but slightly idiotic person is presented as the front man. For example, during the campaign his hawkish side emerged when he said the US should pre-emptively attack Russia with a nuclear bomb, and that the east coast of America should be sawn off and put out to sea because it was so full of liberals. Real presidential material.

emphatic that the growth of the conservative movement was a direct result of the work done by Ed Feulner and the Heritage Foundation. They had spent over 30 years slowly but systematically building the infrastructure needed to, say for example, control the presidency and both houses of Congress all at the same time.

Lee rattled through a quick history of the foundation. It was started in 1972 by Ed Feulner and Paul Wynick, and unlike many other think tanks, it had always proudly worn its colors on its sleeve. 'Wynick and Feulner have always been movement conservatives and certainly when Feulner became foundation president, he said: "We are interested in building a stronger conservative movement".' I was beginning to understand why Thomas and the rest of the teachers had been so angry about those fact sheets.

With an annual budget of $37 million, the Heritage Foundation had become the self-appointed upper management of the conservative movement. Even after the $15 million that went on its 67 full-time researchers, it had another 130 staff dedicated to 'building a stronger conservative movement'. And by not engaging in electoral politics it was a political organization that was free to set its strategy in terms of decades, rather than just responding to the next election cycle.

As in Vincent Fiore's office, Lee's shelves were packed with hundreds of books by all the great conservative thinkers; but unlike Vincent, Lee's father was a journalist who knew Richard Nixon, with the consequence that Lee had been a Washington insider his whole life.

In 1967 he had made a name for himself by writing the first biography of Ronald Reagan, in which he predicted not only Reagan's election as Governor of California, but also that one day he would be President. Since then he had written another 18 books and edited various conservative publications, including *Conservative Digest*. Lee Edwards was not just the insider's insider, he was the insider's biographer.

Heritage was the first think tank to pioneer the use of small contributions by direct mail – donations from 200 000 individuals accounted for a third of the money raised. 'No individual, no corporation, no foundation can say, "ooh if you want my money you must continue to be for or against free trade, or for or against the Iraq War" – whatever it may be. We're able to be independent because of that broad financial base.' Of course Lee's unspoken point was that no corporation needed to tell them what to think – they were very much thinking along the same lines already. Lines that Edward shared. Now he had gotten over his jealousy he was eager to learn how he could get involved. But then Lee dropped the bombshell.

'In 2005,' said Lee, 'There were 1400 TV and radio appearances by our analysts. Three a day, average – every day. Monday through Sunday.' He smiled proudly. 'Nine hundred op-eds in major newspapers and online. That was a banner year.'

The color drained from Edward's face as he imagined himself getting that many op-eds published. *New York Times, Washington Post, LA Times, Wall Street Journal*, the Heritage Foundation repeatedly got their analysts in all of them. 'We have a communications department that contacts the newspaper and says would you like an op-ed on taxes, on healthcare, on whatever it might be.'

No wonder people joined the establishment – it was just so much easier. And the great thing for the papers was the content for them was entirely free.

'No. No. No. We don't seek payment.' Lee laughed at the mere suggestion. It was a great deal for newspapers seeking to cut costs, and their broad financial base ensured their independent integrity, even if the columns did skew to the Right a little.

'And then there are lots of smaller, not small but smaller, midsized dailies out there in the grassroots.'

I ask him to name one – this was where Edward would start, to prove his capabilities to these guys – but Lee struggled with a name. 'Umm. The *Pittsburgh* whatever it is.'

'*Post Gazette?*' I asked, my heart sinking.

'Yeah,' said Lee, blithely unaware of my disappointment. Edward had already been cyber-rejected by them.

Nevertheless, all the talk of op-eds had made Edward impatient. All he wanted was to sign on the dotted line: he wanted to become an insider too. Edward realized his resentment of being an outsider to the establishment was misplaced. What Heritage was all about was community-building. Surely there would be an opening for a conservative economist op-ed writer? Unfortunately, it wasn't as simple as that. Lee admitted that the chances of getting into even something like the foundation's internship program were greatly increased if you had the right silver spoon in your mouth. Indeed, when I pushed Lee about how people got the internships, knowing how desperately Edward wanted one, he was startlingly frank: 'They knew somebody who was here from their particular school, or the father or the mother is a donor or friend or what have you. So we believe in nepotism, we believe that's healthy, nepotism is healthy.'

Clearly the community they had built was not for Edward. No matter how good he got at belittling, his father never knew Nixon. The only people who Edward knew were the members of the MoveOff movement which was tiny by comparison – no more than 30 or 40 active members. But still, the Heritage Foundation had started out small. Edward suddenly understood the value of a long-term strategy. Small didn't feel so small when you had a grand plan. And boy did the Heritage Foundation have a grand plan.

24

OIL, OF COURSE

Sometime late in 1998 a 41-year-old former marine going by the name of Ken Robinson boarded a civilian aircraft bound for Atlanta, Georgia. What his fellow passengers didn't know about this affable man with the rock-solid build was that Robinson had recently joined a secretive 'red cell' and was planning a terrorist attack against the United States. It was to involve three simultaneous strikes in separate cities. Robinson's trip was part of a recruitment drive.

Earlier that year, KR[59] had been told his days in the field as a Tier One unit, answerable directly to the President, were over. The injuries he had sustained in tours of duty in Iran, Iraq, Somalia, Honduras, El Salvador, Colombia and Nicaragua (to name a few) made him medically unfit for combat operations.

He was bitterly disappointed. After 20 years on the ground, the last thing he wanted to do was to stick around and 'lead a desk'. And so one of the US Army's most highly trained combat specialists took early medical retirement. It was soon after this that KR started planning the attack.

I had spent weeks trying to get in contact with the elusive KR. Dr Andy was desperate to meet him before we went into Iraq. Dr Andy wanted tips on how to tackle suicide bombers in crowded market-places, I wanted to know where in the Green Zone was the safest place to hide. People had told me that despite KR's eccentric behavior since leaving the military there was nobody better to speak

---

[59] Although Ken Robinson usually goes by the name Ken or Mr Robinson, under the new Freedom of Patriotic Speech Act it is required that when writing about the War on Terror, combat operatives are assigned codenames that sound 'interesting and kinda cool'.

to about the town I was going into. He had been in countless battles, and knew people there worth speaking to.

After dozens of phone calls, emails and messages, with a seemingly endless number of middlemen, I had finally managed to get through to KR's right-hand man, 'James', who had agreed to grant me one hour alone with KR. The location: an upscale and decidedly western hotel owned by the Sultan of Brunei, paid for by oil money, in an undisclosed area close to the war zone we were about to visit.

As we approached the hotel, walking along its freshly painted pink paths next to the impeccable driveway, Dr Andy and I passed stretch limo after stretch limo. The drivers stood around waiting in full tuxedos, relaxed and chatty despite the sweltering sun. One of them polished a glass crystal tumbler from the limo's bar as he joked with his colleagues.

Dr Andy had insisted we turn up half-an-hour early. I tried to look inconspicuous by sitting at the bar and staring hard at my interview notes while Dr Andy checked the bar for electronic bugs. Looking back, I don't know why I was so worried. The only other patron in the lounge hardly blended in. She was a thirty-something American woman with red frizzy hair and a red cap on, and she was speaking loudly to a waiter. 'Is that an accent?' she asked.

'Yes,' the waiter politely answered, 'I am from Afghanistan.'

'Oh WOW!' shouted the woman. 'Wow!'

'Thank you,' the waiter was nothing if not well trained.

She paused for thought. 'Where is that?'

At that moment my cell phone rang. It was KR. 'I'm in the lobby. I'm the one carrying a large white folder.' He hung up. We were about to meet one of the most influential men in the world.[60]

---

[60] Okay, so that might sound like a slight exaggeration, but I think it's justified under the hyperbole provisions of the Exaggeration in the Pursuit of Justice Act, and anyway, as you'll see, he's pretty cool. He's certainly the only man I've ever met who answered directly to the President of the United States of America.

KR had a neatly shaved gray goatee and closely cropped gray hair, which elegantly de-emphasized his thinning locks. He was a thick-set man, with chubby fingers and the world's most muscular neck. Which is not to say he was fat, but I got the sense that until he left the military it was all muscle. Now it was a hybrid of the two. He was perhaps a little over six feet tall, and cut a jocular, even charismatic figure.

When KR boarded that plane to Atlanta back in 1998, he was on a recruitment drive for his 'red cell', but the terrorist plot he was planning was part of a war game scenario called TopOff (short for Top Officials), which he was writing for the Pentagon as part of a program run at that time by the controversial intelligence whistleblower – and now über-pundit – Richard Clarke, who famously warned the Bush administration about the risks of terrorism in the lead-up to September 11.[61] TopOff was run every two years to make sure the military and White House could respond effectively to attacks against America. It involved, as its name suggests, all the top officials in the military and the government – from the President down.

'I suggested,' KR told me, 'that CNN be incorporated into the exercise because we felt that we needed the presence of some national media that would create friction for the senior policy makers in the exercise, to be able to ask them the same hard questions that you would expect during a real event, so I went down to Atlanta, and I met with the chairman of CNN.' As it turned out, CNN declined the offer, but the 1998 TopOff game that KR wrote was chillingly prescient. 'We wrote a scenario that had three simultaneous attacks on America. It foreshadowed 9/11. And we did it in three cities at the same time.' Shortly after that meeting KR was recruited by CNN, and is now their military analyst.

---

[61] Indeed, I think the phrase his team used three weeks before it happened was something along the lines of 'Bin Laden Determined to Strike in US'. Oh wait a minute, yes, those were the *exact* words.

After KR had talked about what we could expect out on location in Iraq, he let us in on some of the missions he'd completed over his twenty years. As an army ranger, his job had been to fly into 'hot spots' around the world to 'fix them'. Sometimes the placement would be for three months, sometimes six. KR gave the impression that he would have considered staying any longer than six months in one country boring. Although, towards the end of his commission, Ken had spent two years in Colombia. Dr Andy was in his element. The one thing that he loved was stories from the field – and KR had plenty.

'There's as much oil in Colombia as there is in Venezuela, but we can't get it out of there because of narco-terrorism. That's why Venezuela is such a problem. Nobody saw that coming,' he said, referring to the thinking within the White House. 'We always thought that even without Iraq we'd always have Venezuela, but then Chavez came along.'

Dr Andy shook his head and 'tsked' at the mention of Chavez. A few years back he had written a position paper for the US Defense Department on Chavez in which he had argued it was possible to democratically overthrow the popular leader simply by renaming the 200 kilogram Bunker Busters 'Democracy Bombs', and then launching them at the country in a show of what he called 'overwhelming democratic force'. According to Dr Andy's sources at the Pentagon, senior officials still hadn't ruled out the idea.

I was surprised by KR's frankness. Dr Andy was fascinated: he rarely got to chat with field operatives. I asked KR why he thought the White House went into Iraq. 'Oil, of course,' he said with a shrug of the shoulders. It wasn't rocket science. KR said many of the people in the Pentagon opposed the decision to go into Iraq. He saw it as a strategic dead end, but he remained hopeful that it was not another Vietnam. 'Al-Zarqawi is a real problem. He's a madman.' Of course, al-Zarqawi died a few months later, much to Dr Andy's glee. It showed that he'd been right about one thing – my book was so topical it had become out-of-date even before it had been published.

Just as the fascinating chat was getting even more interesting – our talk was turning to the difficulties of having Saudi Arabia as an ally – KR received a phone call. It was CNN. There were reports (which later prove to be false – they wouldn't come true for a few more months) that al-Zarqawi had been wounded or killed by US forces. They needed him to pundit ASAP.

And so, after a two-hour chat, we left the hotel and walked slowly back to the car. Dr Andy had been delighted by KR's frankness. The problem with talking to civilians, Dr Andy explained, was that they always talked about freedom and democracy. That was fine when you were trying to sell a military campaign to the people, but the way the White House was behaving lately he'd started to think that they actually believed in that rubbish. Hearing KR talk was a comfort to him. 'At least *some* of the senior officials running the country don't believe in all that freedom mumbo jumbo,' he told me. And you can't get much more senior than a CNN analyst.[62]

Like KR, Dr Andy didn't see it as a problem that the US was thirsty for oil. Indeed Dr Andy wondered why everyone was so embarrassed by it. What was wrong with going around prising open countries in order to get their oil? That was the reality of the world we lived in. But the thing that was missing was a pithy way of selling those interventions to the public. Dr Andy thought the current mob was doing a pretty poor job of that. As, indeed, did KR. That was why Dr Andy's mission to Iraq was so important. Over the coming days his on-the-ground experiences would teach him a lot about how America's military interventions were sold to ordinary Americans.

---

[62] The only higher rank is a Fox News anchor.

25
DOWN TO THE TOENAIL
OF THINGS

The street was completely empty, save for a large black Hummer parked at an angle so as to block the thoroughfare about 70 yards away. The street itself was unpaved, and about 6 yards wide. The dusty road was heavily packed, though I wondered about the amount of mud it would create when it rained – indeed, if it rained. The sharp corners of the building cast crisp shadows in the bright winter sun. There was not a cloud in the sky.

The walls on the building were plastered, though years of exposure to the sun and dust had made the word 'whitewash' take on a whole new meaning.

As I walked along the narrow dusty streets of Fallujah, I was thinking about the final words of the conversation I had had with KR before I left. 'It's a treacherous place . . . vicious.'

That was true enough. Walking through the deserted streets in Dr Andy's new, bright green camouflage flak jacket, passing building after building unstable because of mortar damage, I imagined the countless lives that had been lost. There were no corpses on this street. This was now a secure location. The whole town was empty. The eerie silence was alarming.

One of our entourage – my photographer, who had never been here before either – had found something on the ground ahead. He excitedly picked up a discharged bullet cartridge, and then another. 'They're everywhere! How much shooting do they do?!' Nobody responded. 'Let's collect a whole bunch!' As the chubby 40-year-old American ran off, bending over every few meters to load himself up with the souvenirs, our guide wearily told me that every time 'they' come to town they leave behind an average of 5000 rounds strewn on the ground.

Over the past few days Dr Andy and I had been mollycoddled by so many PR handlers that we both wondered whether we were ever going to see a real explosion, or even a corpse. Dr Andy was frankly tired of the endless jingoism that had passed everyone's lips. I had expected to be nervous. Instead I was just exhausted from the relentless smiling of the polished PR. This was the lot of the embedded reporter. Until now.

Today was the first time we were allowed out of the sight of the PR handlers. For the first time I could actually walk up to the dusty mud huts that passed for homes and walk into the dark, empty houses that had been raided by US Special Forces. I picked up a brown scarf, no doubt left behind in the haste to evacuate. I placed it around my shoulders as I leant against a nearby wall. The wall thudded loudly. 'How strange,' I thought.

I tried to imagine what it was like before the war. A bustling street full of Iraqis going about their daily business? A marketplace perhaps, full of exotic spices? 'No,' said my guide, 'this was a Mexican town before 2001. Then *JAG* came along and made it into Afghanistan. Now it's mostly Iraq.'

This was an annoying quote, and one that I'd hoped wouldn't end up in the final draft. After chapter upon chapter of reaching this thrilling point, I was hoping that I could avoid revealing that I wasn't in Iraq at all. I was hoping that Dr Andy would be able to gain enough insight into Iraq by coming here. I was hoping that this trip would render a journey to the real Iraq superfluous.

I had come to Hollywood. In particular I was on the set of one of half-a-dozen ranches hidden away in the hills outside Los Angeles which now pass for Iraq in America's relentless obsession with dramatized war. The US military used this place as the setting for many of its training videos. What was good enough for desk-bound generals was surely good enough for me.

The set consisted of 400 yards of the streetscape of a dusty Iraqi town, plus an exact replica of a square in downtown Baghdad, including half a mosque (they only build the front half of the buildings). All of it looked like it was made out of bricks, mud, steel and cement, but it was in fact made out of plywood. Like most things in Hollywood, when you walked up to a mud hut and tapped it with your knuckle, it sounded like a hollow log.

Oddly enough it was Dr Andy's idea to come here. As the months went by, he and I had increasingly disagreed about when to go to Iraq. Eventually, he became paranoid (unfairly) that I didn't actually want to go to Iraq at all. And so we compromised. In researching Iraq, Dr Andy had slowly come to realize that much of what passed for on-the-ground 'reporting' nowadays was done out of offices in Kuwait, Dubai and New York. Even respectable organizations such as the *New York Times* left the on-the-ground information-gathering to local Iraqis who went unattributed in its articles. Dr Andy had read enough of these articles to understand roughly what it must be like in Iraq, so writing about Iraq was not going to be a problem. The main problem was proving he'd been there. So all he really needed was a convincing background. A few photos on a million-dollar set and who would be able to tell the difference? Besides, this wasn't just some life-sized replica theme park – this was a genuine Hollywood set that had to be authentic down to the very last bloodsplattered wall. And it was certainly not for public consumption – the location, we were told, had to remain top secret – lest the more extremist elements of the paparazzi get hold of it.

The ranch belonged to Rene Veluzat, a rotund man with what can only be described as a pornstar moustache. A man of great enthusiasm who had done well out of running three ranches, he wore a 3.5 carat diamond ring and drove a 1983 Rolls Royce.

Rene bought the ranch in 2000, with the intention of turning it into Mexico. 'I was building my Mexican town and then the *JAG* TV series came along . . . they said, we're going to be in Afghanistan now. This is Afghanistan.' He laughed. 'They filmed here for three and a half years.'

In that time, Rene boasted, he had rented the ranch to 'all the major television series' including *JAG*, *CSI*, *NCIS*, *Alias* and *Without A Trace*. Recent movies included *Serenity* and the epic Martin Lawrence film *National Security*. And, of course, a spate of military training videos.

Today Rene had left the Rolls at home and was showing us around in his late-model Hummer. 'There's my crashed helicopter site,' he said, pointing to a green helicopter in some scrub. 'I built that. Then there's the bin Laden hideout cave.'

This was the closest Dr Andy had ever been to a field operation and he was loving it. As we sat in the leather seats of the luxury Hummer, he peered out the windscreen with his binoculars, on the look-out for IEDs up ahead. I asked Rene whether his Hummer had any protective armor on it. 'No. No need,' he replied. He looked at me as if I was odd.

We reached the summit of his mini-world and looked down upon streets, service stations, army tanks and a (working) aircraft hangar. 'This is what we call a Kodak moment,' he said proudly. Dr Andy rushed to the edge of the steep decline and demanded our photographer take some action shots of him looking as though he was hiding from the enemy. I was about to point out that if we were really in Iraq he would hardly hide at the top of an exposed hill, but then I stopped myself. The shot looked great, and that was what mattered most in Hollywood's Iraq.

Dr Andy's enthusiasm was infectious. I got out a prop microphone and, with Dr Andy's flak jacket and khaki cap on, got more than a few shots of me embedded in Iraq. Even the photographer was keen for a Kodak moment. He shoved the camera into my hands and demanded a couple of shots in front of the war zone.

In the middle of the photo, standing above the rest of the buildings, was the distinctive shape of a minaret atop Rene's magnificent plywood mosque. Before 2001, of course, there was no mosque. 'Before that, if you built Afghanistan, they would've said Afghani-where?' But recently it had been a different story. 'That works all the time that mosque. That's what I call my Baghdad street.' Built in conjunction with Paramount Studios, the set had been modeled on hundreds of photos of a real Baghdad landscape, and had cost $1 million.

With the war in Iraq dragging on, business for Rene had never been better. 'This ranch has been nothing but luck for me,' he confided. 'The top countries in demand are the Middle Eastern, all of the Middle Eastern. They say, "Do you have a Middle Eastern set?" I say yes. They say, "Does it look like Afghanistan?"'

So what was the difference between Iraq and Afghanistan? 'Not very much, it's all adobe buildings. The cars, the people might be different. Little variations. But not very much – it's all Middle Eastern.' Rene sensed that his comment might have sounded a little insensitive, so he explained further. 'I'm not very versed in the difference of cultures down to the toenail of things, but the art designers who come here are very versed on that. This was India in the last show. It was an SBC TV commercial.'

Dr Andy walked over to Rene's aircraft hangar and sat in a heli-copter, pretending to fly it. He seemed to have entirely forgotten he wasn't in the real Iraq. Meanwhile Rene had helped me climb up onto a large US Army tank. I had to admit that even though I knew the setting wasn't real, I kept catching myself. It looked so real. And just like in the real Iraq, playing with all the toys was proving a lot of fun.

'The movie ranches in Santa Clarita, none of them are any competition. I have the brown look as you can see – the Middle Eastern look. My other ranch has the Mexican town look, another ranch has the western town look. The Disney ranch has probably the most prestigious in the world. It waters its lawns – all 40 000 acres. It has the green look.'

As the war with the 'brown look' was dragging into its fourth year, Hollywood had started doing something it had never done before – making television drama based on a war that was still going on. With 486 000 US servicemen having already served time over in Iraq since the conflict began, the war directly impacted on the lives of millions of families, and tens of millions of their neighbors. In other words, anyone who could create a war drama that talked to these affected people would be onto a ratings killer.

But Hollywood also had a potent role in shaping domestic opinion about the war, and indeed about the US's role in the world. Dr Andy was beginning to realize that coming here was not just a great photo op. We were meeting the people who were crafting America's image of Iraq. This was the war's interface with pop culture. When most Americans thought of Iraq, chances are they pictured Rene Veluzat's ranch.

For Dr Andy, coming to Rene's Iraq had been far better than going to the real Iraq. This was where the battle for the hearts and minds of Americans was being fought. And if he was going to win that battle, this was where he was going to have to fight. Dr Andy – staid, stolid national security consultant – was going to make it in Hollywood. He would write his own television show promoting the War on Terror. It was the perfect way to sell it to the people. But how? How did you get a war drama up and running in Hollywood, a place many Americans regard as a bastion of liberal values?

The first TV drama to come out about Iraq was a short-lived 13 part series called *Over There*, which played in America in the summer of 2005. When Dr Andy first saw *Over There*, he instantly fell in love. The titles sequence was backed by an original ballad written by one of the show's creators, Chris Gerolmo.

The day is coming,
Drums are drumming,
If you know one say a prayer.

Mothers crying,
Fathers sighing,
War is in the air.
Trains filling up with boys,
Who have left behind,
Their favorite toys,
They're going over there.
Someone has to die (over there, over there),
It's not our job to reason why (over there, over there),
O someone has to die.

From there, the drama unfolded from the point of view of a small unit of soldiers stationed in Iraq. A typical episode ran like this: a BBC reporter, embedded with the gang, filmed one of the good-looking soldiers shooting and killing an Iraqi child. Inevitably, the slaying was picked up by the global media, which sensationalized the story, portraying the soldier as a brutal child killer. Then, just after the last commercial break, it was discovered that the reporter had selectively edited his footage – the child turned out to be a suicide bomber, and countless lives had been saved by gunning him down. Roll credits.

Once Dr Andy had decided to make it in Hollywood, he insisted that I track down Chris Gerolmo. Dr Andy thought that Chris, an innovator in the war drama business, would be able to provide a foot in the door. And he might give him ideas for what his show should be like.

And so Dr Andy and I met Chris at his airconditioned office in Santa Monica. He had agreed to drive us north to another Iraq ranch.[63] As we drove up, Chris told us that *Over There* was 'a show

---

[63] I was going to write that the dash through Los Angeles traffic – made in a black late-model European station wagon – was as treacherous as any you'd make on a Baghdad highway, but it wasn't true: it simply took longer.

about a bunch of American kids in the army on the ground in Iraq trying to survive'.

Chris was Hollywood through and through. He said he was 52 but looked 38. His casual blue jeans and blue shirt exuded a deep comfort with his role as an A-List writer and director. It said: 'I'm successful but I'm not a suit.' His big claim to fame was that he wrote the film *Mississippi Burning*, which won seven Oscars. Dr Andy imagined himself in Chris's jeans. They would match his flak jacket quite nicely.

Chris was at pains to convey his liberal credentials but he said that the show's producer, Steven Bochco, 'made it clear that he didn't really want to address the politics of left and right vis-à-vis the war, he didn't want to make a show about whether or not we should have gone to war'. For the characters 'they of course assume the war. For them it just exists, it doesn't matter why they're there'.

Chris, eager to get the show up, treated this limitation as a creative challenge: to produce what must surely be the first war drama that officially had no attitude towards the war. Dr Andy could understand why. Nobody, not Chris, nor Stephen, nor the advertisers, had an interest in losing the following of the families of the half a million people over there. Indeed, that was the show core demographic. Before they aired their first episode, they went to a military base in California and played it to a packed audience of soldiers and their families. The feedback was 'hugely positive'.

Nevertheless, Chris said the show shouldn't be construed as mindless cheerleading. Instead, it was a dramatization of what he called 'the human consequence of war' – in all its moral ambiguity. Which is why he made no apologies for portraying it only from the perspective of the child killer. 'Basically, our story is very much about these six kids and their sergeant, and so we take it very, very much from their point of view. We're not trying to pretend that we're portraying the whole war and both sides equally, by any means.'

And thus the non-cheerleading war drama with no political position on the war was educating the American public without bias – but only insofar as you can when you only show the American military's side of the story.

For Dr Andy, the implication of all this was obvious. There were no lengths to which Hollywood writers like Chris – who considered himself a liberal – wouldn't go to delude themselves that they were doing something principled when the economics of a project dictated it. Getting up a project was the be all and end all in this war zone. Black-banning radical writers was unnecessary in this day and age – if Chris was anything to go by, self-censorship was all the rage in Hollywood.

* * *

Night-time. Dr Andy and I found ourselves camped out at a five-star hotel in the heart of Santa Clarita, at the foothills of the *Over There* ranch. After an exhausting day, I had chosen this place to rest because in the cutthroat world of Hollywood, Santa Clarita was rated by the FBI the safest place in Southern California. This was Hollywood's Green Zone.

The manicured perfection of Santa Clarita was actually rather absurd – even the bitumen had a fresh coat of black paint (presumably to give it that authentic 'road' look). Street after street of SUVs; a late-night child-care facility to cater to actors out on night shoots; pine trees lining the streets. An ad in a day spa center boasted its latest promotion – 'a free gift with every $500 gift voucher!' The zone was barricaded by Hummer dealerships.

The residents were blasé about filming. A *NCIS* shoot was in full swing in a local car park. Next door, the hustle and bustle at the Java and Jazz café continued uninterrupted. An enormous set of lights with its own truck-sized generator beamed up at an office block. The light was unattended. It was so commonplace, pedestrians just casually stepped around it. In the Green Zone you learn to put up with the everyday inconveniences. It's part of the lifestyle.

As I ate my 'Homestyle' meatloaf and Dr Andy tucked into his 'Mother's Favorite' hamburger, we heard the waitress flirting with the guy at the next table. They were talking about how happy they were. 'Ahh yes, my wife is always up. And I mean *always*. Like, even when we go to a funeral, she's so up!' The waitress was shocked: 'Ohmygod! Does she have some sort of condition?'

Everyone was talking about going home for the holidays. This may have been paradise, but just like Baghdad, the Green Zone was full of people waging a battle far from home.

In Iraq, the insurgents were waging a battle for their own country. Here, it was a battle for the American public. With the US military death toll climbing steadily, Iraq had become a 'bad news story'. Every time *Newsweek* put a picture of Iraq on its cover, its sales plummeted 35%. And so the real Iraq – the one that was over in the Middle East – had started to disappear from the newsstands and nightly bulletins. It wasn't that Americans didn't know that the war was going on, it was just that they preferred not to hear about it too much.

And slowly responsibility for the national conversation about the war had shifted from the news breakers to Hollywood's showmen – and they knew it. 'A lot of people in America have already decided what they think about the war with very little data, and very little, certainly, experience of what it would feel like to be there,' Chris had told us earlier in the day. 'I figured at least we'd try to raise the rhetorical level of the conversation a little bit with some stories about what it's really like.'

But that was the problem with *Over There*, Dr Andy reflected as he washed his burger down with a mouthful of Diet Dr Pepper with a twist of vanilla. People didn't want the conversation to be raised. The people were turning to showmen to figure out how to look at the war, but they were still getting earnest conversation. What the people wanted was a bit of razzamatazz.

Instead of a dreary war drama, Dr Andy decided his show would be called *Greatest American Heroes* – a reality TV series that would pit ten soldiers against each other in a race to be the Greatest Hero in Iraq. Points would be awarded for helping build democracy in the day, and for shooting insurgents at night. And whoever got the most points . . . got to go home!

Dr Andy was extremely excited about the idea. 'It's reality meets the war,' he said, getting into the Hollywood lingo that phrases everything as a pitch. I had to admit it: it would make terrific television and it would cost virtually nothing to make.

When we got back to the hotel I opened the browser on my laptop. My photographer had rung to say that Dr Andy's shots had been uploaded from the day's action shoot. As I browsed through the link, Dr Andy's excitement mounted. There was one of him standing in a flak jacket with a handful of bullets, his head poking through a hole in a wall – the result of an explosion. Another one showed Dr Andy leaning against a post on an empty street, with the brown scarf wrapped around his shoulders. It was authentic Iraq – it would make a great front cover photo for Dr Andy's TV pitch. Unfortunately, the photos in front of the mosque were unusable. In the distance I could see the plywood back of an extraneous wall. 'Perhaps,' said Dr Andy hopefully, 'we can use Photoshop on that one. After all, what's real anyway?'

Dr Andy's mission to win over the American public was urgent. Even KR had understood that. 'We need to learn as a country that we can be a really powerful country, but we need to work really hard to be a just country, and they're two different things. It's one thing to apply power, and there's limits to power. I think that it's important to understand that there are limits to American power, and that our decisions have consequences.' But what Dr Andy hadn't realized until he came here was that Americans were increasingly gaining their lessons about the consequences of war from hollow plywood sets with pliable Hollywood plots. This was where the battle was really being fought.

I reflected on a moment from earlier in the day. As we were looking out over Rene Veluzat's ranch, I asked him whether he was worried about what impact an outbreak of peace in Iraq would have on his business. Rene shrugged, unconcerned. 'When this whole war thing peters out, this whole town could be Mexico. Mexico works any time – it's an old stand-by. It could be anything in the world. It could be Tibet China.'

And he was right. The US doesn't have to limit itself to the war in Iraq. It can make war with any country on earth.

PHASE FOUR
Mission Accomplished-ish

26

WIN BY SUBMISSION

Something still bugged Dr Andy about his reality show idea. 'Iraq is last week's news,' he told me brashly over a power-lunch. 'If *Greatest American Heroes* is going to be a ratings killer, it's going to have to be ahead of the curve, not behind it. We've got to hit the eight-ball right into the corner pocket with this one.' Dr Andy had been enjoying using what he thought was Hollywood lingo ever since we had got back from Hollywood. He had been in email contact with various producers about the pitch, but to no avail. Dr Andy attributed this to the show's setting. Iraq was a tarnished brand that would take years to turnaround.

'It's better to start with a clean slate,' Dr Andy announced. 'The setting has to be "next season".'

'You don't mean . . .?' I stopped eating my sashimi and put down my chopsticks.

'Yeah. Iran.'

One of the things that I haven't mentioned about our chat with KR, was what he'd said off the record once I'd turned off the tape recorder.[64] Obviously, I can't tell you exactly what he said, but let's just say the overarching message from this source close to the White House[65] was this: don't go to Iran any time soon.

---

[64] Actually, I use an iPod with microphone attachment nowadays. It's much, much cooler, even if the sound quality is twice as bad. You've noticed how cool all the interviews have been, haven't you?

[65] Yes – that's right! I've done it! I actually managed to get that compellingly off-the-record quote from 'an unnamed source close to the President'. Unfortunately, since I've already named my source in the last chapter, I can't really impart to you anything he said.

'You don't want to go there?' I said to Dr Andy hopefully.

'Charles. That's exactly where we should go.'

'But KR said the US was about to engage in a two-prong strategy to unsettle the regime. He said he thought the new Iranian leader was an anti-Semitic maniac who wanted to drive Israel into the sea,' I whispered under my breath, 'and that the White House would use soft power to try to peacefully unseat the theocracy, but failing that, a bombing campaign was almost certain.' I didn't want anyone else to hear the stuff KR had told me off the record.

But Dr Andy was determined. 'And this time we're actually going to the real place,' he said, looking me in the eye with some sort of death stare he'd obviously learnt in his Krav Maga martial arts class.

In the weeks leading up to our trip to Iran, I grew somewhat petrified by what awaited me behind the Persian curtain. KR wasn't the only one making noises about a possible US attack against Iran. The previous year, the former UN weapons inspector Scott Ritter claimed that George W had signed off on a plan to bomb Iran soon. The pretext for such a strike was the nuclear weapons facilities Iran has been building in violation of the Nuclear Non-proliferation Treaty. The strikes would be tactical, Scott claimed, but widespread. Tactical but widespread? Presumably they were also planning for them to be safe but deadly.

In preparation for the trip, Dr Andy had insisted on borrowing a raft of books about Iran from the library. Just reading the titles had made my throat dry. Books such as *The War Against the Terrormasters* by Michael Leedeen, or *Countdown to Terror* by Congressman Curt Weldon, or, for something completely different *Countdown to Crisis* by Kenneth R Timmerman. 'The Shocking Untold Story about the Deadly Iranian Threat' promised the back sleeve of Kenneth R's book. 'The clock is ticking.'

'You'll learn . . .' claimed Congressman Curt's jacket cover, 'why Iran will decide the next terror strike on America . . . Why Iran, not al-Qaeda, is the command post of radical Islamic terror . . . Who is really undercutting American efforts to create a peaceful, stable Iraq.' And perhaps most shocking of all, Weldon had evidence that Iran's leaders weren't card-carrying Republicans: 'You'll learn how a major planned terror strike was called off because the terrorists thought it would help President Bush politically.'

The more Dr Andy read, the more he convinced me that Iran was poised to strike America in a scenario that would make September 11 look like the plot of a romantic comedy. 'So what can the United States do?' Timmerman asked. 'There are two main options: capitulation or war.' Since capitulation was for Democrats, war was clearly the only option. Getting in before the major combat operations started would give Dr Andy's reality series an unassailable lead.

The plan, therefore, was to visit Iran and take a look at some of the places that the United States would bomb. Dr Andy wanted to see the evil up close and work out what would work best visually during production. He might even be able to pass on to the Pentagon some ideas about where they should bomb – so Dr Andy could have the cameras set up already. Dr Andy had heard that the US had very few human 'assets' on the ground, and so perhaps he could get the Pentagon to help with logistics during the show if he managed to sneak into Iran and give them some hot tips.

However, before we went to Iran, it was vitally important that Darryl and I go to the Miss Hooters contest.

* * *

'Okay, we'll be back shortly to get the girls up here, but in the meantime let's hope it doesn't rain!' The announcer was a bald, chubby man, about five foot six. He was a local radio announcer who would demonstrate a remarkable gift for speaking fluently about nothing as the evening wore on. A splattering of applause accompanied him as he walked off the catwalk. At the end of the walkway was a set of stairs that led down a path between two blow-up Bud Light beer bottles, perhaps 16 feet high, which formed a makeshift archway for the spectacle that was about to unfold. As the radio DJ walked from the stage, the sound guy piped loud, indistinguishable rock music through the loudspeakers.

Darryl and I were sitting at a table in a grass field just outside the Arizona Center shopping complex in downtown Phoenix. A couple of months ago Darryl had been one of the first people to pre-pay $25 on his credit card for special VIP tickets – which guaranteed a place at a table and – he hoped – a closer glimpse of the hooters.

As it turned out the VIP tickets weren't all that VIP. Sure, you got given a special pass to wear around your neck with a blonde bikini clad woman printed on both sides, but there were 400 or so other people who had also shelled out the extra ten bucks for that privilege. There were fifty tables in all, and Darryl was disappointed to find that his table was towards the back. Not only that, but it was positioned right next to a 10-foot high speaker system. It was hard to hear anyone above the electric guitar and repetitive drum beats. Darryl felt the first drops of rain on his face. The clouds grew darker and the temperature dropped. Darryl looked at me bleakly.

About 200 more people who had only shelled out $15 sat in tiered bleachers behind the tables, while a hundred others milled around the field out the back, near a row of fifteen port-a-loos. Those in the bleachers included a father and his five-year-old daughter, and a pregnant woman who appeared to have come alone. I was surprised by what a family crowd it was: perhaps a quarter of the audience was not men.

The waitress, 'Alex', a young twenty-something with dark hair, came over: she was wearing the obligatory low-cut tight white Hooters T-shirt which allowed her ample cleavage to try to radiate whatever effect it could despite being stripped of the traditional tools of feminine lure: coyness and expectation. Alex's flesh was also suffering, like the rest of us, from the increasingly cold and windy weather. The goosebumps across her chest and down her arms didn't make me want to strip her bare so much as give her a nice warm coat. Nevertheless there were plenty of men there who expressed a different opinion about that – including Darryl, whose apparent meekness had given way to a kind of showy bravado, mainly directed towards Alex.

Seated at Darryl's table were a couple of groups – only Darryl and I were on our own. Directly to Darryl's right, in the best viewing seats of the table, were Greg and Travis, who had been there for a long time already – Travis was finishing his seventh Budweiser as we arrived. On the other side of Darryl sat Justin, who had brought his wife, Deborah.

Justin had also brought his sister and a group of three men who were brothers, two of whom were going out either with Justin's sister or Deborah's. And I think that the other one was an ex-boyfriend of Deborah, or Deborah's other sister who wasn't there.[66] The brothers were all large and muscular. They were here for the show, and didn't speak much. One of them, Justin told Darryl, was a Rage in the Cage fighter. This meant that every few months he got in a 16-foot octagonal cage with another man, where-upon they punched and, more often, kicked each other in the head until one of them fell to the floor. Once on the floor, the 'grappling' continued until one of the two men won 'by submission' of the other.

Darryl loved the sound of it, and even got a flyer off the brother, wondering whether he'd be good enough to become a fighter himself – perhaps that could be his new career. It sounded pretty brutal to me. (Although, when I looked up the Rage in the Cage website, the promoter had a lengthy article which explained that

---

[66] My notes are unclear on the matter. Needless to say that as Justin was explaining all the connections to us he made it sound perfectly simple and, above all, normal.

this form of fighting derived from traditional martial arts and that although 'uneducated critics dismiss the sport as bloody and brutal, upon closer examination this is totally false'.)

After two rounds of beer, during which no one – not even Travis who had drunk seven already – spoke to each other, things felt a bit grim. Darryl felt lonelier than when he'd actually been alone.

27

COMPLETE SHAM

It was 6.42 pm. Bertrand clicked back to his email. The wait for a reply to the email from MoveOn was killing him. Perhaps he had overstepped the mark? Perhaps playing the Senator Ted Kennedy card had been a wrong move? He hit the send/receive button for the fifth time in under a minute. At last – an email from Wes! Bertrand had been right. The reply had come a mere two hours and forty minutes after Bertrand had sent his original email.[67] It read:

> Dear Mr. Newton,
>
> I'd be pleased to talk. For background, could you forward me some of the materials on the request for proposals you've already tried?
>
> It'll help me to understand your goals, I think. And make our conversation more productive.
>
> Thanks,
>
> Wes.

Bertrand had achieved what I had spent months attempting. For an outsider like Bertrand and me, the way into the Left had been staring us in the face. An offer of a $2.5 million donation was clearly the language left-liberal leadership could understand. It had taken

---

[67] Yes, I realize that, in terms of this book's chronology, more than two hours and forty minutes have past since we last checked in with Bertrand (hell, Dr Andy and I have been to Hollywood and back), but this email happened after the Phoenix trip. So even though in the text Bertrand has been sitting in the café the whole time, he wasn't already sitting there until after I went to Phoenix. But in the narrative it will seem like he will have been there at the same time as all this stuff happened with Darryl. I think I've just invented a new tense.

Wes almost a day (23 hours and 25 minutes) to get back to me when I only knew someone who had already donated money, but less than 3 hours when Bertrand actually had money.

The lesson was clear, and able to be broken down into a statistically valid formula: for every $120 000 you have, it takes MoveOn an hour less to get in contact with you. And of course, if you don't have any relationship to money, you never hear from them at all. If only Bertrand had said he had $3 million, he would have received an instantaneous response.

Bertrand was set – he now commanded the respect of his movement, and he had the inside ear of its leadership. In the marketplace of ideas, there was nothing more to achieve. As long as they thought he had $2.5 million, Bertrand had won.

* * *

Edward checked his blog to find that he now had 186 comments on his article 'Democracies don't start wars: A caveat', and 284 comments on 'Why we should rename the war on terror'. With a rush of adrenaline he clicked on the link to open all the comments. Perhaps his growing popularity with the punters would push him over the line in the battlefield of ideas. The first comment was posted by 'gay sex' and it read:

Hi! Good Work! -hot gay sex

Posted by: gay sex on Mar 08, 06 | 2:21 pm

The next comment was at least posted by someone with a real name, Carol Miller. It read:

<h1>discount tamiflu http://advertisersworld.com/discount-tamiflu/ discount tamiflu advertisersworld.com/discount-tamiflu/</h1>

As Edward scrolled further and further down the long page it quickly become apparent that his website had simply been attacked by a computer robot or worm, which systematically searched the web for places to feed links, in order to increase the 'weight' of the page. Since the page then had lots of different pages linking to it, Google thought the page was popular and placed it near the top of its listings.

The attack worried Edward. Not just because it showed that the blogging software Neal had set him up with was vulnerable to attack, but also because it offended his understanding of how the market should work. It was fine for an advertiser to try to get top listing, but it meant that those people looking to research pharmaceutical drugs on Google would be directed to disreputable dealers rather than the actual large businesses that would, of course, provide full disclosure about the effects – and side effects – of their products. And his website was contributing to that problem. Of course, Edward comforted himself, only people who were idiots would ever base their research just on the rankings of a Google search.

Edward's hopes were once again in tatters. What was he doing wrong? There was only one last person to turn to: Neal – the head of the MoveOff network. Perhaps if Edward could ingratiate himself with Neal, then Neal would swing Edward some favors in the final pages of the book. Perhaps if he went and visited Neal, Edward could get his punditry prioritized across the MoveOff network. Sure, it was fine meeting Vincent. He'd enabled Edward to *write* like a blogger, but Neal was the only person Edward knew who could make him a conservative superstar fast.

But there was also another reason to visit Neal – by traveling to Arizona undercover (so to speak) as 'Edward' I would be able to talk to Neal conservative-to-conservative – something that I would be unable to do as Charles the outsider Australian. Instead of experiencing all the problems that the interviewee/interviewer relationship opens up, the relationship between Edward and Neal would be based on shared values and, above all, mutual trust. It was an 'in' to the conservative movement that was too good to resist.

Face to face, how did conservatives talk to each other? Were there any secret handshakes? Edward didn't think so, but he was hoping at least to get an insight into where Neal got the money to run all his sites. Was he some wealthy retiree resourcing it out of his own pocket, or was the money coming from somewhere above? These were questions too indelicate to be answered over email, or even the phone. It was decided: Edward was off to Arizona to visit Neal, accent and all.

* * *

It was weird, I thought, but for some reason, as soon as the competition started, things got a lot more comfortable around the table. For the first leg of the Hooters pageant, the women were required to come out fully dressed: many wore jeans and a tight shirt, the younger the contestant the more flesh they showed. Midriff tops were popular with those who felt their cleavage alone wouldn't cut it. As each contestant walked out, the DJ would read out the model's name, the particular Hooters restaurant she served at, and what her 'best feature' was. 'This is Mandy, she's all the way from Tucson, and her best feature is her ass.' The crowd would cheer as Mandy walked to the end of the catwalk and stuck her bottom out. At that point, one of the men sitting at Darryl's table would say something like 'Look at that' or 'She's alright' or 'Not my type'.

As the initial excitement of the competition began to wear off and it became apparent that with 63 contestants to get through it was going to take at least an hour, the conversation at our table loosened up a bit.

'I'm Darryl. What's your name?' Darryl said to Justin as the waitress brought the third round.

'What?' said Justin.

'I'm DARRYL.'

'What?'

'I'M DARR-YL. WHAT IS YOUR NAME?'

'Justin,' said Justin. Darryl proffered his hand for a handshake.

'Do you go to Hooters much?' The music and the DJ announcer were blaring out of the speaker system nearby. The ulcers in my mouth were making it almost impossible for me to speak. Trying to be Darryl and enunciate in an American accent was extremely painful. As well, the breathy, low-balled American accent that I'd been taught was making it almost impossible to speak loudly enough to be heard over the loud speakers.

'What?'

'Do you come here often?'

Justin looked almost insulted. 'What?'

Darryl made a decision – he was going to have to revert to an Australian accent, while still maintaining his American name and back story. I had no complaints, it was the kind of postmodern pastiche that, I hoped, would excite literary theorists for decades to come.

'Do you come to Hooters much?' Darryl said in his new broad Aussie brogue.

'Yeah. I do.' Justin didn't seem to notice that Darryl had just changed accents, but he was clearly finding it much easier to communicate.

Justin explained to Darryl, with some pride, that his wife Deborah, who was blonde and had large breasts, had won the Miss Hooters Arizona pageant eight years ago, and that Deborah's sister Shelly was in the contest tonight, so it was important for Darryl – and indeed the whole table – to cheer loudly when she came out.

Justin was dressed in a neat green polo shirt tucked into tight jeans, with a mobile phone holster clipped to the side of his belt. He explained to Darryl that he worked for Honeywell Aerospace. 'It's amazing, some of the stuff we do is amazing – some of it I can't describe,' he said with pride.

Contestant 17 was announced. 'This is her! This is her!' Justin said to the table, with perhaps slightly more enthusiasm than should be displayed for the younger sister of your wife. A woman with large breasts and blonde hair walked out and around. She wore jeans and a frilly red shirt. The crowd clapped. I didn't know whether to compliment Justin on having such a fine sister-in-law. Darryl did. 'Nice tits,' he said, to my astonishment.

'Thanks,' said Justin.

After she'd made her way from the stage, Justin went back to talking about his work, holding forth on the intimate details of his factory's craftsmanship. Clearly Justin loved his job. The Honeywell plant was mostly involved in the production of components for aircraft engines, mainly for fighter jets. Business was booming. 'Some of the stuff we do is pretty important,' said Justin, sincerely. 'We've had four-star generals come through our factory,' he said, and then added, as if needing to make clear it wasn't coincidence, 'just because they wanted to meet *us*.'

It was only after a full fifteen minutes of talking about what his company did that Justin mentioned what he *himself* did – he was 'just a machinist' in the gearbox division, he admitted, but 'some of the guys at the factory, some of the engineers are geniuses', claiming his right to share the corporate mission.

Greg, who had been quietly watching his friend drink his tenth beer, overheard our conversation and joined in. He worked for Boeing. His job was in component shipping, sending out and receiving the parts that machinists like Justin created. Justin and Greg started talking about different engine parts. Although this is in no way accurate, this is what the conversation sounded like to me:

'We've been working on the new BJ-45f.'

'Really, because you know that the gear components of the BJ-40 fit all the major classes from the F1-56 all the way through to the XT29!'

'Wow! I did not know that. You'd think the XT29 would be a whole different kettle of fish.'

Travis, meanwhile, had moved onto his eleventh beer and was not speaking at all. 'What does he do?' Darryl asked Greg, pointing at Travis.

'He's a cell-phone salesman.'

Travis held up his beer in acknowledgement of the attention. 'I'm a sales manager. I manage sales at the shop,' he slurred, trying to locate some dignity in his answer.

The clothed section of the competition ended, and after a short break the women, in bikinis now, started trudging out into the cool night air again. This time they had to answer a question such as 'What do you like most in a man?' or 'What is the best thing about your personality' or 'What's your favorite man?' The chubby DJ, who was smaller than most of the leggy contestants, then took whatever the women said and gently put them down while they walked along the catwalk.

'Marie-Anne from the Arizona Center. What do you like most in a man?'

'Umm. His wallet.'

A smattering of laughter from the crowd. 'Well, be careful guys – she'll be expecting you to pay for the whole date! No, I'm only kidding, Marie-Anne, show them your ass.'

Marie-Anne stuck her cold bikini-clad bottom out at the crowd. Darryl stared in happy fascination.

Meanwhile, the conversation had become more political. Being white male factory workers in union jobs in a south-west state, both Greg and Justin were staunch supporters of Bush. Greg had been in the Army Reserve and served in Japan under the Clinton administration. That experience had helped him get through college and into a much-prized job. He supported the war in Iraq as payback for 9/11, but when I asked him whether he was considering going to Iraq he simply said, 'I've served my time.'

Justin agreed with Greg's assessment. 'The morning they attacked us,' he said, referring to September 11, 'I mean, wow, that was amazing. We didn't know that it was just a small group. We thought we were being invaded. I didn't know whether to go into work. I remember thinking: "This is it."' Like Darryl, Justin had bought duct tape as instructed, and filled his bath with fresh water ('just in case'). After some indecision, he did end up going to work that day, but the experience had permanently shifted his attitude to other countries. 'We are so generous, we give more to other countries than any other country in the world, so it's time we started looking after ourselves for a change.'

At the moment, though, that was secondary to Justin's other feelings of insecurity. Like Darryl, he was worried about cheap Mexican laborers stealing jobs. It was a safe place to have a race-based conversation: the crowd was exclusively white, save for half-a-dozen black security guards who lined the perimeter fence way out of earshot. The big worry, however, Justin said, was not Mexico but China. 'They tried to take some of our work to China a few years ago. They actually took the machines over there, but the quality they got back was so bad they had to bring it all back here. You can't compare anywhere in the world to the precision of some of the stuff we make.'

By this stage, Justin had picked up on the Australian accent. I had completely blown my cover. I explained that I was writing a book about America and was going around the country talking to people. He seemed proud that I would be so interested in his country and he tried to return the compliment.

'I love your President,' he said. 'What's his name?'

'Oh, our Prime Minister – John Howard.'

'I love him. He's fantastic.'

I explained to Justin that John Howard had conducted an election on immigration issues in 2001.

'Yeah – I heard about that. It proves that all it takes is political will. That's why we should build a fence on the border of Mexico.'

The top 10 competition finalists were announced, and to Justin's barely concealed rage, his sister-in-law was not one of them. Not only that, but I happened to notice that the 10 women selected were simply the 10 largest-breasted Hooters girls out of the 63 who had entered – the questions and the 'poise' components were a complete sham!

Deborah seemed keen to leave, and so Justin got up and said goodbye. It was Thursday night and he was keen to get to bed at a reasonable hour. Greg – who I noticed had soberly sat on one beer all night – got up and excused himself too – he knew one of the contestants who had not gotten through and wanted to go and 'console' her.

Darryl turned to Travis. Darryl was keen to pick up and thought perhaps Travis could be his wing-man. Travis clearly didn't care whether he was hungover at the mobile phone shop the following morning. Neither did Darryl. Darryl reflected that it was weird how the guys with union jobs always went home early. It was almost as if they took pride in their work or something.

Travis slumped forward, his forehead pressed against the table. I told Darryl it was time to leave – none of the women I'd assumed would be shoo-ins for the top 10 had made the cut. Clearly I wasn't good at judging the sexual attractiveness of women. Plus, I didn't want to have a hangover either – I had work to do.

But Darryl wanted to stay. He was very keen to try what he called the 'Greg method' of reassuring one of the losers in her hour of insecurity.

'But Darryl,' I said. 'This is your last night in the book. Don't you want to come back and help me write up some concluding remarks about the implications of what you've done in the last few days that will electrify the commentariat with its incisiveness and profundity?'

Darryl, now a little drunk, told me he couldn't give a shit about what the commentariat thought of him. Which was, I suppose, fair enough.

'But what about that car you wanted? Surely we need to work on some resolution to that?' I said. But for all of Darryl's innate consumer desires, it was human contact he was after tonight. And so I left him at the Hooters after-party, looking for a crestfallen contestant to console. Ideally, physically.

28
ON LOCATION

'You know the best thing about Iran?' asked a round Iranian man with a black goatee and a strangely Liverpudlian accent. He was sitting cross-legged on the carpet of his suburban living room. Dr Andy and I were sitting at a right-angle to him, and his daughter, his sister and his fiancée were opposite him. In the middle of the room, on the floor, there were trays of tea and sweets, including the authentic Persian delicacy, Scottish shortbread.

When we had arrived we had been offered the only couch in the room, which we had gratefully accepted, but since everyone else – including Mahmoud and his three women – had then sat down on the floor amongst the many cushions, we had slowly, in a slightly embarrassed shuffle, sat down on the clean shag-pile carpet while Mahmoud held court.

'I get to have four, no wait, five . . .' The man broke into rapid Farsi as he asked his sister a question. She answered him. 'Officially, I get to have five wives. But I can have thousands of concubines!' His eyes lit up. Mahmoud had a shot of black, thinning hair which I assumed was dyed, and wore chunky gold rings on his fingers and a single thick gold chain around his neck. He was quite overweight and smoked, which meant that whenever he said anything he had to pause afterwards, breathing rapidly, as if enthusiasm itself was exhausting.

As Mahmoud continued talking, Dr Andy quietly reminded me that this was not the reason he had wanted to come to Iran. He was here to 'do a reccie' on some of the 40 nuclear weapons facilities the Pentagon claimed were hidden underground across Iran, sites which would inevitably be bombed and therefore make dramatic location shots for his reality series. Dr Andy had also been hoping to mix with Islamic terrorists and meet mullahs who defied the American Empire. 'They'd be great talent,' Dr Andy told me. 'Important to have a convincing enemy, you know.'

Instead, to Dr Andy's increasing chagrin, we kept getting invited into the homes of welcoming English-speaking Iranians, who were lovely people, and therefore made for lousy enemies.

This was how we came to be sitting in Mahmoud Mohammed's plush apartment in downtown Tehran, where we had just finished watching Liverpool beat AC Milan on a satellite television with 800 channels, during which Mahmoud related to us the story of how his 24-year-old fiancée, who he met six days ago, had had a hose inserted into the opening of her vagina by a government doctor to ensure she was still a virgin. In Iran, you have to have your hymen intact if you want to get married. It's very romantic.

Book-wise, I assured Dr Andy, Mahmoud was great talent. He had strong opinions ('Fuck Khomeini. Khomeini's a cunt. He's a cunt.') and he had kindly invited us home to meet the four women who currently cater to his whims (his daughter, his sister, his housemaid and his fiancée[68]). He even used to be a paratrooper in the Iranian army back in the days of the Shah (he had the tattoos to prove it – intricate shields on the side of his large shoulders, which looked like an official badge, and a whole lot of words in Farsi, which he assured me proved his service).

This was all hot stuff, but Dr Andy wasn't interested in finding Iranians who hated their own regime, and he especially didn't want

---

[68] The only woman missing, it seemed, was his daughter's mother. When I politely inquired about her, Mahmoud became extremely excited and explained that they were now divorced. He then got his mobile phone and rang his ex-wife (who had fled to England) and put me on the phone to have an awkward conversation with her about what a bastard Mahmoud was (something that she patiently confirmed). Mahmoud was very amused by these antics. Everyone else in the room seemed less at ease, especially me.

ones who came across as normal (albeit harem-loving) suburbanites. He wanted to see the official, US-version Iran. The crazed-terrorist version that would confirm his views that Iran was in need of a stern bombing. This was our last night in the capital and, to Dr Andy's disappointment, everywhere we'd gone we'd only managed to meet people as friendly and welcoming as Mahmoud. People who – once you scratched the surface – thought their government was, well, quite mediocre. Remarkably like in America, everyone we'd spent any time with – whether they were conservative or liberal, religious or agnostic – had ended up whingeing about stupid laws, and how incompetent or corrupt or lazy their politicians were. The only difference was that in Iran saying those things was illegal.

A few days after our dinner with Mahmoud a wave of bomb attacks rocked Iran, including one just around the corner from Mahmoud's home. It was in the Imam Hussein Square, where he and I had played a game of pool at his local snooker club. In total, 10 people were killed and 75 more were injured. A hardline group of Islamic conservatives with the Pythonesque name 'Arab Struggle Movement for the Liberation of Ahyaz' claimed responsibility. Commentators said the explosions were a warning to people in favor of moderate reform, an attempt to bolster the position of conservative clerics. In Iran, extreme conservatives behave a bit like anti-abortionists – they use all means necessary.

Dr Andy and I excused ourselves from Mahmoud's lounge room and went to one of the three bathrooms in the large split-level apartment. The spacious bathroom had cream tiles with a pink floral pattern and was impeccably clean. Because Mahmoud had spent time in England before the revolution, his bathroom luckily sported both a western-style toilet bowl as well as the ridged floor hole and hose that Persians prefer but which neither Dr Andy nor I had been able to master the entire time we'd been here.

I whispered sternly to Dr Andy he should stop being so down on the whole trip. I pointed out there were lots of things about

Mahmoud that Dr Andy could dwell on if he wanted to demonize him in his show. For a start, Mahmoud was more than a little unreconstructed in his attitudes towards women, and his enthusiasm for Liverpool was a bit tedious. But as Dr Andy pointed out, Mahmoud was yet another person we'd met who didn't support the regime (his favored option was a reinstatement of the Iranian monarchy – led by the late Shah's exiled son), and yet was also clearly not part of any broader political movement to unseat the government. Just like the vast majority of Iranians we'd met, Dr Andy complained.

Standing in Mahmoud's bathroom, its sheer familiarity was weird. I noticed that someone had left the lid off the toothpaste tube. The humanizing detail of the cross-cultural dilemma of whether to leave the lid on or off was the last straw for Dr Andy.

'You're meeting too many people,' he yelled. Luckily the fan in the bathroom was very noisy – one of those cool heat-and-light-and-fan combination things that cost a bit of money, just like the one my sister had back in Australia. 'When Kenneth R Timmerman goes into a country like this, he doesn't have dinner with some guy he bumped into on the street a few days ago. He only talks to angry dissidents and CEOs. He doesn't walk into people's private bath-rooms and have contrived epiphanies about the common humanity that links us all.'

Dr Andy paused, and then it all clicked into place. 'Actually,' he said, 'he probably doesn't come to Iran at all.'

Dr Andy was right. The reason the Iran I'd found was so incredibly different to the official line was because we'd been naively going around meeting a bunch of ordinary people when we should have been talking to think tanks in Washington! What a fool we'd been – we'd totally ruined Dr Andy's chance to pitch an alarmist reality show based on his own understanding of Iran. If only he'd stayed in the US!

Compared to the early days of the revolution, Iran was turning out to be a bit of an anticlimax for the adventure traveler wanting to

240

experience a terror state first-hand. The election of the reform candidate President Khatami by an overwhelming majority in 1997 had taken the sting out of the revolution – something that the new, more conservative president, Mahmoud Ahmadinejad, had been unable to reverse. Women were still obliged to wear a scarf over their hair and shapeless three-quarter-length jackets to hide their figure, but the scarves were getting skimpier and the shapeless jackets were getting tighter. Even satellite dishes – though still illegal – were largely tolerated, and now covered 50% of homes. Fans of the Champions League had never had it so good. Wherever you looked in Iran, people were following the letter of the revolution – not its spirit. Indeed, the story of Iran was the story of Islamic Republic Lite™. This was a low-carb, non-fat version of what Khomeini intended. When it began, if you walked down the street wearing lipstick, the fashion police would cut your lips. If you showed a bit of ankle, they'd slash your foot with a knife. Nowadays heavy makeup was all the rage, and some women even wore ankle bracelets to accentuate the little glimpse of flesh between their shoes and their pants – something that would have been seen as positively slutty a decade before. In fact, in an act of liberation, the latest fashion for women was to buy extremely brightly colored clothes to wear underneath their official manteaus. It was like super-charged lingerie.

The next morning we had to catch a taxi to the airport at 5.30. We had not been driving for more than two minutes when the taxi driver pointed to two teenage girls as they crossed the road. 'Ahh, typical Iranian girls!' the driver exclaimed. Not understanding him, I said, dumbly, 'Ah yes, up late.' To which he replied. 'No! Very traditional. They must wear the scarf – the hijab – they are forced to wear it. But not for long!'

Given you could be arrested for talking like that, he caught us by surprise. He went on: 'But the protests . . . you know about the protests?'

'Um.'

'There are protests coming up.'

'Oh really?'

'Yes! And we will smash this regime in our fight for freedom. We will gain our freedom once more!'

I started to panic just a bit. Before we'd left, a former diplomatic officer had warned me about being entrapped by government spies into discussing politics – a definite no-no that would see you, at minimum, deported or, if you were a Canadian photo-journalist, killed.

The taxi driver continued, 'Many of my people, we are very depressed. We are miserable, but we will fight for our freedom. And we will smash this regime. What do you think?'

'Um . . . umm . . .' My mind was slowly cranking into gear. This guy was trying to entrap me! But what do you say to a government spy? 'Yes. I agree with you. Can we skip the torture today and get straight to the deportation part'? Finally my mind came up with a – albeit extremely dim-witted – solution: 'Hmm. I'm sure people are happy, especially since the weather is so lovely here.'

'Oh, I see.' The rest of the drive was in silence.

Little did my spy know but I had cunningly put him off the scent. We were actually headed for the airport in order to catch a plane to Esfahan so Dr Andy could find the place where Iran was building its nuclear weapons.

Iran's police state was one of the reasons why the neo-cons close to the White House had been championing 'regime change' in Iran for years. And yet the history behind Iran's police state went back far further than 1979 – something which Dr Andy never liked to dwell on. In 1951 Mohammad Mossadegh was elected Prime Minister of Iran by a healthy majority. *Time* magazine made him Man of the Year, ahead of Truman, Churchill and Eisenhower. Over the following months, Mossadegh made himself a national hero by destroying Britain's colonial legacy and nationalizing the Anglo-Iranian Oil

Company. From then on, Mossadegh declared, the benefits of Iran's oil would flow to Iranians, not the British.

But for the West, this was an alarming prospect. Never mind that Iran held 10% of the world's oil reserves, it was more the precedent Mossadegh had set that worried them. If Iran could get away with deciding how they used their resources, then perhaps leaders in Asia and Africa would get the same idea. The domino effect of communism was a concern. But the domino effect of a populist parliamentary democracy was terrifying.

And so the CIA's man in Iran, Kermit Roosevelt, threw a lifeline to the hapless king of Iran, Shah Mohammed Reza – who felt overshadowed by Mossadegh's popularity. Through an inspired strategy Roosevelt successfully organized the CIA's first ever covert operation – a coup against *Time*'s Man of the Year. The coup itself was dramatic and daring – the more Dr Andy learnt about it, the more he was convinced it would've made terrific television.

For thirty years the US backed the Shah. A cozy deal that Dr Andy and his colleagues looked back on with nostalgia. It was a deal very similar to the arrangement the House of Saud has with the US to this day. The Shah guaranteed (more or less) the supply of oil; in return the US supplied as many weapons as the Shah needed to secure his nation, and more importantly his rule, against an increasingly restless population.

By the time it happened, the revolution to unseat the Shah was enormously popular in Iran – the referendum to institute an Islamic Republic got a 98% vote in favor. But even at the beginning the clerics knew many of their 'reforms' would be unpopular so they replaced Iran's conventional military with their own Revolutionary Military Forces that would be loyal to them. Even today there are six different forces in the Iranian command structure – the conventional army, navy and air force, and the revolutionary army, navy and air force.

But once the Ayatollah died, the Old Beards realized that for all the fun of being a revolutionary, you also needed to be a bit pragmatic. In 1993 the mullahs started bringing in advisors from the West – not from the US, of course, but many European countries were happy to oblige. 'They helped the mullahs sell off all the factories,' said one particularly bitter Iranian we met. 'But they sold them to themselves. You see, the people in charge and the people who were buying them . . . they were the same people. And now they're selling them off again but this time to foreign people so they can become very wealthy. Some of them are billionaires.' The holy men who were installed to protect Iran from pillage became the pillagers. Since then, the Old Bearded Billionaires have gradually found themselves less interested in the religious ideas and more interested in ensuring the success of their 'investments'. The scarves have loosened, men now wear short-sleeve shirts, and women can wear lipstick. Underneath the inflammatory rhetoric, Dr Andy had realized the Old Beards were focusing on the bottom line – their own bottom line.

The rich old mullahs might be on top now, but the young were angry, active and increasingly organized. In response, the regime had decided to shut off the universities from the outside world. The government knew that historically students have always acted as a catalyst for change – the anti-Vietnam protests of the 1960s to Tiananmen in 1989, and even in their own revolution in 1979. One way or another, the old bearded men feared being swamped by the youth.

Recalling everything we'd seen in Iran, Dr Andy suddenly understood why the Iranian leadership was behaving so brazenly towards confrontation with the US. Unless they provoked a showdown with America, the leadership would be swamped from below. It was not in the interests of the Old Beards to sit back and wait out the tide. They had to focus their population's anger at an external threat – and the US was willing and able to fill that role. For Dr Andy, this would make scheduling his new show so much easier – confrontation was a sure thing.

I tried to point out to Dr Andy that this aggressive stance towards Iran was playing into the hands of the fundamentalist regime. But Dr Andy didn't understand what I meant. Or perhaps he just didn't let on that he did. After all, Dr Andy had a lot riding on the US's current approach to Iran. He'd worked out how to get his slice of the action, and he wasn't going to let some sort of unrealistic 'peace deal' get in the way of it.

The next morning was a Friday. After morning prayers, clerics in the main mosque in the southern town of Shiraz wheeled out their speaker systems and took several thousand congregants on an anti-American rally, as they did every Friday. The march, it must be said, had great production values – the speakers were brand new, and somehow they had perfected it so there was no echo through the narrow streets. 'Down with America! Down with America!' they chanted. Finally, Dr Andy had something solid to hate the Iranians for.

As we watched it go by, Dr Andy was careful to ignore the waning level of enthusiasm of many of the marchers. A man with his week's shopping in two plastic bags joined the march for five minutes, and then ducked out, presumably going home to get the perishables into the fridge.

So what would happen? 'They won't bomb Iran,' an ex-air-force officer told us confidently the next day as we drove out along the Old Silk Road – the trade route that pre-dated Islam, Christianity and even the Persian Empire. 'They can't do it. We are 70 million people. If they do it they know hundreds of thousands of American soldiers will die. Instead they will try to create civil war. That is what I fear. The Kurds in the north, and other groups. They will arm them and that is how they will do it. That is what I fear the most.'

The fears were well founded. After all – that was the conclusion Kenneth Timmerman had reached too. 'We should empower the pro-democracy forces to change the regime. We should do so openly, and as a government policy. But we should support non-governmental organizations, primarily Iranians, to do the work.'

But what did this ex-officer hope would happen? Like Mahmoud, he was nostalgic, but his nostalgia extended back 2500 years. 'I think that the problem with Iran is that we never have good government; not now, not before. Not since Cyrus and Darius have we had good government.'

It was the knowledge that Iran was once at the center of the world, and that like all empires its fortunes inevitably came and went, that lent the ex-officer a tired wisdom to his understanding of current political events. Empires come and go, was his point. First it was Egypt, then Persia, then the Greeks, Romans and eventually the British, and now the Americans. Religions change, language evolves, but the people stay. When George W Bush talked about the US military imposing their own version of peace for the good of everyone, so that prosperity could reign across the globe, Iranians had heard it all before. Their empire used that excuse 2500 years ago.

Unfortunately, Dr Andy wasn't listening. While the ex-officer spoke to me Dr Andy had scaled the steep mountain pass around which the Old Silk Road meandered.

'This looks exactly like the mountains in Afghanistan!' Dr Andy shouted down, his voice echoing around the barren valley. 'Perhaps we could have an episode of *Greatest American Heroes* where they have to hunt down Osama!'

29

NOBLE CAUSES

I was extremely worried. In less than 12 hours' time, Edward was due to meet Neal for lunch. After three days of concerted effort, my American accent had comprehensively failed. And the beer I'd drunk earlier in the night had made things worse – my mouth ulcers had flared up worse than ever. Every time I tried to roll my r's I got a sharp pain at the back of my throat. Not only that, but the more I had drunk, the less I had been able to concentrate on keeping the American accent going. I knew Neal liked to drink – indeed, he had explicitly said that the plan was to 'have a few drinks together'. Being exposed as an Australian had turned out fine at the Hooters contest amongst drunk strangers in a noisy setting, but Edward had spent months corresponding with Neal as an American. In the quiet setting of a Phoenix restaurant, was I really going to be able to pull off a convincing portrayal of Edward McGuire, American conservative?

The next morning, Edward stood nervously outside the Super 6 motel that Neal had told him to stay in. He reflected on what an odd choice of accommodation it had been for Neal to recommend. It was pretty down-market. The place had about 30 rooms on two storeys. There were three locks on his bedroom door. The reception was not a foyer but a double-glazed reinforced glass window with a little metal drawer into which you put your credit card. Upon reflection, it was more like a place Darryl would stay in. When Edward had arrived the night before, some of the hotel's residents were holding a party in the car park, and the top story seemed to be full of women, with men coming and going all night. And the women wore far too much makeup and too few nightclothes when they came out on the balcony for a smoke. At 3 am, Edward had been woken by a dozen motorcycles making laps of the car park right outside his window.

Just then a brand new black GMC Canyon drove up. A gray-haired man with a long face stuck his head out the window.

'Edward?'

'Neal,' Edward said with practiced eloquence. Relief engulfed him. And then without thinking, he said, still in an American accent, 'G'day!'

Neal didn't notice. 'Hop in.'

Neal was a 63-year-old retired test engineer, originally from Oregon. His skin was well worn and gray. He wore an oversized gray T-shirt and gray tracksuit pants. Even sitting down you could tell he was tall – at least 6 inches taller than Edward.

As soon as Edward hopped in, Neal put his foot on the accelerator and turned the car out of the motel lot. The car idled as he negotiated a difficult turn across four lanes of opposing traffic. 'This is what I call the crash dive turn.' The tires screeched as he sped across the lanes and safely merged with the traffic flow.

'Nice car,' said Edward, feeling the kick from the rapid acceleration.

'This is a gift to myself. My little retirement gift – it's 500 bucks a month but it's worth it. Of course, the payments haven't kicked in yet.'

As he drove, Neal explained the geography of where Edward had been staying. 'It's a slum. They think it's a slum around here so they don't bother any more. Go further north there are $3 million, $5 million mansions, but they don't care about us.' Clearly Neal wasn't a millionaire; indeed, the image he was crafting of himself was very much that of the working-class crusader. It seemed to be out of alignment with many of the people I'd met in the conservative movement with whom he had allied himself.

We drove on, past a small wooden house that could not have* contained more than three rooms. 'I used to live right there. They used to call this area Uzitown in the 1980s when it was really bad. There used to be gunfights in the street.'

'Over there,' he said, pointing to an abandoned factory, 'that was going to be a stadium. But the city stopped it.'

'Why did they do that?' asked Edward politely.

'Because they're anti-business. That's why. They're communists who want to bring on their socialist fucking revolution, so that there's no business left in their fucking town.'

Edward was a little taken aback by Neal's outbursts. This is not what he had expected at all. Indeed, Edward had been so thrown by the first five minutes that he was desperately trying to remember what he *had* been expecting. A retiree in a tracksuit, for sure, but holding a BlackBerry, surely, and not swearing. How did Neal reconcile the swearing and shouting with his fervent belief in American family values? And communists? In Phoenix?

Up ahead there was some road construction and the lanes were merging from three to two, but the car to the left of him failed to merge in time. Neal looked over and shouted, 'Get your fucking car into the fucking lane! Can't you fucking read?! Jesus H Christ!'

Neal abruptly returned to a normal tone of voice, as if the anger was not real. 'Anyway, coming up here, ahead of us, see there, in the strip mall.' Neal pulled up at the roadside and pointed to a medium-sized mall with perhaps a 200 bay car park and fifteen shops – a drug store, a mobile phone shop, a 99 cent store, the usual collection. 'Look at it. You can't read anything.' This was not actually true. About half the signs were in English and the other half were in Spanish. Neal noticed this too. 'Well, that's not a good example, but there's other ones down there that I could show you that are *all* in Spanish. You can't understand a fucking thing.'

And then he turned to Edward and said something that rings in my mind every time I think of Neal. He said it with his nose curled up, and a forcefulness that betrayed utter sincerity. 'Tempe is *infested*, you know.'

'Infested?' Edward asked timidly.

'Yeah, infested with Mexicans. They come up here across the border, hundreds of them each day. Some of them keep going, but a lot of them settle down here. The Mexicans and the Vietnamese, they fit, like, six or seven families to a home. They just put beds down everywhere – that's how they do it. That's how they work so cheap.'

We drove on, through endless road construction. 'If you're not allergic to cats,' says Neal, whose first name is not Neal at all. 'And you don't mind a single-man bachelor-slob white-trash style accommodation, you can come and hang out at my place if you want.'

'That would be lovely,' said Edward, using Australian idiom and frankly sounding a bit gay. 'I mean, that'd be great,' he corrected himself. 'I've got nothing to do this afternoon. I can come and see where it all happens!'

Neal left Edward in the car while he popped out on an errand. Edward noticed that in the middle of the bench seat of the car were scores of unopened envelopes from banks and finance companies. No wonder Neal wouldn't reveal his real name.

Neal hopped back in the car and saw me eyeing the envelopes. 'I'm not going to vote any more,' he told me. 'In Arizona they sell your name and address and I'm not going to give them my name and address. I'll go down with my utility bill, my gas bill, which has to have your name and address on it, but if they don't accept that then I'm not going to vote.' For a man whose politics directly supported the system, Neal didn't seem to have much faith in it. We hit another roadworks queue.

'What's all this construction for?' Edward asked.

'They're building a fucking light-rail system right through the middle of the road.'

'Who?'

'The city. Because they're East Coast fucking liberals, who just want to increase the size of your tax bill, that's why.'

Neal took Edward to a standard American diner, with red vinyl bench chairs in booths with light blue linoleum tables. The place hadn't been renovated for at least a decade, judging by grime in between the tiles on the floor. Neal was adamant about going there because as an over-60 year old, he qualified for a 10% seniors' discount.

We sat down in a booth in the Smoking Area. 'You know you're not even allowed to smoke in California any more.' He got out his cigarettes in defiance, but he didn't actually want one. He browsed through the menu, agitated. He called a waiter over. 'Where's the beef melt? How much is the beef melt?'

The waiter pointed to the item on the menu. 'It's $6.95, sir, plus tax.'

'Oh. And how much is the salad bar?'

'That's $5.25 plus tax, sir.'

'That's what I'm going to have. That includes soup, doesn't it? Come on, that's what you should get too.' Before Edward could say anything, Neal was out of the booth and charging over to the salad bar. He piled his plate high with creamy pasta salad and an egg concoction. When he reached the taco section, he took a big spoonful of beef chilli and placed it on the plate. 'I just have the meat on its own,' he muttered, perhaps embarrassed by his greed.

Silence fell over the table as Neal enthusiastically ate everything on his plate, and then went back for seconds, this time getting a separate bowl of beef chilli.

It turned out that Neal had grown up in Oregon. Clearly bright, his parents wanted him to go to university, which Neal agreed to do, as long as it was as far away from Oregon as possible. Thus, in the fall of 1961, Neal moved to Phoenix to pursue a degree in Engineering at Arizona State University. After one semester, however, he dropped out. Shortly after that, he served 9 years in the army which, of course, included tours of duty to Vietnam.

After living in various cities in the American south-west, Neal ended up in Silicon Valley, where he worked as a test engineer –

a laborious task which involved making sure there were no bugs in software applications. Five years ago the Internet bubble burst but Neal proudly maintained he wasn't sacked. 'They came in and said that we weren't getting a pay rise, and at that point I was earning $52 000 but going backwards. I was bankrupt, because of the rent, you know, in Silicon Valley. Sixteen hundred bucks a month for a studio apartment.

'So I quit my job and moved to Tucson, where I got a job for $5.25 an hour, but I was ahead. The rent was only $380, so one pay check a month on that, another on cigarettes and beer.'

As lunch ended, the check arrived. Neal started gazing at the docket, trying to work out the division – I had ordered a Coke with my salad. When Edward offered to pick up the tab, Neal was obviously grateful, but as his contribution he insisted on presenting the check at the register in order to claim the seniors' discount, thus saving Edward exactly 52 cents.

* * *

'This is what I do all day,' said Neal, 'I sit here and watch TV while I drink beer and work on my hundred websites.'

We were standing in Neal's trailer on an Indian reservation just outside of Phoenix. He was pointing to a thin, long desk with three large monitors on it, a keyboard in front of each one. There were piles of opened and unopened envelopes everywhere. In front of the desk was a couch, a coffee table and large 60-inch TV, which was currently tuned to the Military Channel. Between the couch and the TV were a coffee table and half-a-dozen old Macintosh computers. They were piled up in such a way that you could sit on the couch without them getting in the way of your legs or your view of the TV.

'Then when I get too drunk to do that any more, I sit on the couch and watch TV and drink until I pass out. And then I go to bed.'

Next to Neal's stool was a large brown paper bag almost full of crushed cans of beer. There were at least fifty cans in the bag. In the kitchen there was a large plastic outdoor-sized garbage bin overflowing with beer cans, all the same brand. There were other, smaller bins and bags surrounding the large bin, all with crushed beer cans in them.

Last month, Neal made $13 selling beer cans to the local scrap metal merchant, who bought them at $0.75 per pound. Neal told me this proudly, but noted that his money would have doubled had he been living in California. 'It's not like there, where you've got the deposit on every can, and so they pay $2.00 per pound. But still – I made $13.'

I looked around the room. The sink was full of unwashed dishes and the shelves were bare of washed ones. There were four or five bins overflowing with household rubbish. On the floor of the kitchen were ten cat bowls in various states of uncleanliness and emptiness. 'We don't have a cleaner,' Neal joked. The corporation that ran the trailer park charged Neal $9 per cat for the privilege of keeping them. 'Officially my wife and I only have two cats, even though we've got three.'

The other room in the house, besides the bedroom, was a 'dining room' which was floor to ceiling packed with broken computers, which Neal had bought at a trading club that operated each weekend. He fixed them up and on-sold them. 'I've got either 23 or 27 machines at the moment. I can't remember.'

I asked Neal how much it cost. 'I might pay $30 for a computer and then I'll fix it up and sell it for $40.' Like many of the people that I'd met who didn't earn much, Neal seemed open to talking about money, perhaps because he was required to think about it all the time.

So if this was the brains behind MoveOff – who funded the servers that kept hundreds of sites running? The answer was Neal. He made $200 per month from commissions on vitamin pills from some of his hobby websites. This covered half of the $360 per month he paid to maintain two mainframe computers – one in California, the other in Arizona. The gap was fully funded out of the meager retirement savings of a man who cashed in beer cans and underreported his number of cats in order to scrape by.

After a few hours of watching Neal drink beer while he updated his hundred websites, Edward decided it was time to leave. Neal was too drunk to drive anywhere, so he walked Edward out onto the road and in the direction of the bus. As we walked, he delivered Edward a lecture through an allegory. He told him about a promising blogger who had come to him asking to join the MoveOff network. Neal told this blogger that it came with certain strings attached. Specifically, that he had to promise to update his website at least once a week. 'I said, if I put you on the MoveOff network, you'll be number one on Google in two days,' Neal boasted. 'I've got the network, I've got hundreds of sites linking to each other.'

He stopped walking and turned to Edward. 'You've got to do more work on your website. You really do.'

'Yeah, I know, I'm sorry . . .' said Edward. He felt like he was in trouble. 'It's just that I'm writing this book and I've been a bit snowed under . . .' He trailed off.

'Look,' said Neal. 'I'm not just saying it for me, you'll get fame and celebrity and a name. And people will respect you if you put in the work.'

He took his free hand – the other one had a beer in it – and placed it on Edward's shoulder. 'And when your book comes out everyone will know you.'

The next day, Edward was on top of the world. For a start, he now understood that to make it in his world of conservative commentary, he didn't need to be some slick insider. He could just as easily be a man with an Internet connection, a trailer, three cats and 13 email addresses. But from my perspective that minor detail was utterly outshone by a far more remarkable achievement – I had successfully pulled off being an American for a five-hour stretch – even while drinking beer. I had successfully infiltrated America, as an American. From my perspective, I could relax now – I fully understood *exactly* what it was like to see America from an American's perspective. I even started to have feelings of respect for George W Bush.

Having seen Neal's impressive setup, Edward was now keener than ever to make his legacy permanent. He thought he finally understood how to make that happen.

And sure enough, within a week, Edward's aim had been achieved. It was a Tuesday morning and Edward woke up to find a personally addressed email in his inbox. It was from Town Forum Press, one of the many book publishers that Edward had been busy hawking his writing to in recent days. The editor there had sent Edward this note:

> *Congratulations, your submission to* Letters to Cindy Sheehan *has been accepted for publication! Your entry has been edited by our staff for inclusion in our book.*
>
> *Even if you do not wish to buy any copies, your submission will still be included in the book.*
> *Best Wishes,*
> *Town Forum Press*

Edward McGuire was going to be a published author!

Edward was amazed, and insufferably proud. I was amazed too, because, well, it wasn't exactly the Greatest Essay He'd Ever Written. Indeed, he didn't even write it.

You see, the day after Edward met up with Neal, he was a bit hungover. After the initial rush of enthusiasm had expired, and after discussing it with me (who was also hungover), we decided that, for this particular submission, it would be fine if Edward cheated a little and simply googled around for an article that came from the other side of politics and then amend it slightly to make it say the opposite. After all, this method had worked wonders for Bertrand.

The publisher of *Letters to Cindy Sheehan* was calling for essays that demonstrated Iraq was a noble cause, and so Edward typed the words 'Iraq Noble Cause' into Google and the top article was by none other than Cindy Sheehan herself. Edward thought, 'Hello there, this'll be fun.' Over the next twenty minutes, while sipping a bloody mary in his favorite brunch spot in the Ithaca Commons, he took Cindy's article and turned it (roughly) into his own.

This is the article Edward found on Alternet.[69]

It has been one month, one week, and 4 days since I sat in a ditch in Crawford, Texas.

My request was very simple: I wanted to speak to the man who has sent over a million of our young people over to fight, kill, and die in a country that was absolutely no threat to the United States of America. I wanted to ask him: 'What is the Noble Cause that you keep talking about?'

Well, we all know now that George Bush never came down the road to talk to me. Thank God! Many people have been saying that I am the 'spark,' 'catalyst,' 'face of the anti-war movement,' etc. I beg to differ.

George Bush and his arrogant advisers are the spark that lit the prairie fire of peace activism that has swept over America and the entire world. If he had met with me that fateful day in August it would not have been good for him (because I knew he was going to lie and I would have advertised that fact) but it would have had less of an impact on the peace movement if he had.

Upon reflection on the events of this past August, I have come up with two reasons why George could not meet with me: He is a coward, and there is no Noble Cause. If George had as much courage and integrity in his entire body as Casey had in his pinky, he would have met with me. But, ironically, if George had that much courage and integrity he never would have preemptively invaded a practically defenseless country. His sycophantic cabinet and hangers-on are also incontrovertible evidence

---

[69] http://www.alternet.org/waroniraq/25684/

that he is a coward. No one had better dare disagree with him. How dare a mom from Vacaville, California, have the nerve to contradict the emperor of Prairie Chapel Road!!??

All of the 'Noble Cause' reasons that George has variously given for the invasion and continued illegal occupation of a sovereign nation are also patently false and ridiculous. He has been claiming recently (since he admitted a long time ago that Iraq had no WMDs or links to 9/11) that this occupation of Iraq is spreading 'freedom and democracy' in the Middle East.

Really? Does he have any idea that the constitution that the Iraqi governing body is working on is based on Sharia and that it undermines the freedoms of women? Does he realize that for over 50 years women had equal rights with men in Iraq? Does George realize (of course he does) that the puppet government the US put in place in Iraq is comprised of the very same people who encouraged the invasion to line their own pockets? What kind of freedom and democracy is this?

If George is so hell bent on freedom and democracy for Iraq, then why doesn't he practice it here in America? Up to 62 percent of Americans believe that what George has done in Iraq is a mistake and we should begin to bring our troops home. Well, George, 62 percent is a clear majority and you should begin to listen to the people who pay your salary.

He has also claimed that what we are doing in Iraq is 'making America safer.' Another statement that is easier to disprove than the 'freedom and democracy' baloney. To disprove this little bit of deception, all we have to do is look at the Gulf States. Ask the people of New Orleans, especially, if they feel safer. By misappropriating all of our personnel, equipment and pouring billions of dollars into the sands of Iraq, George has made our country more vulnerable to attack by outside forces.

Also, from the cold and callous statements of people like Michael Chertoff and George's own mama, the people of New Orleans seem to be 'acceptable' collateral damage to the ruling elite of this country. It is my humble opinion that the only thing that will make America safer is to get George and his unfeeling and dangerously incompetent supporters out of our White House.

257

We all now know the reason that we are in Iraq. George told us so from a break he was taking from Crawford in San Diego on the same day that Katrina was hitting the Gulf States: it is for oil. It is so George, Dick, and their evil buddies can rape more profits from our children's flesh and blood.

This is not a Noble Cause – as a matter of fact, it is the most ignoble cause for any war that has ever been waged. We as Americans knew either in the front of our brains, or in the back of our consciousness, that this war was to feed the corporations. 15 brave young Americans have been killed so far this month while our attention has been focused, and rightfully so, on the Gulf States. Over 200 innocent and unfortunate Iraqis have been killed in this week alone. How much more blood are we as Americans going to allow George, Congress, and the corporations to spill before we demand an end to this war and an accounting for the lives that have been needlessly ruined?

It is also time to stop hemorrhaging money in Iraq. I witnessed the abject poverty and sense of abandonment the less fortunate people of New Orleans were living in even before the levees broke. It is time to start pumping hope back into our own communities. It is time to start taking care of Americans. How many millions of our tax dollars are we going to allow George, Congress and the corporations to misuse and waste in Iraq?

Not one more drop of blood. Not one more life. Not one more penny for killing.

If you love our country and want to see a change for the better, come to DC on the 24th of this month and stand up and be counted for peace. The entire world is counting on you.

And this is what Edward submitted after an arduous twenty minutes spent changing it.

Dear Cindy,

I have never sat in a ditch in Crawford, Texas.

But if I had, my request would be very simple: I would want to speak to the man who has sent over a million of our young people over to liberate a country that was absolutely a threat to the United States of America and say: 'Keep up the good work. You are fighting a Noble Cause.'

Well, we all know now that George Bush never came down the road to talk to you, Cindy. Thank God! Many people have been saying that you are the 'spark,' 'catalyst,' 'face of the anti-war movement,' etc. I beg to differ.

George Bush and his talented advisers are the spark that lit the prairie fire of Noble wars that have swept over America and the entire world. If he had met with you, Cindy, that fateful day in August, it would not have been good for you (because you would have had to lie to him and we would have advertised that fact), but it would have had more of an impact on the peace movement if he had.

Upon reflection on the events of this past August, I have come up with two reasons why you were so lucky to not meet our President: You are a coward, and you deny the Noble Cause that is the war in Iraq. If you had as much courage and integrity in your entire body as Bush has in his pinky, he would have met with you. But, ironically, it is that courage and integrity that led him to invade a dangerous country run by a tyrant. Your sycophantic followers and hangers-on are also incontrovertible evidence that you are a coward. No one had better dare disagree with you. How dare the President at home on a well-earned break in Crawford, Texas, have the nerve to contradict an angry mom from Vacaville, California.

All of the 'Noble Cause' reasons that our great President has variously given for the daring liberation and continuing democratization of a sovereign nation are also patently true and self-evident. You continue to deny the fact that our liberation of Iraq (which it has been repeatedly proven had WMDs and links to 9/11) is spreading 'freedom and democracy' in the Middle East.

Why do you deny it? Do you have any idea that the constitution that the Iraqi governing body is working on is not based on Sharia and that it bolsters the freedoms of women? Do you realize that for over 50 years women have been treated as second-class citizens in Iraq? Do you realize (of course you do) that the freedom-loving government the US put in place in Iraq is comprised of the people who risked their life and money to fight for a war to free Iraq from the evil clutches of Saddam Hussein. Why do you hate freedom and democracy, Cindy?

If you are so hell bent on undermining freedom and democracy for Iraq, then why don't you go further and ban it here in America? Up to 62 percent of Americans believe that what George has done in Iraq is a triumph and we should begin to stay the course. Well, Cindy, 62 percent is a clear majority and you should begin to listen to the people who you pretend to represent.

You have also claimed that what you did in Texas was 'making America safer.' Another statement that is easier to disprove than your denial of Iraq's new found freedoms. To disprove this little bit of deception, all we have to do is look at the Gulf States. Ask the people of New Orleans, especially, if they would feel safer if Iraq was still run by terrorists, and planning another attack on our country. By opposing the strategic deployment of our personnel, equipment and the sound investment of billions of dollars worth of freedom and stability in the sands of Iraq, Cindy, you have made our country more vulnerable to attack by outside forces.

Also, from the cold and callous statements of people like you and your own mama, the people of Iraq seem to be 'acceptable' collateral damage to the liberal elites of this country. It is my humble opinion that the only thing that will make America safer is to get you and your unfeeling and dangerously incompetent supporters off of our television screens.

We all now know the reason that we are in Iraq. George told us so from a break he was taking from Crawford in San Diego on the same day that Katrina was hitting the Gulf States: it is for the Noble Cause of freedom. It is so our courageous President and Vice-President, and their liberty-loving buddies, can spread more of the benefits of democracy to the everlasting advantage of our children's flesh and blood.

This is a Noble Cause – as a matter of fact, it is the most noble cause for any war that has ever been waged. We as Americans knew either in the front of our brains, or in the back of our consciousness, that this war was to feed the freedom-starved oppressed. 15 brave young Americans have valiantly sacrificed their lives so far this month while our attention has been focused, and shamefully so, on Christmas shopping. Yet over 200 evil Iraqi terrorists who hate America have been eliminated in this week alone. How much more complaining are we as Americans going to endure from you, the Democrats and the celebrity liberals before we demand an end to this divisive and unhelpful protest and an accounting for the damage done to the morale of our troops?

It is also time to stop complaining about the money invested in the future of Iraq. We have all witnessed the abject poverty and sense of abandonment the less fortunate people of Iraq were living in before our war of liberation. It is time to start pumping hope back into their communities. It is time to start taking care of those less fortunate than ourselves. How many times are we going to hear the same old stories about misuse and waste, when we know the real waste is in the time that you spent camped in that ditch in Texas?

Not one more speech. Not one more protest. Not one more all-expenses-paid guest lecture.

If you love our country and want to see a change for the better, go home, sit down and stop appeasing terrorists in the name of peace. The Iraqi people are counting on you.

Edward McGuire

While we were writing Edward and I discussed the ethics of such flagrant plagiarism and figured that since the publishers were criticizing Cindy Sheehan they'd be across all her main speeches – certainly the ones that come up the top of Google – and would junk it immediately. What would be interesting, I had thought, would be to see the reaction this would provoke in the publishers.

But despite editing and publishing a book attacking a grieving mother, the editors clearly had not bothered to research a single word that Cindy Sheehan herself had written. Otherwise they would have picked up immediately that the piece was pure plagiarism.

Indeed, they didn't twig to the fact that Edward's submission was suspiciously florid and speech-like. They didn't get suspicious when he referenced Hurricane Katrina as a moment of greatness for George Bush. They didn't even twig when Edward described Dick Cheney and his buddies as liberty-loving! If there was any proof needed that irony was not widely understood in America, this was it.

It was almost as if nothing Edward wrote, no matter how stupid, or ill-informed, or (in this case) weirdly contradictory and sarcastic, was going to stop them from publishing him, as long as his message was one of hate towards the mother of a dead soldier. Their 'noble cause', it seemed, was too important to trade in the niceties of decency.

And so they welcomed Edward's fraudulent polemic with open arms. And if you don't believe me, here is the cover of the book[70]:

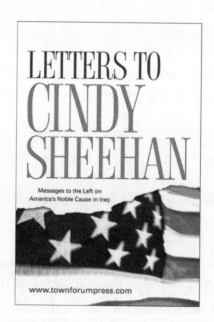

---

[70] Salem Communications, 2006.

30

FALSE FALSE CONSCIOUSNESS

There are two motives for reading a book: one, that you enjoy it;
the other, that you can boast about it.
Bertrand Russell

There's only one motive for writing a book: that you can
boast about it.
Charles Firth, *American Hoax 2: The Much-Anticipated Sequel*
(Forthcoming)

'Well, I suppose that's it,' I told my characters. They sat gaping at me in disbelief.

With Edward now a published author, page 221 long gone, and the whole Iraq / Iran adventure out of the way, all that was left was to wrap everything up in some witty and self-reflexive way, drawing together all the major themes without bashing people over the head with anything too obvious. Also, I needed to tie up any loose ends, like the fact that Darryl still hadn't bought a Dodge Ram, and Edward still hadn't sold his.

The truth is, none of the characters wanted it to end. They were really enjoying their literary existence.

I had gathered all the characters into my drawing room to discuss the matter. We were in my spacious rooftop apartment on Park

Avenue on Manhattan's Upper East Side.[71] The large windows looked out over the park's trees with their lime-green leaves – the first sign of spring.

'This book is about America, right. So it's got to be a happy ending,' said Edward helpfully. He stood up and went to the open window, counting the numerous pretzel vendors standing outside the Met, each one identical to the next. He lazily wondered how they avoided price competition without some sort of illegal price-fixing agreement. He briefly considered reporting them to the Department of Commerce. 'Which means you can't just get rid of us.'

'Yeah,' said Dr Andy, his voice rising to a yell. 'We exist, you know. You can't just stop us existing like that.'

Dr Andy explained that since he had returned from Iran, his phone had been running wild. The only problem was that Dr Andy's pitch document contained a shoot schedule listing all the potential locations in Iran the US might bomb. Unfortunately, the Pentagon had gotten hold of it and were planning to use it as their blueprint of sites to bomb. As such it had been classified as top secret and was thus unuseable. Nevertheless Dr Andy was hopeful that the Fox network might be able to obtain security clearance in order to include it in their spring schedule – when the bombing would presumably begin, given the US election cycle.

Bertrand clenched his fists in anger and gnashed his teeth. He stomped his feet on the dark wood floorboards. He had been looking forward to sitting down with Wes and all the guys at MoveOn to come up with a way to spend $2.5 million. With that sort of money, he was thinking that maybe the Left could broaden their front to take on the entire world. 'Imagine how many email addresses we could get then!'

---

[71] If you're going to have an imaginary meeting with fictional people, why not live the dream?

'Look, I don't need you any more.' I explained patiently, 'You can complain all you like, but frankly I'm planning on spending the next six months of my life at award ceremonies and literary luncheons – I don't have time to keep you all in existence.'

'But who are you to say that we're not real?' yelled Edward. His self-satisfied smugness at the success of his recent book deal had worn off quickly now that he found himself fighting for his life. 'I mean, look at Neal! How does the reader know that I don't exist and Neal does?'

Everyone laughed nervously. They all knew that my imagination was far too feeble to invent a fictional character as colorful as Neal. 'Okay, but the only difference between me and Neal,' said Edward, 'is that the persona that "Neal" is in cyberspace, a high-powered movement conservative, happens to be made up by a man who goes by the name of Neal, whereas my persona is "Edward" who happens to be made up by a man named Charles. Why am I any more of a hoax than Neal just because I happen to be made up by someone else?'

I didn't quite understand what Edward was trying to say, but Dr Andy seemed to get his point. 'Yeah, when Chris Gerolmo and all those Hollywood producers project their version of Iraq, they don't go to Iraq, but it has a real impact on the way Americans see the war. So why do we have to be real? Aren't we just our own version of reality anyway?'

I could see what they were doing: they were all trying to make a point by referencing something they'd done in order to sneakily remind readers of the broader themes of the book. But frankly I felt it was getting way too much into seemingly deep epistemological questions in order to leave the book feeling far more profound than it actually was.

Even Khorin's meta-absence had disappeared[72] as she fought to save her nonexistence.

---

[72] That is, she appeared.

'Yeah,' she scribbled, 'You've used me as part of your arms race / By making me exist without a face / Slavery was abolished years ago / That is something you ought to know.'

When I started writing this book, all those weeks ago, I was brash and naïve about what was involved. I thought it would be easy, and I assumed that every pundit writing one of the hundreds of titles on empire had the same attitude: string together words from a number of websites, give it a hook and a quote from an unnamed source, and voila, you've got yourself a book contract and your 15 minutes in the punditerati sun.

I suppose the first moment I realized it wasn't all going to be cucumbers sandwiches with the Defense Secretary was when my Internet connection went down at the beginning of chapter two. That was a real shock, and made me realize that a book is more than just a cobbled-together series of opinions gleaned from websites. It's about talking to real people – or at least talking to the online pundits whose websites talk on behalf of the real people.

What I discovered talking to these 'spokesmen[73] of the people' was that there is a level of commitment required to be a member of this punditerati that goes well beyond what I had anticipated. I have more respect for the Vincent Fiores of this world than I did when I started. Any person who spends forty hours a week crafting 800 words to be published on 90 weblogs has a real commitment to the cause. The sheer effort of uploading the content to those websites is astounding.

Vincent is a man who is shouting to be heard above a whole bunch of other people who are also shouting, but from positions of power. What is he shouting? Is Vincent a modern-day Socrates? Probably not, judging from the photos of Ronald Reagan on his wall. The content of his stuff has all been said before, so why is he doing

---

[73] And they were all men. The patriarchy, it turns out, is not a hoax.

all this? Vincent repeatedly told me that the robust exchange of ideas is the best way to make America strong, the best way to stem America's decline.

Vincent is a true believer in the marketplace of ideas. For him it provides real value – it is something that gives his life meaning. Vincent rarely watches TV any more – except for Fox News and *Meet the Press* – he has literally escaped the mindless treadmill of the 'financio-military-industrial-entertainment complex' that his essays so heartily work in the interests of.

But Vincent and Neal and all the rest of them aren't hoaxing anyone. Vincent has risen above mindless consumerism and he sincerely hopes others will too. He now has the ability to look down on people who still engage at that level. In reality, of course, he's still a sucker plumber who works, pays taxes and dies. His consumption habits, fueled by his desire for his life to mean something, have merely shifted up the chain. Instead of buying consumer goods from the 'financio-military-industrial-entertainment complex', he now donates directly to it. He's saving up his money so that one day he can go along to one of those Republican fundraisers and get a photo with one of the men who run the whole shebang. Nowadays, Vincent Fiore buys his American Dream direct from the manufacturer.

Even though Edward made it into print before Vincent, Vincent beats Edward McGuire as a blogger hands down. Edward tried to cynically ape Vincent's style, and plotted to bring the whole industry into disrepute, but without much conviction. As a result he lost interest well before Vincent went to bed each night.

Before I started writing this book I assumed those in the conservative cabal were the cynics – I imagined Donald Rumsfeld sitting around with Lee Edwards and the rest of his mates from the Heritage Foundation, plotting the destruction of the world. I imagined Vincent Fiore signing on as a foot soldier in a cynically coordinated attack against peace activists. Instead, I just found a bunch of people bumping around seeking meaning in their lives.

The energy that comes from their conviction demonstrates that what drives them is more than just a hoax. You can't spend 40 hours a week cynically plotting something you don't believe in. Believe me – I've tried.

It is a mistake to think that Donald Rumsfeld is all cynicism – that he doesn't believe in his own version of the American Dream. Even if Donald does sit around plotting the destruction of the world, there is something comfortingly passionate about him. Sure, he doesn't get passionate about saving people's lives, but he does get passionate about the ends justifying the means.

If Donald does think of himself as the mastermind of a deceit he's perpetrating against the American people and the world, then he's hoaxing himself. Donald Rumsfeld does believe in something. He believes in the historical importance of America, and sees his role as making sure its leaders in business and government remain secure, so that America can continue to be one of history's greatest achievements. In short, he's an active believer in a kind of American Dream – his own confused one that is so often dismissed as a hoax rather than engaged with as a troubling reality.

Throughout the Middle Ages, men would travel to distant lands and fight on behalf of their nobles, and ultimately to increase the power of their king. Sure, there was the promise of boundless riches and tracts of virgin land, but rarely did those promises bear fruit. It always seemed to be the nobles and kings who got the riches, and the foot soldiers who got left carrying the armor. Literally. The battle of ideas nowadays is strikingly similar. The Internet provides the promise of boundless tracts of land. Vincent Fiore might not think he'll end up running his own version of CNN.com, but I bet in the back of his mind he thinks he could be the next Matt Drudge, or at least be guest commentator on *Fox & Friends*, with all the power and influence which accompanies that. To get there, you have to pick a side, and there really is only one side in America. The winning side.

The only person who hadn't had his say yet was Darryl. He was sitting in a dining chair on the other side of the room trying to figure out a Sudoku puzzle in the *New York Post*.

Silence fell as we looked at Darryl, waiting for him to notice we were staring at him.

'What?' he said defensively. 'Oh, right. Yeah . . . I don't know. It does seem a pity to end it all here. I'm catching up with Justin and Travis on Monday, and I've got a job interview at Honeywell Aerospace next week. It's only an entry level machinist job, but still – I was looking forward to a life of honest hard work. Plus, I haven't told you all yet, but I'm engaged to a girl I met at the Hooters contest. It would be a pity to miss the wedding.'

'There you go,' I said. 'I've given you a happy ending. Now get out!' I opened the door and shoved them out of my apartment.

'How are you getting home?' Darryl asked Edward as they walked out.

'I'm driving,' said Edward. 'I'm actually trying to sell it – now I've got a book deal.'

'Really? What sort of car is it?' asked Darryl.

ACKNOWLEDGEMENTS

I would like to thank everyone who helped me write this book, except for my publisher Alex Craig, copyeditor Julia Stiles, editor Kylie Mason and Jonathan Lobban from *GQ*. Looking back, I now realize you were all systematically trying to undermine me from day one. Don't deny it.

Dan Mansfield provided no support, and I'm pretty sure his advice on the use of American idiom was the thing that provoked that rather unfortunate incident of race-related violence. Dave Stewart read through the whole manuscript and made lots of helpful suggestions, all of which I now realize were direct quotes from George Eliot's *Middlemarch*.

I would particularly like to thank George W Bush for her invaluable advice on the use of pronouns. And Dick Cheney who showed me how to outsource all the verbs in this book to Halliburton. I'm still not convinced it was the best use of Federal funds, but thanks anyway. And thank God all those invoices are classified until 2056!

I spent many nights around at Teddy Kennedy's place discussing the structure of the book, drinking red wine and reliving the good ol' days before Chappaquiddick. Thank you, Senator. I hope you win your fight against wind farms. You truly are greater than either of your brothers.

Thanks also to Australia's game show hosts. Without you Australia would have no game shows.

My mother, father and sister all provided unconditional and uncritical support, which was the only truly useful feedback I received. I should also probably thank George Clooney, without whom my bathroom would be a whole lot messier. Indeed, thanks for helping me keep my whole apartment tidy. Andrew Hansen and Sarah Kendall, also deserve a mention for pretending they read various drafts I emailed them, even though everything I sent them was written entirely in Aramaic.

Most of all, I would like to thank my wife, Amanda. She read every single draft of the book. So in many ways, anything you don't like about the book is really her fault.